Management for Professionals

More information about this series at
http://www.springer.com/series/10101

Stefan Heissner

Managing Business Integrity

Prevent, Detect, and Investigate White-collar Crime and Corruption

Springer

Stefan Heissner
Ernst & Young
Cologne
Germany

Translation from the German language edition:
"Erfolgsfaktor Integrität - Wirtschaftskriminalität erkennen, aufklären, verhindern"
by Stefan Heißner (2. Auflage)

ISSN 2192-8096 ISSN 2192-810X (electronic)
ISBN 978-3-319-12720-0 ISBN 978-3-319-12721-7 (eBook)
DOI 10.1007/978-3-319-12721-7
Springer Cham Heidelberg New York Dordrecht London

Library of Congress Control Number: 2015930081

Printed on acid-free paper

Springer is part of Springer Science+Business Media (www.springer.com)

Preface

White-collar crime and corruption keep the economy in a state of constant unrest. Hardly a day goes by without some form of manipulation, fraud, bribery, price fixing, or other misdemeanor being revealed to the world and developing into a serious scandal in the full glare of publicity. White-collar crime and corruption are themes that can no longer be avoided by any manager or company.

However, no one really seems to have a precise understanding of what white-collar crime and corruption actually mean when viewed from a company's perspective. Similarly, within the world of business, there also appears to be no real awareness of how misconduct originates in companies or how it is possible to protect against it.

The affected CEOs, supervisory boards, managers, and managing directors appear altogether too surprised when confronted by these incidents or, in the worst-case scenario, suddenly find themselves in the dock. This happens because they have been made directly liable for either their own actions or even for the misconduct of their employees or business partners.

The legal and regulatory environment at a national and international level makes this possible.

Yet what is liability all about? At what point do you become liable yourself and for what? How can you eliminate the risk of liability—or even more importantly any claims for damages—due to fraud, bribery, or all of the other types of offenses? And what aspects of white-collar crime and corruption need to be addressed in order to achieve this goal?

Only a small minority of German managers are likely to have the answers to these questions in hand. Nevertheless, they feel a genuine sense of panic about their own liability. And they are quite right to feel this way, especially as the legal straightjacket has now been tightened to a frightening degree for international business dealings. This has been accompanied by increasingly professional criminal investigations in the area of white-collar crime. It must not be forgotten that misconduct within a company does not only impact on those people actively involved, but it also results in assets totaling billions of dollars being irretrievably wiped out every year.

The answer often given when dealing with these urgent questions about misconduct and personal liability is compliance—a hot topic and yet a real mystery in equal measure. This is because there are few people who can provide a clear explanation in broad terms of the organizational, specialist, and methodological factors behind this often overused phrase—despite the fact that a great deal has been discussed about this subject in interviews, business briefings, circulars, specialist articles, and libraries full of specialist literature.

It is often decision makers in the world of business, however, who have trouble getting to grips with large sections of this specialist literature. These publications on the relatively modern management discipline of compliance are consequently described as being too large, too difficult, too technical, too complicated, or excessively legal.

This book focuses on precisely this point. It is aimed at those managers, executives, and entrepreneurs from small and medium-sized companies who have previously had little or even nothing to do with the subjects of white-collar crime, corruption, and compliance. This book wants to be understood and to offer even newcomers to the field an understandable overview of these subjects. And in their search for corporate success, it has never been more important for companies to actively tackle these issues than it is today.

As a result, this book will not cover legal texts and judicial rulings in great detail. It will instead look at the stories behind the laws and regulations, as well as at their actual impact on the different players in the business environment.

It will also seek to provide practical explanations for how white-collar crime arises in a sociological sense, what motives and types of perpetrators are really concealed behind these offenses, and the various types of damage their actions can cause using examples and cases from criminal investigations, forensic audits, and compliance consultancy.

It is only those who understand this criminological background can make decisions in an emergency situation for comprehensively dealing with damage claims. By providing the most authentic insight possible into the methods used in a forensic audit, this book aims to ensure that processes and procedures can be better evaluated and understood.

However, reacting appropriately is only half the battle in a practical sense. This is because only those who also take preventative action to protect their company, in the form of a fully functioning compliance management system, are able to effectively minimize corporate and personal risk. Therefore, this book concludes by presenting and explaining the model-based functionality of a compliance management system that has also proven effective in reality.

It is nevertheless still important to cast a critical eye over the subject of compliance management, because these types of system form only part of the solution from a practical point of view. A core message in this book is that both corporate and personnel managers have a clear obligation to actively promote, reward, and practice the themes of integrity and compliance. Of course, every system of control has its limits and this makes concepts such as "tone from the top" and the leadership maxim "walk the talk" important elements of a holistic approach for sustainably reducing deviant behavior—and thus also limiting the damage caused by white-collar crime and corruption.

With this in mind, a word of warning at the very beginning: the battle against criminality and corruption can never truly be won despite all these practical insights, tools, and systems. It is a constant game of cat and mouse that will probably continue for all eternity, even in commercial enterprises.

An appropriate response to crime and corruption, and intelligent preventative measures, will nevertheless help the cat make the game significantly more difficult for the insatiable mouse—or, in other words, will effectively protect corporate assets. This book is specifically designed to assist in this process.

Cologne, September 2014 Stefan Heissner

Acknowledgments

I would like to express my sincere thanks at this point to the team at komm.passion who were actively involved in the creation of this book.

Contents

1 Drivers and Trends 1

1.1 Basic Features of Manager Liability 3

1.1.1 Basic Principles of Compliance Obligations 5

1.1.2 Liability Based on the Regulatory Offenses Act and Stock Corporation Law 8

1.1.3 Criminal Liability 9

1.1.4 Civil Liability 10

1.1.5 Labor Law and "Political" Responsibility 11

1.1.6 Digression: Protection in the Form of D&O and Fidelity Insurance 12

1.2 Relevant Legislation and Its History 14

1.2.1 The Beginnings: Tulip Mania and the South Sea Bubble 14

1.2.2 Foreign Corrupt Practices Act: Starfighter and Bananagate 16

1.2.3 Sarbanes-Oxley Act: Criminal Energy and Creative Accounting 18

1.2.4 Dodd-Frank Act: Shackling the Banks? 23

1.2.5 UK Bribery Act: Well-Oiled Arms Trade 24

1.2.6 Legislation in Germany 26

1.3 Social Conditions and Drivers of White-Collar Crime 28

1.3.1 Deterioration of Social Control 30

1.3.2 Increasing Complexity 31

1.4 Trends in Regulatory and Liability Law 32

1.4.1 Completing the Legislative Framework for Combating Fraud 32

1.4.2 Stricter International Regulations for Combating Corruption 33

1.4.3 Regulating Access to Resources 34

1.4.4 Regulating Social Factors 35

Literature 35

2 Perpetrators and Offenses 37
2.1 White-Collar Crime: A Practical Definition 38
2.1.1 Different Aspects for a Comprehensive Understanding of White-Collar Crime 38
2.1.2 Alternative Term: "Deviant Behavior" 41
2.1.3 Overview of the Relevant Offenses Included Under "Deviant Behavior" 42
2.2 The Development of White-Collar Crime 50
2.2.1 White-Collar Crime: A Necessary Evil of the Market Economy? 50
2.2.2 Sociological Aspects in the Development of White-Collar Crime 51
2.2.3 The Fraud Triangle: A Standard Instrument for Explaining White-Collar Crime 52
2.3 Motives for White-Collar Crime 54
2.3.1 Motive: Pursuit of Social Status 54
2.3.2 Motive: Feeling of Obligation and Emergency Situations 55
2.3.3 Motive: Obedience to Authority 55
2.3.4 Motive: Pragmatism 55
2.3.5 Motive: Ignorance 56
2.3.6 Motive: Career Ambitions 56
2.3.7 Motive: Boredom 56
2.3.8 Motive: Pressure to Perform 57
2.3.9 Motive: Revenge 57
2.3.10 Motive: Social Recognition 57
2.3.11 Motive: Peer Pressure 57
2.4 Perpetrator Typologies in the Area of White-Collar Crime 60
2.4.1 An Overview of the Perpetrator Typologies 61
2.5 The Consequences of White-Collar Crime 64
2.5.1 Extent of the Damage Caused by White-Collar Crime . . . 66
2.6 Conclusion: Management Bears the Responsibility 71
Literature 71

3 Forensics 73
3.1 Commissioning a Special Investigation 75
3.1.1 The Trend in Public Prosecutor's Offices: The American Model 77
3.1.2 The Public Prosecutor's Office and Companies: Divergent Interests in the Investigation of White-Collar Crime 79
3.1.3 The Crime Enforcement Authorities and Companies: An Increasing Level of Cooperation 80

3.2 The Process of a Forensic Investigation . . . 81
3.2.1 Assessing the Current Situation and Tactical Considerations for the Investigation . . . 82
3.2.2 Three Basic Rules at the Start of an Investigation . . . 85
3.2.3 Concealment and Cover-Ups: Examples from Purchasing and Sales Departments . . . 87
3.3 The Criminalistic Process and the Formulation of Hypotheses . . . 89
3.3.1 Physical Documentation as a Source of Information . . . 91
3.3.2 Electronic Data Analysis as a Source of Information . . . 94
3.3.3 Background Research/Business Intelligence as a Source of Information . . . 99
3.3.4 Interviews and Audits as a Source of Information . . . 103
3.4 Investigations in the Future . . . 106
3.4.1 Offenses and Investigations Are Increasingly Driven by Technology . . . 106
3.4.2 Investigative Work Is Becoming Increasingly More Specialized . . . 107
3.4.3 Investigation and Prevention Are Becoming More Closely Linked . . . 107
Literature . . . 108

4 Systems for Combating Criminality . . . 111
4.1 Critical Preliminary Remark on the Design of Compliance Management Systems . . . 114
4.2 Methodological Principles for Compliance Management . . . 118
4.3 Compliance Culture, Compliance Objectives, and Compliance Communication: Elements of Strategic Corporate Management and the Management of Personnel . . . 121
4.3.1 Examining Employees and the Corporate Culture . . . 122
4.3.2 Harmonizing Compliance Objectives and Compliance Communication . . . 123
4.4 From the Risk Assessment, Through the Compliance Program and Compliance Organization to Constant Improvement: The Control Loop for an Effective and Sustainable System . . . 124
4.4.1 Compliance Risk Assessment . . . 124
4.4.2 The Compliance Loop . . . 136
4.4.3 Organizational Principles: Responsibilities, Reporting Channels, and Setting the System Up as a Company Department . . . 160
4.5 Testing and Evaluating Compliance Management Systems . . . 164
4.5.1 IDW PS 980: A Calibration Tool for Fully Functional Preventative Systems? . . . 165
Literature . . . 172

5 A Look Ahead to the Future 175
5.1 Compliance in Germany: An Overview of the Current Situation . . 175
5.1.1 The Control Paradox of Compliance and Its Negative Effects 176
5.1.2 The Danger of Pro-Forma Solutions 178
5.2 The Next Step: Protecting Corporate Values with Integrity 179
5.2.1 Compliance as a Strategic Management Theme 180
5.3 The Requirement for Compliant Business Practices in Global Competition 181
5.4 The Path to the Future: Good Corporate Governance 182
Literature 184

About the Author

Stefan Heissner is head of the highly specialized division "Fraud Investigation and Dispute Services" (FIDS) at EY, the global professional services firm, as the Managing Partner responsible for Central Europe and the CIS countries. Heissner's background means that he is familiar with the phenomenon of white-collar crime from more than one perspective. Before being engaged for the last 15 years in the field of forensic auditing, Dr. Heissner also worked for the police force for 15 years—most recently holding the rank of Detective Superintendent.

Additionally, Heissner explored the economic analysis of white-collar crime and corruption in his dissertation and several other scientific publications.

Heissner is an internationally renowned expert in the fields of criminalistics and compliance, as well as being the author of numerous specialist papers and a popular guest speaker.

Education and Career Experience Economics Degree (Diplom-Ökonom), Dr. rer. pol., Detective Superintendent (retired), Certified Fraud Examiner.

Publications/Committees "Die Bekämpfung von Wirtschaftskriminalität—Eine ökonomische Analyse unterschiedlicher Entscheidungsoptionen" (Combating White-Collar Crime—An Economic Analysis of Various Decision-Making Options), Publishing Company: KPMG, 2001.

Coauthor of the "Handbuch der Korruptionsbekämpfung" (Handbook for Combating Corruption), Publishing Company: C. H. Beck, 2007.

Member of the Compliance Working Group at the Institute of Public Auditors in Germany (IDW)

1 Drivers and Trends

The Development of the Social Conditions and Legal Basis for Dealing with Liability Issues

The deal appeared quite simple when the "1st Amendment to the German Stock Corporation Law" (1. Aktienrechtsnovelle) was adopted on June 11, 1870: The state would, at the King's mercy, forgo their existing right to monitor every incorporated company personally. At this point in history, the state was still the North German Confederation—the country of Germany did not yet exist. In return, commercial enterprises promised that they would independently ensure that everything was being conducted in the correct manner. And the institution responsible for doing so was a newly created body called a "supervisory board." In order to demonstrate that they were taking this due diligence seriously, the members of a supervisory board were also made personally liable at the time, in addition to the entrepreneurs themselves. For example, anybody who was aware of false statements concerning the "assets of the company," yet did not report them, was threatened with 3 months' imprisonment (see Endemann et al. 1870, Article 206).

The King's representatives could not have known at the time that this legal innovation would take on a life of its own over the coming years and instill anxiety and fear into future generations of businessmen and women. As early as the 2nd legal amendment in the form of the "Law dealing with companies limited by shares and incorporated companies" (Gesetz, betreffend die Kommanditgesellschaften auf Aktien und die Aktiengesellschaften) in 1884—this time issued at the mercy of the Kaiser—the liability of the supervisory board and their shareholders was increased for the first time. The law contained a total of seven paragraphs dedicated to the duties of due diligence and supervision. The next legislative reform in 1937 contained 14 paragraphs relevant to this subject. In the Stock Corporation Law (Aktiengesetz) of 1965, which is still valid today, there are approx. 55 paragraphs dedicated to the management, control, indemnity, and personal liability of management personnel and supervisory board members for incorporated companies. These articles nearly always deal with white-collar crime and corruption. In order to be held technically liable, it is not even necessary for CEOs, managing directors, and supervisory boards to perpetrate any crime themselves, or hand over a proverbial briefcase full of cash. It is merely sufficient for them to have failed to take sufficient

S. Heissner, *Managing Business Integrity*, Management for Professionals,
DOI 10.1007/978-3-319-12721-7_1

care for protecting the company's assets against fraud, manipulation, corruption, and the many other existing forms of white-collar crime.

Naturally, there are similar liability regulations dealing with every other form of business under German commercial law. These are supplemented by numerous other regulatory interventions into the world of business that govern the personal liability of those individuals actively involved. These regulations are mostly hidden behind unwieldy abbreviations. Here is a just a small selection: AnSVG, BilReG, BilKoG, APAG, VorstOG, KapMuG, BilMoG, ARUG, UMAG, and KonTraG. In addition, there are other non-legislative or quasi-legislative regulations to which companies submit themselves, such as UN conventions, corporate governance codes, or OECD ethical standards. If a company also conducts business transactions abroad or holds branches in the USA or Great Britain, the regulations dealing with liability can be multiplied many times over.

It is thus safe to say that those management boards, managing directors, and supervisory boards with only an average grasp of the legal regulations no longer have a sufficient overview of the situation. And as an example of the current level of complexity found in modern liability regulations, the "Handbook on Manager Liability" (Handbuch Managerhaftung: Risikobereiche und Haftungsfolgen für Vorstand, Geschäftsführer, Aufsichtsrat) by Gerd Krieger and Uwe Schneider (see Krieger and Schneider 2007) comprises over 1,000 densely printed pages. It is not for nothing that the management and supervisory bodies of incorporated companies today employ whole legions of lawyers, auditors, compliance consultants, and self-styled governance experts in order to master the highly complex issues surrounding personal liability for their own or third-party misconduct. This is because the risk is real, and the possible consequences can prove fatal. A series of recent cases have demonstrated this point. As a result of the bankruptcy of the Austrian bank HGAA, BayernLB—the regional bank of Bavaria—is demanding 200 million euros from each one of the eight members of the company's old management board. The reason being that they are liable in the legal sense for losses totaling billions of euros. Håkan Samuelsson, the former CEO of MAN AG, and five former colleagues on the management board are being sued for damages totaling 237 million euros as the result of a corruption scandal. In truth, it is now barely possible to calculate the potential judgments for damages against CEOs who are found responsible for antitrust infringements linked to billions of euros in fines. The possible consequences of this liability include personal bankruptcy and the end of a career. However, the consequences are even worse when viewed objectively. If it can be proven that those at the helm were aware of the risk (for example, based on the minutes of management board meetings) but nevertheless negligently, or to a greater or lesser extent intentionally, ignored the possible damages, they could face criminal prosecution and, in the worst-case scenario, end up in jail due to complicity or a breach of trust. This scenario is not impossible based on German and international law, but is now a fact of life and an everyday reality.

The financial crisis in 2009 has greatly increased the pace at which regulations dealing with manager liability are being tightened—this is also evident at a statutory level. The German Bundestag passed a comprehensive package of laws in May

2013 (see Federal Press Office 2013) that, alongside the introduction of a so-called "separate banking system," greatly increased the criminal liability faced by company managers, and explicitly prescribed imprisonment for breaches of duty in the area of risk management, as well as fines of up to 10.8 million euros.

The radical reaction of politicians towards credit institutions is not least due to the fact that it was in the banking sector that primarily tax payers had to pay for the losses resulting from fraud, manipulation, or the lack of risk awareness. This catapulted the issue of manager liability once and for all into the public eye.

The consequence of this public pressure is that existing laws are now being more strictly interpreted and implemented. Naturally, only very few managers can afford to pay hundreds of millions of euros in damages from their own coffers, or are able to settle the fines issued by international antitrust divisions. The fact that companies issue these demands for damages in the first instance, and the speed with which they act, indicates a clear change in mentality—which should provide every corporate player holding a position of responsibility in an organization with food for thought.

This change in mentality is evident in two recent quotes from prominent German supervisory boards—which were actually not issued that far apart. In connection with the corruption scandal at Siemens, the Chairman of the Supervisory Board Gerhard Cromme spoke of "not taking the last shirt off the back" of the responsible CEO. Yet only a few years later with regards to the recently announced corruption case in their HGV Division, the MAN Supervisory Board and top manager Ferdinand Piëch commented that the CEO should face the "full force of the law" (see Ott 2011).

This fits into the overall picture. There is increasingly less scope for negligence, supervisory boards are becoming more stringent, and criminal investigations ever more professional. It is simply no longer possible to ignore the areas of corporate governance and compliance. Only concrete and credible action ensures that liability risks can be excluded. This book describes how this can be precisely achieved.

In this context, the focus will be placed initially on the basic features of manager liability.

What needs to be done in terms of white-collar crime and corruption in order to exclude the risk of liability? Which legal regulations make company managers liable and in what form? How did these laws originate and how will they develop in the future?

1.1 Basic Features of Manager Liability

Anybody who purchases a food truck and sets it up in a pedestrian zone finds themselves—at least in terms of liability law—in a simple and clear situation. Ownership of the company and control over it lie in the same hands, and while the owner pockets the profits made from their activities, they are also personally liable for the consequences of any legal violations, or the failure of the business. However, if we are dealing with 100 food trucks that are operated by a GmbH (a company with limited liability in Germany) with an employed managing director, or with a stock corporation that serves the whole of Europe with hot dogs and aims to conquer the world in the medium term, the situation is far more complicated. This is because ownership and control lie in different hands. Accordingly, errors made by managing directors, management boards, and supervisory boards do not directly impact on these corporate players, but rather diminish the profits made by members or shareholders of the company and, in the worst-case scenario, wipe out their assets. The same is naturally also true if managers manipulate balance sheets, misappropriate funds, consciously disregard business risks, or bring ruin to their employers in other ways.

For a long time it was not necessary for executives, managers, or management boards to give much thought to the idea of personal liability. In the worst-case scenario, they lost their job or generously made their positions "available" by stepping down, often, where possible, combined with lavish severance packages—or a "golden handshake." The legal hurdles that needed to be overcome to make somebody liable for their misconduct were high. This was despite the fact that the obligation for "proper corporate governance" in the case of incorporated companies had long been part of German commercial law [see Article 93 of the German Stock Corporation Law (Aktiengesetz) and Article 43 of the Limited Liability Companies Act (GmbHG)]. However, it is very difficult in practice to provide clear evidence of misconduct or a violation of the duty of supervision. Questions such as what is actually classified as corporate error, and whether and in what circumstances a manager can find protection under the scope of "general corporate risk," are such complex issues that in reality they are almost impossible to answer. "Could he really have prevented it?" "Nobody could have seen it coming." "The fraudsters managed to deceive us all."

Up to now, experience has shown that a manager must have acted extremely negligently and demonstrated their incompetence or negligence multiple times in order to be made liable for the resulting damages to any notable extent. Although the situation was, to some degree, otherwise if criminal offenses in the area of white-collar crime or corruption had been committed, this did not change the high legal hurdles that had to be overcome to prove manager liability in general for quite some time. And the legal processes against white-collar crime and corruption themselves were certainly not noted for their lack of clemency in the past. The case of Thomas Middelhoff and the Arcandor bankruptcy is symbolic of a series of legal processes in which managers escaped leniently from cases of liability. Klaus Lederer, who as Group Manager of Babcock Borsig covered up the disastrous predicament of the group for many months, was only handed a suspended sentence, a 250,000 € fine, and 1,000 h of community service for delaying insolvency proceedings. In comparison to his salary at the time, the fine amounted to nothing more than pocket money and he was even permitted to carry out some of his community service in sunny Florida.

But, to be absolutely clear from the very start, the days when management boards, members of the company, fully authorized representatives, managing directors, authorized signatories, trade representatives, departmental managers, managers, and other executives of companies had nothing to fear in the area of personal liability are well and truly over. At the latest since the events surrounding the banking and financial crises in 2009, much stricter rules have been introduced for the many existing business regulations on the international stage. The processes of law enforcement and the assertion of liability claims are rapidly becoming more professional.

And what applies to those "executive bodies" responsible for the operative business of the company is also true at the level of the supervisory board. The liability of members of the supervisory board or members of the audit committee in relation to the company has also been tightened. For example, in the form of extended reporting obligations according to Article 107 of the German Accounting Law Modernization Act (Bilanzrechtsmodernisierungsgesetz—BilMoG). The obligation of the supervisory board to provide advice and monitor the management of the company as stipulated in the German Stock Corporation Law (Aktiengesetz) is currently being scrutinized ever more critically in criminal investigations. The supervisory board can be found guilty of so-called "negligent supervision" (see Habersack et al. 2010, Articles 76–117) if, for example, it does not critically challenge and check unusual or frivolous payments. In such cases, the supervisory board would be considered personally liable—and face compensation claims against their own private assets—or deemed to be guilty of a breach of trust. The "minimum standard" expected of the supervisory board in terms of how consciously and actively they scrutinize the subjects of compliance and corporate governance is also rising. However, it remains much more difficult in practice to hold the supervisory board liable than is the case with an executive body actually involved in the operative business of the company. It still remains to be seen what effects the change in the law in the form of Article 107 of BilMoG will have in reality.

The changes in the legal and liability-related evaluation of misconduct, negligence, and malicious intent are also causing a shift in our understanding of white-collar crime in general. Because the administration of justice in the area of white-collar crime has long since ceased to merely focus on cases of fraud, but now also treats non-observance or underestimation of risk as an almost equivalent offense. Using corresponding compliance management systems, this transforms the battle against white-collar crime and corruption from being the duty of individuals to being an obligation for all.

1.1.1 Basic Principles of Compliance Obligations

The rules relating to white-collar crime and corruption for the purpose of protecting a company's assets have thus multiplied, and this trend is set to continue. Criminal investigations and cases of liability are becoming less and less constrained by national boundaries and probe ever deeper into both the digital and analog inner workings of companies. Even a small review of the relevant cases such as that found at the start of this chapter clearly demonstrates this trend.

One of the core tasks of the management of a company is to ensure that corporate activities are carried out in accordance with existing laws. This type of conformity with relevant regulations has become commonly known as "compliance," which has become a dominant management buzzword in recent times. Therefore, compliance management is actually nothing more than a systematic attempt by the management of a company to implement legal regulations in the company for the purpose of excluding their own liability in the event of loss. This is supplemented in many cases by their own, internal "quasi regulations" that go above and beyond the requirements set by the legislators. In a purely legal sense, the responsibility of the management of the company for ensuring compliance results from the legally stipulated duty of supervision and due diligence, as well as the correspondingly defined sanctions in the event of misconduct. The following legal principle is valid: It is possible to delegate the compliance tasks themselves but not the legal duty of supervision and due diligence (see Moosmayer 2012, p. 5 ff.).

If you consider German legislature and the corresponding legal judgments, which will be examined in more detail later in the book, it is possible to identify fundamental compliance obligations that no management board, manager, managing director, or supervisory board can avoid any longer.[1] If a company is internationally active or represented by subsidiaries in the USA or Great Britain, the legal framework dealing with cases of liability is also extended to include the laws valid in these countries. How operative solutions can be developed and implemented to meet these obligations in the form of an effective management system for the prevention of white-collar crime, corruption, and other deviant behavior is discussed in Chap. 4. However, the management of a company is also legally responsible in general terms for the following compliance obligations (see here Kreft et al. 2011, p. 14):

- Identifying and evaluating corporate risks.
- Setting up a compliance organization with an internal control system and developing a compliance program to counteract these risks.
- Integrating compliance measures into day-to-day business operations.[2]

Even though it is never possible to provide complete protection against fraud and misconduct by individuals, the liability of members of company management is evaluated based on the effectiveness of the systems they have introduced to prevent these offenses. Today, their personal commitment also plays a role in assessing responsibility. The criteria according to which personal liability is evaluated by the judiciary in serious cases are by no means set in stone. Instead, the legal

[1] There is a comprehensive range of literature on this special aspect of compliance: a good overview is provided by Moosmayer (2012, p. 3 ff) and Hlavica et al. (2011, Chap. 6).

[2] Looking at the situation from a practical perspective and through experience in compliance consulting will show that there are massive pitfalls especially when integrating compliance into normal operations in a company, which are barely covered in the relevant literature or by consulting services.

interpretations remain fluid and are based on the experience of the judges or public prosecutors and comparable cases. Moosmayer—Compliance Officer at Siemens AG—is quite right, for example, to speak of a "minimum standard" (see Moosmayer 2012, p. 5) in the implementation of compliance measures, whose fundamental conditions are the exclusion of liability risks in a variety of different dimensions. These currently comprise:

- Duty of organization[3]: Preventative measures need to be organized and backed up by clear responsibilities and processes. This also applies to an increasing extent to the institutionalization of anonymous whistle-blowing systems.
- Duty of control[4]: In terms of internal control systems (ICS), regular organizational controls must be carried out, for example, in the form of forensic data analysis.
- Duty of investigation[5]: Serious indications of misconduct must be investigated—whether it is by an internal auditing department or, for example, by commissioning an external auditing company or law firm. It is important in this process to comprehensively resolve these cases—above and beyond the clarification requirements set by the state—measure and limit the losses, and recover any lost assets as far as possible.

A special duty of supervision also exists after the identification of any confirmed cases. The management in those companies where corruption or white-collar crime has already been identified is also obligated to permanently maintain corresponding preventative measures in a transparent and believable manner. If any subsequent cases are discovered, management boards are faced with immediate criminal liability, and already make themselves guilty of complicity and a breach of trust if the judiciary is of the opinion that more could have been undertaken to prevent the losses.[6]

How precisely can supervisory boards be made liable for their negligence according to German law? What consequences must managers take into consideration? A detailed examination of this area demonstrates that managers are at risk on a multi-dimensional scale, not only for their own misconduct, but also for the misconduct of third parties—and are increasingly faced with the loss of their private assets, the threat of imprisonment, and damage to their own reputation that could last practically a lifetime.

[3] See OLG Stuttgart NJW 1977, p. 1410.

[4] See BGH GmbHR 1985, p. 143 and OLG Koblenz ZIP 1991, p. 870.

[5] See BGH GmbHR 1985, p. 143 and OLG Koblenz ZIP 1991, p. 870.

[6] See the case of Anton Weinmann (MAN) in Sect. 5.1.2.

1.1.2 Liability Based on the Regulatory Offenses Act and Stock Corporation Law

In Germany, the liability of managers is historically anchored in laws dealing with regulatory offenses. This situation provides much cause for irritation. When you think of regulatory offenses, you primarily think of driving too fast in a car, illegal parking, or disturbing the peace. Despite this, the size of the fines possible for regulatory offenses already corresponds to the levels of damage associated with white-collar crime: According to the German Regulatory Offenses Act (Ordnungswidrigkeitengesetz—OWiG), fines of up to one million euros are possible for malicious acts. When it comes to the disgorgement of profits gained from criminal offenses, these fines can reach significantly higher levels.

Articles 30, 130, and 9 of OWiG stipulate that a company is liable in the case of attributable misconduct by a supervisory body. These articles also define who these supervisory bodies may be. They include, among others, company bodies, fully authorized representatives or authorized signatories, and trade representatives in management positions, as well as those people charged with monitoring company management in an executive position. Furthermore, Articles 130 and 9 of OWiG stipulate that it is precisely these persons who are liable in the event of a legal violation. They carry the sole responsibility for the fulfillment of their duty of supervision and are solely accountable for this task. In view of the high level of complexity involved in this task, it is possible and normal to delegate the establishment and implementation of a compliance management system to a single managing director and, in the next step, to a single company department. However, as already described, it is important to note that only the task can be delegated and not the responsibility.

Infringements against the minimum requirements for compliance described above result in liability in accordance with OWiG. If legal violations are uncovered, this indicates the complete failure of the compliance management system without any further investigation into the individual circumstances and results in liability according to Article 130 of OWiG. If a compliance management system has been established, it must be monitored by the management of a company in the form of an institutionalized reporting and monitoring system. Should weaknesses in the system become apparent, the management of a company is itself required to intervene. When already identified compliance risks are not minimized, the management of a company can also be held liable in accordance with Article 130 of OWiG (see Moosmayer 2012, p. 17 ff.).

There are still managers even today who believe that they can avoid liability based on the regulations in OWiG if they involve intermediaries or "advisers," who pay bribes in their place or undertake fraudulent manipulations. Naturally, it is not possible for them to avoid liability—even if they have been taken by surprise when a service provider has committed the offenses. An institutionalized prevention system—as prescribed by OWiG—also includes checking the integrity of third parties.

In the case of incorporated companies, such as stock corporations, the liability of corporate bodies is also anchored in other laws. The requirements placed on compliant corporate governance have become increasingly stricter as a result of the recent economic crisis. The management board of a stock corporation is thus expressly obligated to establish and implement a risk management system by the German Law on Corporate Governance and Transparency (Gesetz zur Kontrolle und Transparenz im Unternehmensbereich—KonTraG) 1998 and Article 91 Paragraph 2 of the German Stock Corporation Law (AktG). Article 116 of AktG also makes the supervisory board liable for the fulfillment of this obligation. If due diligence obligations are infringed in the management and supervision of a company, the company is entitled to make claims for damages. Although this right to claim damages is limited by the German Law on Corporate Integrity and Modernization of the Right of Rescission (Gesetz zur Unternehmensintegrität und Modernisierung des Anfechtungsrechts—UMAG), which supplements Article 93 Paragraph 1 of AktG 2005. In a similar way to the American Business Judgement Rule, there is no breach of duty if the member of the management board "could reasonably assume when making a business decision on the basis of appropriate information that he/she was acting in the interests of the company." However, by using the term "reasonable information" in the wording of this limitation—which is even applicable in the event of objectively negligent behavior—it assumes that a functioning compliance management system exists.

KonTraG and UMAG further tighten the legal situation regarding liability by making it easier for shareholders to enforce their claims for damages. In accordance with KonTraG, even small shareholders owning 10 % of the share capital of a stock corporation can enforce their claims for damages. UMAG reduces this figure further to 1 % of the share capital, or a stock market value of 100,000 €.

1.1.3 Criminal Liability

If there is a case for liability in accordance with OWiG, it is possible that criminal proceedings may be faced. For this to happen, it is not necessary for a manager to have committed a criminal offense themselves, or to have directly benefited from the offense. Article 14 of the German Criminal Code (StGB—Acting as an Agent) stipulates that laws are also applicable to representative corporate bodies or members of the company, as well as to appointed managing directors or executive employees. Article 73 ff. of StGB states that benefits gained from the crime must be forfeited. In practice, this leads to disgorgement measures for significant sums of money, for which the manager may be liable to pay from their private assets. If antitrust violations come into play, the fines imposed can exceed hundreds of millions and even run into billions of euros.[7]

[7] The European Commission imposed fines of 1.4 billion euros against the car glass manufacturers Saint-Gobain, Asahi, Pilkington, and Soliver in 2008 for illicit agreements—the repeat offender

In the case of criminal liability by the management—just like with the laws dealing with regulatory offenses—the failure to apply risk minimizing measures within the framework of compliance management is particularly fatal because it represents willful intent, or at the very least tacit approval. This is all the more important because even existing D&O insurance provides no cover or only partial cover in the event of proven intent or "gross negligence." In contrast to OWiG, the use of criminal law in liability cases for managers and supervisory boards also introduces the possibility of imprisonment.

It may sound paradoxical, but if the management of the company does not even embrace the subject of compliance and fails to carry out a risk analysis, they only commit a violation of the regulations and trigger Article 130 of OWiG. The resulting punishment thus includes fines and sanctions. However, if it is apparent from protocols or internal documents that the management of the company was aware of existing risks but did not react to them in a reasonable manner in the form of compliance measures then it is possible that their misconduct will be investigated under the scope of criminal law. Therefore, this "tacit acceptance" due to the lack of preventative measures turns all management boards/managing directors into almost accomplices or accessories to the act without ever having committed a criminal offense themselves. Nevertheless, they remain 100 % liable and are faced, in the worst-case scenario, with a prison sentence.

1.1.4 Civil Liability

If a financial loss is experienced by a company due to an infringement of the duty of supervision, the management of the company could face a demand for compensation under civil law issued by the relevant supervisory board.[8] In the case of an Aktiengesellschaft (AG—stock corporation) in Germany, the supervisory board is obligated to seek compensation in accordance with Article 53 Paragraph 2 of AktG, while in the case of a GmbH (a company with limited liability in Germany), the shareholder's general meeting is obligated to seek compensation in accordance with Article 43 Paragraph 2 of GmbHG. These bodies are left with little freedom of action[9] because, in accordance with the ARAG/Garmenbeck decision by the German Federal Court of Justice (BGH), in 1997, a failure to investigate and implement claims for compensation would correspond to a breach of trust, which could in turn also be prosecuted under criminal law.

If the infringement against the duty of supervision is interpreted as a case of complicity, this is considered as tortious liability in accordance with Articles

Saint-Gobain alone received a fine of 896 million euros. e.on and Gaz de France Suez were fined a total of 1.1 billion euros in 2009 for an infringement of EU antitrust law.

[8] BGHZ, p. 135, 244.

[9] Ibid.

826 and 830 of the German Civil Code (Bürgerlichen Gesetzbuch—BGB).[10] And if the manager is considered personally liable due to the infringement of a law for the protection of the company—for example, in the event of a breach of trust—there is scope for an additional claim for damages in accordance with Article 823 Paragraph 2 of the BGB. Fines issued in accordance with OWiG, lost profits, subsequent tax demands, legal fees, and, not least, lost profits from any exclusion from participation in public procurement contracts are all added together when assessing the level of damages and the corresponding claims for compensation can quickly run into tens of millions of euros. These claims for compensation are then directly issued to the manager or the management board responsible at the time of the offense and are made against their private assets.

1.1.5 Labor Law and "Political" Responsibility

It is perfectly conceivable, for example, that a banker could cause financial loss due to unauthorized market speculation but cannot be prosecuted under criminal law because they have not lined their own pockets. In this scenario, they have certainly violated their employment contract but have not committed any crime. In terms of the legally prescribed obligation to prevent losses being incurred by the company, only the departmental manager or the management board would have infringed the rules and would be responsible in this case. The handling of these types of cases under labor law incorporates very concrete liability-related elements. A company requires really good reasons not to dismiss the responsible employee—after all, the whole company becomes the focus of special attention following a case of loss—and both the management board and the supervisory board are liable for ensuring that there is no repeat occurrence.

Especially in the case of large companies, infringements against corporate governance are closely followed by the public. The media increasingly delight in reporting on these types of scandal, putting a company and its management personnel into the spotlight, and ensuring a long-term loss of reputation that could last for much longer than the actual case itself. This loss of reputation can be more serious to the company in question than the direct financial consequences of the infringement. One consequence of a failure to comply with corporate governance standards is the threat of exclusion from public contracts. Because corporate governance in a company is now also closely scrutinized, to an increasing extent, outside of the public procurement process, and is graded in ranking lists, it can also have competitive disadvantages for business with other companies—for

[10] The German Federal Court of Justice (BGH) found in the Informatec case in 2004 that the management board were liable to pay compensation due to immoral behavior in accordance with Article 826 of BGB. An incorrect ad-hoc notification had induced shareholders to purchase shares in the company.

example, even in the labor market. What high-potential employee would decide to work for a company in crisis?

One of the most common measures for rebuilding the company's reputation is for the management of the company to assume responsibility. If it can be proven that a manager has committed a culpable act, or neglected to perform an action, then their dismissal is almost unavoidable. Even if they have behaved correctly, these types of scandal often result in the person in question taking "political responsibility"—meaning being dismissed or advised to voluntarily retire in order to facilitate a fresh start, or to satisfy political pressure from shareholders. Such a move satisfies the public need for somebody to be made personally culpable for the offense and impacts on newsworthy personalities who have already been forced into the media spotlight due to the scandal.

The company's loss of reputation often, therefore, results in a loss of reputation for those actively involved and stretches far beyond the actual financial losses. In these times of increasingly comprehensive corporate governance obligations, there is a clear necessity to fill responsible positions only with people of proven integrity. Now, more than ever before, the reality is that becoming entangled in a fraud or corruption scandal will, without fail, result in the end of a person's career. In view of the liability regulations (only partially) described above, what supervisory board wants to risk appointing a "rotten egg" to the management board? Even when it contradicts the legal philosophy of fines and social rehabilitation, involvement in a case of loss and the resulting political responsibility invariably continue to have an effect throughout a person's entire working life.

1.1.6 Digression: Protection in the Form of D&O and Fidelity Insurance

In principle, it is possible to limit the liability of managers through contractually secured exemption. However, as described above, the legislation increasingly promotes the enforcement of liability claims against management personnel, meaning there are limits placed on this approach. Therefore, a common solution is to take out so-called "D&O insurance." In the USA, this type of insurance is standard across the board, while in Germany it is used at least by large companies (see Paetzmann 2008, p. 181). So-called "fidelity insurance" is also, in the broadest sense, a credit insurance like a D&O policy. However, fidelity insurance provides significantly greater offense-related protection in the event of loss due to fraud, embezzlement, theft, a breach of trust, malicious damage, or sabotage—practically all actions that require a claim for damages in accordance with Article 823 of BGB. The term "fidelity insurance" is used here because it primarily provides insurance for those actions carried out by persons in the company who hold positions of trust with corresponding authorization—thus not necessarily the same client base as for D&O insurance.

D&O stands for Directors and Officers, meaning the company bodies and executive personnel, or precisely those people under threat from liability claims in accordance with Article 9 of OWiG. As a personal liability insurance for financial losses, D&O insurance provides cover for cases of internal liability to the company and also external liability, for example, to shareholders in the event of an infringement of obligations by the insured party. In contrast to the USA, the focus in Germany is placed primarily on internal liability to the company. The historical development of D&O insurance policies has not been without some controversy—because they could free managers from their responsibilities and, thus, potentially encourage a lax attitude to corporate governance. On the other hand, a disproportionately high risk of liability can, in turn, result in an equally undesirable preoccupation with risk avoidance. In addition, there is also the fact that the levels of compensation sought are often far in excess of the private assets held by the manager and, therefore, effectively unenforceable. Therefore, a consensus has been reached where taking out insurance has created an appropriate balance between risk and reward, while at the same time covering any possible claims for compensation (see Paetzmann 2008, p. 188). The German Corporate Governance Code recommends agreeing an excess for this type of insurance so that managers are not completely released from all liability.

D&O insurance has some special features in comparison to other types of liability insurance. One feature that should be mentioned, in particular, is the "claims-made" principle. While other personal liability insurance policies are based on the loss-occurrence principle, in which claims resulting from events during the insurance period are refunded, D&O insurance only covers claims that are asserted during the insurance period. In practice, this can result in serious problems. Therefore, it is sensible and normal to also negotiate subsequent insurance and, if required, extra cover for an earlier period within the insurance contract. Experience has shown that D&O insurers are highly unwilling to pay in serious cases. It is only in a rare number of cases that contractually stipulated claims are settled without any problems. A common occurrence in practice is that insurers cite incorrect information that the management board are supposed to have provided during the conclusion of the legal proceedings (see Werle 2006).

Yet even when a D&O insurance policy has been carefully drafted, it never offers complete protection against liability claims. Nobody should fall under this illusion.

The reason for this is that crimes committed through willful intent, gross negligence, or conscious neglect of duty are generally not covered by the insurance. Furthermore, compensation claims can also exceed the agreed insurance cover in extreme cases. As the level of compensation claims for antitrust infringements alone can reach into the hundreds of millions of euros, D&O insurance cover is quickly exhausted and supervisory boards have to make civil claims for the outstanding amount from (ex) members of the management board. After all, they would in turn make themselves liable and guilty of a breach of trust if they didn't.

1.2 Relevant Legislation and Its History

White-collar crime is an inseparable part of economic activity. It is likely that less than a week elapsed following the invention of the scales before the first malefactor contemplated manipulating the weights, or before the first counterfeit money appeared after the introduction of coins. Corruption is perhaps even older still because it doesn't even require any technical skill for a decision-maker to obtain personal benefits by disregarding the well-being of the community. Thus, economic history also chronicles the game of cat and mouse that has endured throughout the ages between deception and honesty, or crime and the law. In this context, it is almost inevitable that crime sets the pace that legislators, enforcement authorities, and, not least, supervisory persons in companies and organizations attempt to follow.

An overview of the particularly relevant legal innovations in the fight against white-collar crime consequently document the history of misconduct, as well as the minor and major scandals that will be presented below.

1.2.1 The Beginnings: Tulip Mania and the South Sea Bubble

As far back as the early eighteenth century, the mechanisms of stock exchange trading were utilized to trigger speculative bubbles and exploit the enormous growth in value just before they burst. The process for creating this type of pre-industrial bubble was apparent at the latest after the Dutch Tulip Mania in 1636/1637. The price of tulip bulbs increased fourfold in the Netherlands between the middle of November 1636 and the start of February 1637, before it then abruptly collapsed again. Those dealers who were left holding their bulbs—which could be as expensive as a luxury property—when the bubble burst, or who were obligated to fulfill "futures contracts" at maximum prices risked losing their entire assets. In the end, a solution was found in which most purchase contracts could be annulled on payment of a fine.

In the case of the South Sea Bubble at the London Stock Exchange (1720), the hope of achieving spectacular profits from overseas trade was maliciously exploited to sell securities that would in reality never yield dividends. The almost simultaneous Mississippi Bubble at the Paris Stock Exchange followed a similar pattern. Prices and demand drove each other reciprocally upwards until the value of shares in the South Sea Company had risen almost eightfold. However, when the bubble burst after the failure to pay the first dividends, shareholders were ruined and a recession was triggered across the whole country. Even the highly learned scholar Isaac Newton was not able to see through the swindle and lost £20,000 of his savings.

Although not quite so broad in scope, the Great Stock Exchange Fraud of 1814 was perhaps even bolder in nature. The value of British government securities was temporarily inflated as a result of deliberately spread reports of the supposed death of Napoleon. The men behind the swindle rejoiced over the spectacular profits, while the popular naval hero Lord Cochrane, who was alleged to have spread the rumor, temporarily lost his aristocratic title and his rank of admiral as a result. Although the markets were constantly faced with irregularities, and corruption in Great Britain at the time of the Napoleonic Wars had reached alarming levels, the legislators still remained largely inactive.

It was only in 1889 with the Public Bodies Corrupt Practices Act[11] that the first law was introduced making any form of bribery of public officials a crime. This law remained the only basis for fighting corruption in Britain outside of common law until the UK Bribery Act came into force in 2010.

It wasn't until the stock market crash of 1929,[12] which started in the USA and triggered a worldwide economic crisis, that a broad range of legislation for controlling the finance sector was introduced. The Banking Act (2nd Glass-Steagall Act) introduced on June 16, 1933, by US President Franklin D. Roosevelt prescribed the institutional separation of deposit/lending business and investment business—precisely the breakup of commercial and investment banking that is currently being discussed again today in Germany. This division was designed to prevent the catastrophic interaction between collapsing stock market prices and defaults on loans, as had been observed in the Great Depression after 1929. The Glass-Steagall Act remained in force for more than six decades and was only replaced in 1999 by President Clinton with the Gramm-Leach-Bliley Act. In combination with a series of other liberalization measures for the financial markets, it laid the foundations for the financial crisis of 2008/2009 that quickly triggered calls for a return to the politics of the Glass-Steagall Act.

The Securities Act of 1933 and the Securities Exchange Act of 1934 were directly aimed at stock market transactions. Stock market legislation had been the responsibility of the individual US federal states up to this point, and was thus inconsistent. Share issuers had only been prevented from promising everything under the sun by the so-called "Blue Sky Laws." However, uniform federal laws now came into effect from 1933. The Securities Act defined comprehensive disclosure obligations in the issuing of new shares and criminalized the provision of incorrect information or fraud in stock market flotations. These regulations were further tightened 1 year later by the Securities Exchange Act. The regulations not only covered stock market flotations but rather all stock market transactions. All stock market and securities traders also now had to be officially registered. A newly created authority was responsible for enforcement and thus for the effectiveness of

[11] An Act for the more effectual Prevention and Punishment of Bribery and Corruption of and by Members, Officers, or Servants of Corporations, Councils, Boards, Commissions, or other Public Bodies, August 30,1889.

[12] The already faltering share prices on the New York Stock Exchange fell dramatically on October 24, 1929 (commonly known as "Black Friday," although it actually occurred on a Thursday). The financial crises triggered a global depression with high levels of unemployment that lasted several years. From the high point of the boom period in September 1929 until the lowest point in summer 1932, the Dow Jones index hardly regained more than a tenth of its previous value.

the law in practice. The United States Securities and Exchange Commission (SEC) still checks all securities transactions to this day for their compliance, and possesses comprehensive legislative, executive, and judicial expertise above and beyond state boundaries, as well as currently employing a staff of 3,000 employees. The responsibilities of the SEC were extended again to include bonds and investment funds in 1939 and 1940, respectively.

1.2.2 Foreign Corrupt Practices Act: Starfighter and Bananagate

While the transparency of securities business in the USA was significantly improved by the Securities Exchange Act, there was a lack of correspondingly tough regulations dealing with the bribery of politicians and public officials. It again required public scandals in this area before the legislators were forced to act. In the case of the Foreign Corrupt Practices Act (FCPA), the trigger was a series of international bribery cases that led to serious problems between the USA and their western trading partners in the 1970s. Many of these cases of bribery only initially became known following the Watergate Scandal during the Nixon administration and the subsequent investigations.

The widespread use of bribery at this time was demonstrated by the fact that more than 400 US companies openly admitted to having used bribery as a tool for promoting their international business. In total, more than US$300 million was paid out in bribes. This would be worth billions of dollars today. As a result of the introduction of the FCPA, the USA was the first industrialized nation in the world to make cross-border bribery and corruption a crime.

In this context, the Lockheed scandal was a particularly important milestone. The aircraft manufacturer spiraled into financial difficulties in 1971 and could only be saved by state guarantees for loans totaling over US$195 million. However, the rescue package included obligatory checks of the company's accounts and transaction history by the Government Emergency Loan Guarantee Board. Once these investigations had been completed in 1976, it became clear that Lockheed had paid millions of dollars in bribes to promote the international sales of the F-104 Starfighter and the C-130 Hercules transport aircraft. A large proportion of the files had already been destroyed at this point so that not all of the money flows could be substantiated. Bribery allegations against Franz Josef Strauß, the German Federal Minister of Defense at the time, were thus dropped and allegations against Prince Bernhard of the Netherlands were also never brought before a court.[13] In contrast, the heads of government in Italy and Japan lost their positions as a direct consequence of this bribery scandal.

[13] The body of evidence against Prince Bernhard was quite overwhelming, there was allegedly even a personal letter from the Prince to Lockheed in which he requested the transfer of a provision to the value of US$1.1 million. However, following a major intervention by the Queen of the Netherlands who threatened to abdicate the throne, the court case was subsequently dropped. In return, Prince Bernhard stepped down from all public offices on August 26, 1976.

In the same period during the middle of the 1970s, the so-called "Bananagate Scandal" also occurred. In this case, a state investigation was triggered by the suicide of United Brands company boss Eli M. Black, who had fallen to his death from the 40th floor of the Pan Am Building in New York on February 3, 1975. It transpired that the fruit distributor United Brands (formerly United Fruit, now called Chiquita Brands) had paid a total of US$2.5 million to the Honduran State President Oswaldo López Arellano in order to achieve a reduction in the export duties on bananas. Honduras lowered the duties from 50 cents to 25 cents per crate, not only saving United Brands millions of dollars but also causing the breakdown of the dominant banana producing cartel at the time "Unión de Países Exportadores de Banano" (UPEB). The investigation carried out by the SEC determined that keeping these bribes secret from the United Brand shareholders was an infringement against the duty of transparency by the company. The bribes themselves were not, however, unlawful according to US law at the time. The signing of the FCPA by President Jimmy Carter on December 19, 1977, introduced one of the most important anticorruption laws in economic history to date and made bribing foreign public officials a crime for the first time.

In its definition of beneficiaries, the law limits its scope to serving officials, although the target group ranges from chairmen of political parties, politicians, and civil service employees through to all employees engaged in public service. All other definitions cast a decidedly wider net. Therefore, the term "payor" encompasses civil service employees, companies including their employees and shareholders, as well as private persons in the USA. The law also covers inciting third parties to undertake bribery. Beyond the borders of the USA, companies from other countries can also be impacted and fall under the jurisdiction of the FCPA. For example, if they have a subsidiary in the USA, are listed on the US stock exchange, or use US communication channels for their activities. In the strictest sense, it is merely sufficient for them to pay bribes in US dollars in order to be liable in accordance with the FCPA.

Those people described above are forbidden by the FCPA to make, offer, or promise payments in order to convince a foreign public official to facilitate the completion of a business transaction for a company or person, continue with a business relationship, or hand over business to a third party. This does not only involve public contracts, but more importantly, covers all forms of business right down to the conclusion of business transactions with private individuals. However, it continues to be permissible—although it may be prohibited by law in the beneficiary country—to make payments designed solely to accelerate legally compliant processes. These are known as "facilitation payments."

A second part of the law is important for the enforcement of the FCPA, and obligates companies to carry out their accounting processes in accordance with 15 USC Article 78 m (Periodical and other Reports). This includes complete and transparent bookkeeping that reflects all transactions made by the company and which is monitored by a suitable internal control system.

Once this law had come into force, a large number of companies both in the USA and abroad were prosecuted for violations of the FCPA. A particularly spectacular example was the action taken against Siemens in which the company was issued with a fine of US$450 million for bribing public officials and the systematic concealment of these payments by its accounting department—this is still the highest punishment handed out to date in an FCPA case.[14] Similar action brought against Daimler AG 2 years later was settled following a payment of US$93.6 million. The FCPA has up to now had a massive effect on business conducted by and with American firms due to the notable consistency with which it has been implemented by the United States Department of Justice (DOJ) and the SEC.

The FCPA was adapted to comply with the anticorruption guidelines of the OECD (Organization for Economic Co-operation and Development)[15] through the International Anti-Bribery Act in 1998. In doing this, the USA responded to complaints within their indigenous economy that they were disadvantaged by the FCPA in comparison to countries with laxer regulations. Instead of relaxing the regulations, the USA initiated a working group at OECD level to harmonize international regulations, which jointly developed the anticorruption regulations. Alongside all of the OECD members, Argentina, Brazil, Bulgaria, and South Africa also joined the convention.

What effect has the FCPA had on the personal liability of managers? According to American corporate criminal law, the maximum possible fine according to the FCPA is US$2 million. Natural persons are liable for a maximum of US$100,000 per infringement of the law and face a maximum of 5 years in prison (see Bitzer in Hlavica et al. 2011, p. 256). Nevertheless, significantly higher fines, prison sentences, and profit disgorgement settlements are possible in individual cases. According to the guidelines issued by the US Office of Management and Budget, action brought in accordance with the FCPA already provides sufficient grounds for permanently excluding individual companies from the American market. For example, in the form of blacklists in the award of public contracts and the withdrawal of export licenses.

1.2.3 Sarbanes-Oxley Act: Criminal Energy and Creative Accounting

The new millennium brought a series of major balance sheet manipulations and fraud scandals that dragged the whole economy both in the USA and abroad into serious financial difficulties. It all began with the Enron scandal in 2001. Enron was formed as a result of the fusion of the natural gas companies Houston Natural Gas and Internorth (Omaha) in 1985. The energy company initially focused on the operation of gas pipelines but later became increasingly active as a gas trader and rose quickly to become the market leader in the USA and Great Britain. The

[14] As of: January 2013.

[15] Title of the regulation: Convention on Combating Bribery of Foreign Public Officials in International Business Transactions.

deregulation of the American gas market in 1992 provided the company with more impetus due to the removal of price controls and quality specifications. Enron earned a reputation as both an innovative and profitable company with a constant stream of new energy-based and financial services products. Enron was considered the darling of Wall Street for a long time and the epitome of a model company—while there was hardly any trace of the criminal forces at work beneath the surface.

However, the situation changed dramatically in 2001. The SEC placed the accountancy department at Enron under the microscope. In October, the company had to admit that they had declared excess profits totaling US$1.2 billion. Enron then filed for protection from creditors in December but not before the company had quickly issued bonuses at an executive management level amounting to hundreds of millions of dollars. The investigation into the scandal clearly demonstrated that the innovative ingenuity at the company had increasingly shifted to its accounting practices. Through the development of an almost bewildering network of countless subsidiaries in stunning offshore locations and the exceedingly creative booking of expenses and profits from forwards contracts, it was possible to simulate fictitious profits and capital growth of billions of dollars. Shares valued at US$70 billion were wiped out by the company's insolvency, while only US$7.1 billion was paid out in settlements. The Board of Directors at Enron was sentenced to make compensation payments totaling US$168 million. Around US$13 million had to be settled from their private assets, while the remainder was covered by D&O insurance. In addition, a number of managers were handed prison sentences. Jeffrey Skilling, the Chairman of the Board, was hit the hardest with a prison sentence of 24 years and 4 months. Enron founder Kenneth "Kenny" Lay died of a heart attack shortly before the pronouncement of the court's judgment. He could probably have expected a sentence of around 45 years in prison. Right up until shortly before the collapse of the company, Lay was still being celebrated as an entrepreneurial genius and the American epitome of a self-made man.

The auditing company employed by Enron also didn't escape scot-free, as they played a key role in the pending legal proceedings. Arthur Andersen LLP, still one of the big five auditing companies at the time, ceased their business activities and the company was disbanded as a result of accusations that they had hindered the investigations by destroying files.

One year after the Enron scandal, a similarly catastrophic bankruptcy occurred at the company WorldCom. The telecommunications company had been founded back in 1983 as Long Distance Discount Services, Inc. The company was renamed LDDS WorldCom in 1995 after the merger with Advantage Companies Inc. and the simultaneous share flotation. The name was then later changed to WorldCom. As a result of its aggressive acquisition policy, the company rose to become the second-largest telecommunications supplier in the USA, and it achieved a similar market position in the growth market of the Internet. The acquisition of MCI in 1998, which was valued at US$37 billion, is to date the largest corporate merger in US history. The planned merger with the Sprint Corporation in 1999 would have been even larger, but it was not possible to finalize the proposed US$129 billion deal due to political pressure in the USA and Europe. In the new millennium, telecommunications companies were faced with considerably trickier conditions. The fabulous profit figures to which WorldCom had become accustomed could now only be achieved through elaborate manipulations of the books and balance sheets—to a level of US$11 billion in total. The first signs of these problems hidden in the balance sheets became clear when CEO Bernard Ebbers requested corporate loans totaling US$400 million as security for the financing of his private activities. Ultimately, the falsification of the balance sheets at WorldCom was exposed by internal auditors and made public, despite the resistance of their superiors who were embroiled in the scandal. Bernard Ebbers had already resigned before the fraud was uncovered, the CFO Scott Sullivan was then fired, and David Myers from controlling more or less resigned voluntarily. Once the problems with the balance sheets became known, shares in WorldCom plummeted, and the company filed for bankruptcy protection in July 2002.

In the bankruptcy proceedings, the company initially paid US$750 million to the SEC to settle creditors' claims. The company later agreed to pay a civil penalty of US$2.25 billion. Bernard Ebbers was also sentenced to 25 years in prison in the end.

Both the Enron and WorldCom scandals demonstrated that the regulatory mechanisms created after the Great Depression of 1929 were no longer sufficient to tame the now significantly more complex economy. And Enron and WorldCom were by no means isolated cases. In the years before and after the turn of the millennium, a multitude of balance sheet manipulations and investment fraud scandals were revealed in the USA and Europe. Here is a just a small selection: AOL—due to artificially inflated prices, the mortgage bank Freddie Mac reported lower profits in their books to evade taxes, and the Italian food corporation Parlamat siphoned off 8 billion euros from their own balance sheet to the Cayman Islands. These scandals and balance sheet manipulations resulted in calls for legislators to take action and attempt to re-establish the trust that had been lost among shareholders and investors.

The accounting transparency demanded by the Securities Exchange Act of 1934—the implementation of which was largely left to the companies themselves—had plainly turned into a farce. The legislators sought to provide assistance in the form of significantly more concrete regulations in the areas of transparency and control mechanisms. The basis for this transformation was signed on July 30, 2002, by President George W. Bush: the Sarbanes-Oxley Act—named after its architects Paul S. Sarbanes and Michael Oxley.

This law was a direct response to the experiences gained from the recent scandals and, to this day, encroaches deep into existing legislation in order to re-establish trust among shareholders in the reporting of listed companies, and the checking of this reporting by auditing firms.

The Sarbanes-Oxley Act applies to all companies whose securities are traded or offered in the USA either on-market or off-market, as well as to their subsidiaries. The 66-page law is divided into 11 sections (titles). The first two sections of the law deal with auditing companies. An independent supervisory authority called the Public Company Accounting Oversight Board (PCAOB) was thus created to supervise the auditing companies. In addition, the act reduces possible conflicts of interest by forbidding the provision of non-audit services and establishing a principle for the rotation of auditors. Section 3 makes the management of the company personally responsible for compliance. For example, the CEO and CFO are required to certify the correctness of the published figures and the efficiency of the control mechanisms every quarter. This declaration holds the same weight as a statement made under oath and is backed up by significant criminal and civil sanctions.

Section 10 supplements section 4 by stipulating that a company's tax return must also be certified by the CEO. The greatest financial and organizational costs for the company are generated by section 4, which deals with extended reporting and control regulations. For example, companies now also have to disclose all off-balance sheet transactions and liabilities with nonconsolidated business units relevant to the company's performance. Furthermore, a "suitable" internal control system must be established that reviews the proper preparation of these financial statements. Management responsibilities now include ensuring the effectiveness of this compliance management system, reporting any possible issues, and certifying the report issued by the auditor of the annual accounts. Sections 5–7 deal with the role of analysts and the SEC, but do not have any direct effects on the organization of the company. In contrast, sections 8[16], 9[17], and 11[18] are once again directly relevant because they classify numerous infringements against the regulations in the law as criminal offenses, and generally increase the punishability of white-collar crime.

The Sarbanes-Oxley Act represents the most radical shift in transparency legislation in the USA since the Securities Act and the Securities Exchange Act of 1933/1934. Its scope stretches far beyond the USA and it has also had significant effects on the reporting and auditing practices in the member states of the EU. In the first instance, all companies active in American financial centers are directly affected by the regulations. Furthermore, after the law had been signed, significant pressure to conform to the regulations developed at a political level leading to comparable legislation being introduced outside the USA. For example, Japan has passed corresponding laws that are known as J-SOX after the common abbreviation SOX for the Sarbanes-Oxley Act. The EU also introduced a directive that is commonly known under the name Euro-SOX (see Official Journal of the European Communities 2006). The initial role of the Euro-SOX directive was to restore the weakened confidence of investors in the truthfulness of company reporting and auditing processes in Europe. In addition, it also had the specific aim of clarifying and strengthening legal standards to such an extent that the European auditing standards would be recognized in the USA by the PCAOB. The newly created regulatory committee called the "Committee on Auditing" supports the implementation of the directive in member states. In Germany,

[16] Corporate and Criminal Fraud Accountability Act of 2002.

[17] White Collar Crime Penalty Enhancement Act of 2002.

[18] Corporate Fraud Accountability Act of 2002.

Euro-SOX was implemented through a series of new laws. In particular, this includes the Auditor Oversight Act (Abschlussprüferaufsichtsgesetz—APAG)[19] and the Professional Oversight Reform Act (Berufsaufsichtsreformgesetz—BARefG),[20] which strengthen the laws governing the auditing profession and its professional oversight. The German Accounting Law Reform Act (Bilanzrechtsreformgesetz—BilReG)[21] is focused directly at company level and stipulates that reporting at publicly traded companies must be completed in accordance with the International Financial Reporting Standard (IFRS); other companies are also authorized to use this form of reporting. Furthermore, BilReG extends the scope of reporting requirements, as well as the role and responsibilities of the auditor.

In the Aftermath of SOX: Whistleblower Protection It is not a rare occurrence for white-collar crime to be deeply embedded within the corporate culture where it is tolerated or even promoted. Loyalty to the company—as desirable as it is in other contexts—leads here to a conspiracy of silence along the lines of the omertà, which is sometimes reminiscent of the infamous "honor-based organizations" in Italy. In addition, there is the fact that it is possible to move significant sums of money through corruption or manipulation of the financial accounts. The pressure to stay silent within these old boy networks is thus immense, even in cases where people are not seeking any personal enrichment themselves. Therefore, detecting and proving white-collar crime depends on the meticulous tracking of business transactions and money flows—a feasible and well-founded process, but one also requiring considerable effort. It would be much quicker to focus the spotlight on dubious practices if concrete information about the affected company or institution existed. It is possible that this type of denunciation can occur due to resentment but, as a general rule, so-called "whistleblowers" act out of ethical conviction or loyalty to their company, whose success and reputation they do not wish to see tarnished. In the previously mentioned major scandals of recent times, internal whistleblowers played a decisive role in detecting the crimes and unraveling the web of lies. For example, Cynthia Cooper (Vice President Internal Audit) uncovered the falsification of the balance sheets at WorldCom and made them public despite considerable resistance from within the company. In the case of the Enron scandal, Sherron Watkins (Vice President Corporate Development) played a similar role. These two women and another whistleblower Coleen Rowley, who publicly revealed irregularities at the FBI, were named as Persons of the Year by TIME Magazine in 2002 (see Richard and Ripley 2002). However, public recognition is only one side of the coin. A whistleblower's career often ends in total collapse. They are bullied, fired, sued, and driven to financial ruin—if not even to suicide. In response

[19] Law to further develop the professional oversight of auditors in the German Law Regulating the Profession of Auditors (Wirtschaftsprüferordnung) of December 27, 2004.

[20] Law to strengthen the professional oversight and reform the professional rules in the German Law Regulating the Profession of Auditors (Wirtschaftsprüferordnung) of September 3, 2007.

[21] Law to introduce international accounting standards and ensure the quality.

to the experiences of these early whistleblowers, the first whistleblower legislation was consequently passed.

The Whistleblower Protection Act introduced in 1989 attempted to resolve the dilemma between these people's image as role models or traitors to some extent. It protects those whistleblowers working in US federal agencies against discrimination when they expose misconduct by their employers such as legal violations, wastage, and abuse of authority. However, the Whistleblower Protection Act has proven somewhat disappointing in practice. In accordance with a ruling by the Supreme Court in 2006 (see Cornell University Law School 2006), the exposed misconduct may not originate from within the direct sphere of the whistleblower's professional duties. In addition, complaints filed due to the discrimination of whistleblowers have been mostly rejected by the responsible agencies (Office of Special Counsel, Merit Systems Protection Board and Court of Appeals for the Federal Circuit). Following a number of attempts, the Whistleblower Protection Enhancement Act (WEPA—p. 743) was finally passed at the end of 2012. It aims to further improve the legal situation with regard to whistleblowers in public service.

Surprisingly, the situation in the private sector is more favorable due to the existence of a very old law. The prevalence of corruption and other white-collar crime during the American Civil War prompted President Abraham Lincoln to introduce the False Claims Act (often also known as the Lincoln Act) in 1863. This law permits a citizen to initiate proceedings in the name of the state if they are aware that a third party has made false claims against the state. In the event of success, the person bringing the lawsuit stands to receive between 15 and 25 % of the recovered amounts as a qui tam payment. A similar method is used by the Whistleblower Informant Award from the US revenue service, the IRS, in which informants are even awarded a premium of up to 30 % of the recovered amount. For example, the banker Bradley Birkenfeld received US$104 million in August 2012 because he supported the agency in its investigations against his employer UBS. The fact that Birkenfeld was himself implicated in the affair and subsequently sentenced to a prison sentence of 40 months as part of a state witness ruling was irrelevant.

1.2.4 Dodd-Frank Act: Shackling the Banks?

The financial crisis of 2007/2008 also demonstrated the urgent need in the USA for stricter regulations in the banking sector. During the Subprime crisis of 2007, the investment bank Bear Sterns initially experienced serious liquidity problems and was taken over by J. P. Morgan. Lehman Brothers then collapsed into bankruptcy in 2008, triggering a global economic crisis—the consequences of which are still being felt to this day. The Dodd-Frank Act[22] signed by President Barack Obama on

[22] Full name: Dodd-Frank Wall Street Reform and Consumer Protection Act.

July 21, 2010, is designed to prevent future financial crises of this type. The law is designed to increase transparency in the financial sector and put an end to the practice—which is also common in Germany—of rescuing banks that are "relevant to the system" using state assistance and, not least, to protect consumers from abusive practices in the area of financial services. The law is extraordinarily comprehensive in nature at almost 850 pages in length. Similar to the formation of the PCAOB with the Sarbanes-Oxley Act, the Dodd-Frank Act created a new agency to monitor the financial market—the Financial Stability Oversight Council. Other institutions were also created for the insurance market. Proprietary trading by banks and their involvement in highly speculative types of investment has been limited, while a state-regulated winding down procedure for those banks that nevertheless experience difficulties has been defined.

Whether the Dodd-Frank Act can sustainably shackle the unbridled speculation engaged in by banks remains to be seen.

1.2.5 UK Bribery Act: Well-Oiled Arms Trade

Another important development in legislation dealing with manager liability was introduced in Great Britain, which had not been spared from its own corruption scandals and was forced to respond with corresponding laws. Europe's largest armaments company BAE Systems came under scrutiny from the Serious Fraud Office (SFO) in 2009, because they were suspected of bribery in a diverse range of international arms deals in the 1990s. Similar accusations had already been made back in 2006 about the sale of fighter jets to Saudi Arabia. However, the court case was dropped due to concerns about national security interests. There were also no prosecutions as a result of the new investigation. BAE reached an agreement with the prosecuting authorities to end the investigation in return for the payment of fines totaling £286 million (327 million euros) of which £257 million was paid to the USA and £30 million to Great Britain. The chief executive of the company Mike Turner stepped down in October 2010—citing age reasons. However, the court case and the relatively generous treatment of BAE created such a sensation that amendments to the legislation were required to prevent any future scandals. Not least due to the massive international pressure from those countries that, in comparison to Great Britain, had already introduced restrictive laws against bribery and corruption. This included, in particular, the USA with the FCPA and Germany with the International Bribery Act introduced in 1999.

Great Britain certainly had some legislative ground to make up at the time of the BAE scandal. More than 120 years after the introduction of the Public Bodies Corrupt Practices Act, the UK Bribery Act was designed to provide new foundations for fighting corruption in Great Britain.

The UK Bribery Act came into force on July 1, 2011. It can be viewed as the British counterpart to the FCPA and is considered one of the strictest anticorruption laws in the world. For example, it includes extremely far-reaching regulations for the punishment of bribery. The UK Bribery Act covers every form of bribery that attempts to obtain or retain business, or to achieve an advantage in the execution of business transactions. In contrast to the FCPA, it also encompasses facilitation payments and is not limited just to the bribery of public officials. Even merely offering to pay a corresponding bribe is punishable by law, while the possible fines are unlimited.

Offenders can be both natural persons and companies, while the scene of the crime could be any country in the world. The only prerequisite for criminal liability according to the UK Bribery Act is that there exists a "sufficiently close business connection" to Great Britain. This is often the case if the person acting in this context is a British citizen or the company is based in Great Britain. However, it is also sufficient for the company to be trading actively in Great Britain or for the business to use British services such as bank accounts or have an Internet presence in the country. If the business connection is deemed to be sufficient, every action that would be liable to prosecution in Great Britain is also punishable worldwide and can thus be pursued globally. This could also include the involvement of British agencies in Germany. Protection against criminal prosecution is solely and exclusively provided by the implementation of a suitable compliance management system. In this context, the Ministry of Justice and the Serious Fraud Office have clearly outlined the requirements they set for the adequate procedures that need to be provided by such a system in two guidance papers. The UK Bribery Act handles so-called "third-party due diligence" in much greater detail than the transatlantic and German legislation. It stipulates that all business partners must be included in an integrity check. As a result, managers are directly liable for the misconduct of third parties in cross-border trade if they infringe against international corruption legislation.

Although the UK Bribery Act is extremely comprehensive and strict in this area, up to now it has not been backed up by the necessary organizational structures that would be required to also enforce this type of restrictive and encompassing law. In the 2010/2011 financial year, the SFO investigated around 300 persons. However, only 17 cases with 26 convictions were brought to court based on the legislation issued in the UK Bribery Act (see The Stationery Office 2011)—and these figures encompassed the whole scope of white-collar crime. In reality, the law is, at the present time, a predominantly political marketing tool that fulfils the international requirements for consistently fighting corruption. The UK Bribery Act will only assume a position of real significance when it is also implemented in practice, and strictly and consequently executed, as has been seen in Germany and, above all, in the USA with the SEC. Nevertheless, even those companies that have only peripheral business dealings with Great Britain cannot avoid the need to align their compliance management systems with this development in British legislature. Because it is only a matter of time before this legislation will be properly enforced.

1.2.6 Legislation in Germany

The German Federal Government started to seriously deal with the subject of white-collar crime in the middle of the 1970s. The 1st and 2nd Laws on Combating Economic Crime (Gesetz zur Bekämpfung der Wirtschaftskriminalität) were introduced in 1976 and 1986, respectively. They represented a response from the legislators to the changing conditions in economic life. For example, they dealt with fraud involving Eurocheques or credit cards, and also covered, in part, the new field of computer crime. Legislators were given a significant push by the International Anti-Bribery Act, which implemented the anticorruption guidelines from the OECD[23] in US law. The Federal Republic of Germany fulfilled its obligations as a signatory of the guidelines in 1998 with the Law on Combating International Corruption (Gesetz zur Bekämpfung internationaler Bestechung). In addition, clear signals were sent out by the legislators in this context with the German Tax Relief Act (Steuerentlastungsgesetz) of March 24, 1999,[24] which put an end to the practice of offsetting bribery payments to domestic and foreign public officials as "necessary expenditure."

However, a law that is significantly more important in practice than the tightly worded and difficult to implement Law on Combating International Corruption is the German Law on Corporate Governance and Transparency (Gesetz zur Kontrolle und Transparenz im Unternehmensbereich—KonTraG) of March 5, 1998. KonTraG obligated stock corporations (Aktiengesellschaften), companies limited by shares and some forms of GmbH (a company with limited liability in Germany) to introduce a risk management system and include risk reporting in their annual reports. Compliance with this requirement is monitored and reviewed by the auditor. Furthermore, the personal liability of the management board, supervisory board and auditors was extended under both criminal and civil law.

The spectacular bankruptcy of Philipp Holzmann AG in 2002—then one of the world's largest construction companies—provided a further reason for action in the area of corporate governance. Shortly after the company's 150-year anniversary celebrations, financial problems were "discovered" in the previously flawless balance sheets and the company was forced to admit a loss of 2.4 billion DM. All attempts to rescue the company failed and Holzmann filed for insolvency proceedings on March 21, 2002. Even when the question of guilt was never publically resolved, the Holzmann bankruptcy revealed clear deficits in the corporate culture in Germany. A government commission[25] was founded in response to these events, which recommended the development of a "Code of Best Practice" as a self-regulatory measure for the economy. This task was entrusted to another

[23] Convention on Combating Bribery of Foreign Public Officials in International Business Transactions.

[24] BGBl I, p. 402.

[25] Government commission "Corporate Governance—Company Management—Corporate Control—Modernization of the German Corporation Law."

government commission[26] also correspondingly financed by the economy, which issued the German Corporate Governance Code [Deutschen Corporate Governance Kodex (DCGK)] on February 26, 2002. This code continues to function according to the "comply or explain" principle to this day—thus its regulations for good company management must be observed or justification must be explicitly provided for any deviation. If a company deviates from these regulations without providing sufficient justification, it can have serious consequences for the company, such as making resolutions issued by the supervisory board invalid,[27] or nullifying the ratification of any acts carried out by the supervisory board or management board.[28] DCGK is checked on a yearly basis by the responsible government commission and is thus regularly amended.

In addition to strengthening the self-regulation of the economy, German legislators also actively introduced a plethora of individual laws in response to the Dotcom bubble of 2000 and the global financial crisis of 2008/2009. The German Investor Protection Improvement Act (Anlegerschutzverbesserungsgesetz—AnSVG), the German Accounting Law Reform Act (Bilanzrechtsreformgesetz—BilReG), the Extension to the German Securities Trading Act (Erweiterung des Wertpapierhandelsgesetzes—WpHG), the German Law on Financial Reporting Compliance (Bilanzkontrollgesetz—BilKoG), the Auditor Oversight Law (Abschlussprüferaufsichtsgesetz—APAG), the German Act on the Disclosure of Executive Board Remuneration (Vorstandsvergütungs-Offenlegungsgesetz—VorstOG), the Capital Markets Test Case Act (Kapitalanleger-Musterverfahrensgesetz—KapMuG), and the German Law on Corporate Integrity and Modernization of the Right of Rescission (Gesetz zur Unternehmensintegrität und Modernisierung des Anfechtungsrechts—UMAG) came into force in 2004 and 2005 with the aim of improving company transparency, investor protection, and the enforcement of legal regulations. Two further laws followed in 2009 in the form of the German Accounting Law Modernization Act (Bilanzrechtsmodernisierungsgesetz—BilMoG) and the Act on the Implementation of the Shareholders' Rights Directive (Gesetz zur Umsetzung der Aktionärsrechterichtlinie—ARUG). BilMoG was especially important in this area because it introduced a comprehensive revision of the processes for carrying out annual reports, financial accounting and annual auditing. Furthermore, the transparency obligations within the framework of corporate governance were extended.

As could be expected from Germany, there have been enormous legislative and regulatory developments over the last 10–15 years. The ability to offset "necessary expenditure"—in other words bribery payments—from tax was abolished, while around the same time the Law on Combating International Corruption was introduced, together creating the fundamental structures within tax and criminal law to make prosecution of any infringements now possible. However, the decisive

[26] Government commission on the "German Corporate Governance Code".

[27] OLG München Az: 7 U 5628/07.

[28] BGH Az: II ZR 174/08.

step was the development of a specialized process for investigating these crimes. This was achieved via a roundabout route—the expertise being initially gained in the 1990s while combating organized crime. The organized crime units in the police force and the criminal investigation bureaus were principally focused on the smuggling of narcotics and any associated criminality, which not least encompassed corruption and money laundering. In this environment, there was no thought given initially to corruption in the issuing of completely legal business contracts. However, the discovery of money laundering activities enabled the financial and crime enforcement authorities concerned to learn how to professionally track money flows in all economic sectors. Stricter control and reporting obligations for the banks further strengthened this very efficient method of investigation.

Even closer monitoring of money flows was introduced following the terrorist attacks of September 11, 2001, in order to trace money used to finance international terrorism. The USA and European countries have since developed a comprehensive catalogue of sanctions that stretch far beyond the original fields of application in narcotics-related crime and terrorism, to now include all areas of the economy. Financial and crime enforcement authorities in Germany have increasingly learned how to effectively implement these standards—it is thus hardly surprising that the key piece of evidence in investigations into white-collar crime is increasingly provided by the financial authorities.

Nevertheless, only a handful of public prosecutor's offices—particularly Munich I headed by Manfred Nötzel, named by Manager Magazine in 2011 as the "keenest sniffer dog around" (see Freisinger and Katzensteiner 2011)—are in a position to uncover complex and comprehensive manipulation of balance sheets or deeply embedded and cleverly concealed white-collar crime. Nötzel's reputation is not without some foundation when you consider the investigations into the activities at Siemens, MAN, Ferrostaal, and BayernLB (Fig. 1.1).

1.3 Social Conditions and Drivers of White-Collar Crime

The social perspective of white-collar crime has changed over the last few years. In particular, the speculative media presence in response to the previously described fraud and corruption cases, as well as those people involved, has led to the development of a very keen social awareness for white-collar crime and corruption. Especially following the financial and banking crises of 2009 and the subsequent currency crisis in Europe, "greedy bankers" have been publicly pilloried and white-collar crime has increasingly become a symbol for social injustice. The manner in which perpetrators of economic crimes are handled has regularly hit the headlines in the tabloid press. Many of these perpetrators ultimately walk away with suspended sentences or go completely unpunished as key state witnesses.

From a consultant's point of view, companies often underestimate the social aspect of this phenomenon when it comes to dealing with these cases themselves. Despite the fact that managers have to deal with a huge number of regulations and

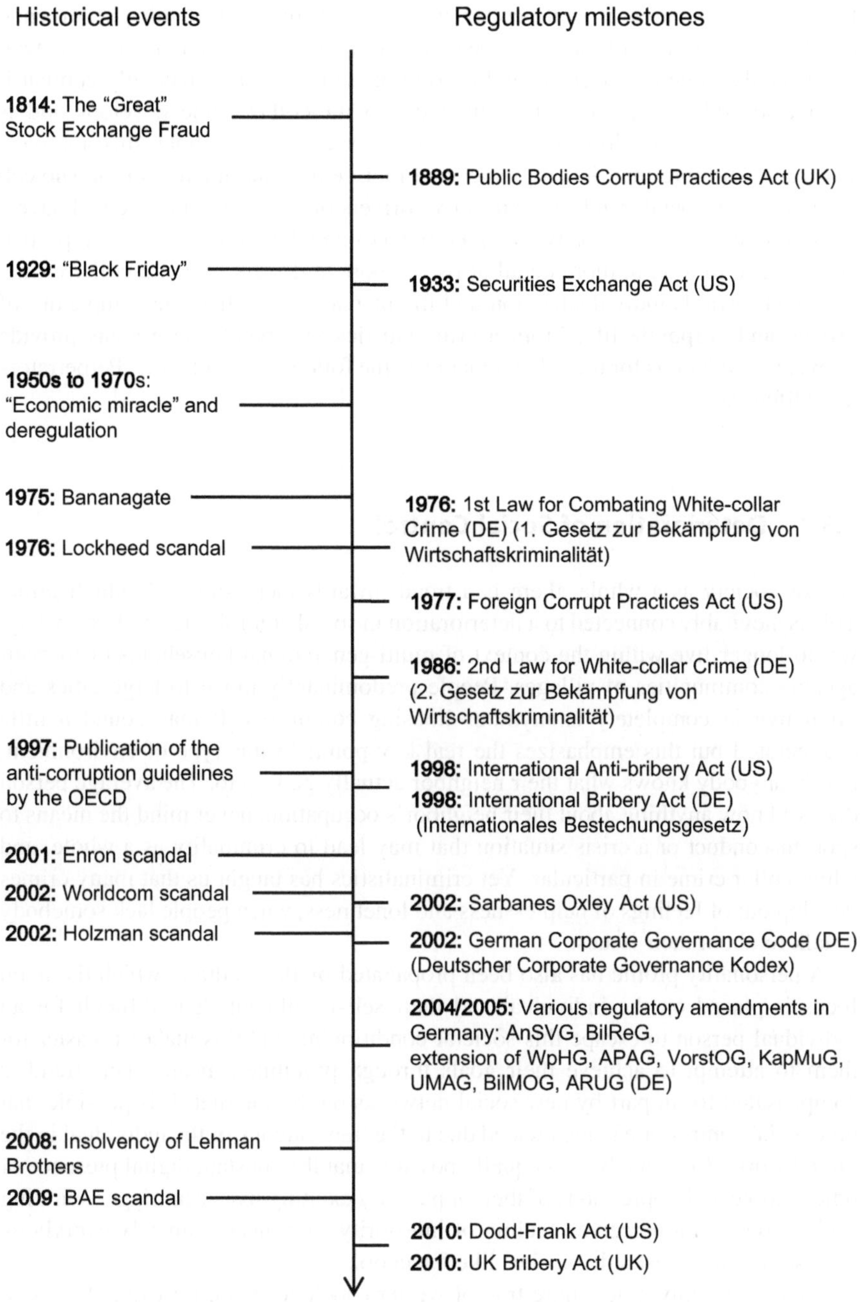

Fig. 1.1 An overview of the regulatory milestones

legislation in the area of white-collar crime and liability issues, this phenomenon also has a very powerful social perspective that shouldn't be ignored. Anybody who understands white-collar crime and corruption and wants to effectively combat it must also address the conditions in which white-collar crime develops and is conceived. If viewed from the perspective of society as a whole, this approach will result in more than just a greater and more emotional interest in the subject. There are also social trends that are active drivers of white-collar crime and have a direct influence on a company's own employees and daily business. It is important at this stage to look in more detail at two important drivers of white-collar crime: the trend towards individualization and the increasingly noticeable complexity of private and corporate life. From a criminalistics viewpoint, these areas provide relevant foundations for the subject matter in the following chapter on "Perpetrators and Offenses."

1.3.1 Deterioration of Social Control

Across society as a whole, there is a trend towards increasing individualization. This is inevitably connected to a deterioration in social control. In a modern society, we no longer live within the context of multi-generational households or in manageable communities of villages. People predominantly move to large cities and often live in completely anonymous housing complexes. It may sound a little exaggerated but this emphasizes the real key point: In this type of environment, hardly anybody knows what their neighbor actually gets up to. The average person doesn't know anything about their neighbor's occupation, never mind the means to spot misconduct or a crisis situation that may lead to criminality as a whole, and white-collar crime in particular. Yet criminalistics has taught us that many crimes develop out of feelings of helplessness and loneliness, when people lack somebody to talk to about their issues.

A personality profile has also been propagated by the media in which the main focus is placed on the individual and their self-fulfillment. It is difficult for an individual person to escape this societal conditioning and this makes it easier for them to attempt to achieve their goals through prohibited means. This trend is compensated for in part by new social networks on the Internet. It is possible that new social controls are being created due to the transparency of the individual in the digital world. Conversely, it is equally possible that the constant digital presence of other people and impressions of their apparently exciting lives can trigger spiraling social envy and a perceived feeling of inferiority—because ultimately everybody only shows their best side on sites like Facebook.

This is certainly much more true of western societies than, for example, Asian societies in which individualization and materialism are not quite so advanced. However, the fact that images of the social dream in advertising, film, and television encourage a clear tendency towards the pursuit of a picture-book career and self-fulfillment is now true for almost every society in the world. Turning to white-collar crime is not an uncommon response for dealing with this social trend and fulfilling the expectations that are omnipresent in the media.

1.3.2 Increasing Complexity

Online registration, tax declarations, general terms and conditions, hundreds of television channels, and seven different types of fish fingers in the supermarket: Life is no longer as easy as it once was. A whole new industry of lifestyle coaching has developed under the motto "Simplify your life." Simplicity is the sales gimmick of our time, from mobile phones to management consultancy.

As banal as it may sound, complexity and excess supply characterize modern life in industrial nations. This has had remarkable effects on the economy. The economist and consultant Friedemund Malik declared in the Handelsblatt newspaper as far back as 2008 that commercial enterprises were "uncontrollable" due to their level of complexity (see Malik 2008). A development that has probably exponentiated even further in the 5 years since the article was published. Why is complexity a driver of white-collar crime? Because complexity creates a lack of transparency. And this lack of transparency offers fraudsters and manipulators niches of uncertainty that they can utilize for their own purpose. How else do literally countless files full of inaccurate technical documentation or manipulated risk assessments reach the hands of supervisory boards and management boards at airport construction companies and major banks? Quite simply due to the complexity and the inability or the lack of will on the part of those people involved to reduce this complexity.

In the case of financial products such as derivatives, the focus is often no longer placed on the actual function of banks—i.e., to provide capital or financial support to companies.

Instead, numerous products are developed with the sole aim of generating more profit margin. Quotations in the industrial sector are also becoming increasingly complex and their concepts have been borrowed in part from the banking sector. A typical feature in this area is the lumping together of sales and financing. For example, there are hardly any offers made anymore for mobile telephones or cars where financing is not directly included in the sale to a lesser or greater extent. This increase in complexity inevitably goes hand in hand with some form of concealment of the qualitative and quantitative characteristics of the product.

Moreover, this level of complexity is exacerbated by the increasing level of networking in the global economy. Inevitably, it is more difficult to monitor a business that is no longer restricted only to the German market but trades globally with a variety of interlinked markets. A range of different legal, and even cultural, conditions contribute to making these structures even more complex.

1.4 Trends in Regulatory and Liability Law

This short history lesson on manager liability and the corresponding legislation has shown that regulatory innovations designed to combat white-collar crime and corruption are almost always reactions to particularly public cases of fraud or corruption scandals. This situation is not likely to change much in the future. More than one horse will have bolted through the proverbial stable door before the most vital areas of the economy become more strictly regulated, on both a national and international scale, and these regulations are also implemented correctly—if this is at all possible. The simple reason for the increasing regulatory pressure is the fact that more crimes are now being detected than in previous years, which are then rapidly made known to the public—not least due to the influence of the Internet—causing quite a stir. Therefore, politicians and governments are simply required to deal with this subject more frequently and pass corresponding legislation.

However, nobody should have any illusions in this area. There is hardly a politician or EU parliamentarian who has placed white-collar crime and combating corruption at the forefront of their agenda—even if public pressure has grown over the last few years. In particular, the global financial and banking crises with their casino-like excesses have raised public awareness for corresponding regulation. Looking ahead to the future, this trend is set to continue—intensified by the many publicized manipulation and corruption cases in recent history, and the continued economic uncertainty across the whole of Europe. This will result in a relatively large number of different fronts where it is already possible to anticipate the need for future regulatory and liability-related innovation. Therefore, the overall focus placed on white-collar crime and corruption, particularly by supervisory boards, needs to be a great deal broader than in the past.

In the medium and long-term, particular attention needs to be paid to the subject areas described below—even if in many cases it is hard to predict the precise legal and thus liability-related implications.

1.4.1 Completing the Legislative Framework for Combating Fraud

Banks have especially suffered from white-collar crime over the last few years, and have often been the subject of corresponding headlines. In particular, the banking sector in London has recently experienced a year of real scandal. Barclays received a 360 million euros fine for the manipulation of the Libor Interbank offered rate, while Standard Chartered and HSBC paid almost two billion euros in fines for money laundering. The bank UBS lost a major part of its management team in London due to the Kweku Adoboli fraud case and was sentenced to pay a fine of 37 million euros—the bank itself lost billions due to the fraudulent activities in its investment sector and was close to bankruptcy.

All of these events suggest that a legislative response can be expected in the area of fraud and manipulation prevention in the future. Practical experience has shown that despite the Sarbanes-Oxley Act, the preventative systems introduced in these companies are not yet up to the standard required to function correctly within highly complex and digitalized company divisions such as investment banking.

While the Sarbanes-Oxley Act places a particular responsibility on auditors, it is to be expected that new legal innovations will introduce stricter regulations for normal operations in companies and daily compliance management—with an increasingly digital perspective. The targeted monitoring of digital company data, in particular, would have certainly made it possible to prevent some of the previously named cases of fraud and money laundering. In Germany, the revised German Data Protection Act (Bundesdatenschutzgesetz) is now applicable in this area.

In the implementation of a preventative system, particularly as part of a compliance management system, a new standard will be established that will have increasing influence on the judicature. Criminal prosecutions will make managers increasingly liable if systems for the early detection of manipulation, money laundering, or terrorist financing are not completely up to date. Even when there is not (yet) explicitly any comprehensive legal basis in this area. This is particularly true for the fight against fraud and corruption, where there is a great deal of catching up to do in the area of legislation and criminal prosecutions.

1.4.2 Stricter International Regulations for Combating Corruption

The rail track cartel, TV and computer screen cartel, interest rates cartel, and TV broadcasting cartel all ensured that the competition watchdogs in Germany and the EU were certainly not left idle in 2011 and 2012. All of these already concluded or pending legal proceedings in the area of international cartelization and price fixing will be reflected to a massive degree in stricter regulations. We can identify a clear trend in this area: international law enforcement is taking the subject of competition seriously. The competition watchdogs across the world are now working in a significantly more structured, professional, and aggressive manner than in previous years. Naturally, they are also motivated by economic policy interests in their home countries.

It is only really the USA and Germany that are currently acting in a consistent manner in this area, although the commitment to combating corruption in Germany is concentrated within a handful of public prosecutor's offices working in line with the American model. The everyday work of management boards will thus be characterized by a significant intensification of the enforcement work as they are increasingly confronted with inquiries and investigations by antitrust officials—for example with so-called "e-discovery" inquiries. According to an EY study (see Ernst and Young 2012) from 2011, only a small fraction of companies are really prepared to deal with these types of inquiries into their electronic data—or are at all capable of handling an investigation. Despite the fact that they are faced with legal consequences and serious fines when there is a delay to the supply of data or if it is not supplied at all.

Stricter criminal prosecutions for antitrust offenses will once again have significant consequences for the whole area of corruption. A long-standing legal hot potato in Germany has been the crime of bribing members of parliament, which is currently regulated in Article 108e of the German Criminal Code (StGB). This states that buying or selling votes is only punishable by law if it is connected to elections or parliamentary votes. This paragraph has been rightly criticized by associations and judges as a blunt sword because it doesn't take into account many other forms of corruption. Politicians offering advantages in the award of public contracts and gaining rewards in the form of money, favors, or donations remain de facto unpunishable according to the current legal situation. As a result of these gaps in the legislation, the Federal Republic of Germany has to this day not been able to ratify the UN convention on corruption from October 31, 2003. Sooner or later there will be calls for further regulation in this area—with businesses now even calling for it themselves.

Another area that will gain importance in the future is combating corruption in business transactions with developing countries and emerging markets, in order to counteract the enormous misallocation of resources. A great deal of money for developing countries has been trickling away into dubious channels for decades without any added value having been created. Cooperation in the area of development projects can only function correctly if this problem is tackled. A similarly urgent goal is to dry up the financing channels for international terrorism. Liability-related innovations are also to be expected, particularly in business relationships in the Middle East and the "Arab Spring" countries, if business partners are not carefully selected in accordance with the concept of third-party due diligence.

As a result of the enduring legal disputes in the area of competition and patent law, legal innovations can also be expected in this field. The dispute between Apple and Samsung is currently setting a precedent in the consumer electronics industry that is sure to point the way forward in future for regulations dealing with the protection and theft of intellectual property.

1.4.3 Regulating Access to Resources

Climate change will create new challenges that will transform the economic framework for nations worldwide. For example, rising water levels could threaten the very existence of some states. And this is no longer only true of idyllic South Pacific atolls, such as Tuvalu or Tonga, but also for more economically relevant countries such as Bangladesh—or even the Netherlands in our immediate neighborhood. In other countries, particularly those near to the Arctic Circle, conditions could, on the other hand, significantly improve if new agricultural land were to be created or if natural resources could be more easily exploited. The global competitive environment will be noticeably changed in the process. Moreover, increasing competitive pressure combined with a simultaneous scarcity of natural resources will in turn become drivers of global white-collar crime that need to be tackled on an international scale. Countries are barely able at present to work constructively together at this level. It has after all hardly been possible to reach a consensus on solutions for the currency and debt crises, even in Europe with its organized community of states. If the problems resulting from climate change become large enough, the Gordian knot will also need to be cut in this area to achieve globally binding laws, along with a system of worldwide enforcement—combined with corresponding regulations and liability rules for managers.

1.4.4 Regulating Social Factors

A further challenge is the development and implementation of social standards. Unhealthy working practices or child labor are still common in developing countries. Many things that are legally prohibited in Germany and are also expressly forbidden in companies according to corporate social responsibility programs still occur at the far end of highly convoluted supply chains. Programs such as the Global Contract from the United Nations represent a first step in the right direction, but they are still overly focused at the level of non-binding declarations of intent for them to prove really helpful in an environment dominated by tangible economic interests. Nevertheless, the hope remains that some binding regulations will soon be drafted in this area—which will then actually be implemented.

Literature

Bundesministerium, der Justiz. (2013). *Aktiengesetz, Sorgfaltspflicht und Verantwortlichkeit der Vorstandsmitglieder (Federal Ministry of Justice: The Stock Corporation Law, Due Diligence and the Responsibilities of Management Board Members)*. Federal Ministry of Justice. Accessed June 24, 2013, from http://www.gesetze-im-internet.de/aktg/__93.html

Cornell University Law School. (2006). *Supreme Court of the United States*, Garcetti et al. v. Ceballos No. 04–473. Cornell University Law School. Accessed June 24, 2013, from http://www.law.cornell.edu/supct/html/04-473.ZS.html

Editorial Team of the Federal Press Office. (2013). *Finanzmarktstabilisierung, Aufbau eines Trennbankensystems (Stabilization of the Financial Market, Development of a Separate Banking System)*. Press Release. Federal Press Office. Accessed May 17, 2013, from http://www.bundesregierung.de/Content/DE/Artikel/2013/02/2013-02-06-trennbankensystem.html

Endemann, Walter, Das Bundesgesetz betreffend die Kommanditgesellschaften auf Aktien, vom 11. Juni 1870, Berlin, aus den Materialien erläutert von Dr. Wilhelm Endemann (The Federal Law Dealing with Partnerships Limited by Shares, from June 11, 1870, Berlin, from material explained by Dr. Wilhelm Endemann) Publishing House Fr. Kortkampf

Ernst & Young. (2012). *Enabling Compliance Welche Rolle spielt Technologie? (What role is played by technology?)*. Ernst & Young GmbH. Accessed June 24, 2013, from http://www.ey.com/Publication/vwLUAssets/Enabling_Compliance/$FILE/Enabling_Compliance_Welche_Rolle_Spielt_Technologie.pdf

Freisinger, G. M., & Katzensteiner, T. (2011). Wirtschaftskriminalität, Die Korruptionsjäger von München I. (White-Collar Crime, The Corruption Hunters from Munich I) *Manager Magazine Online*. Accessed January 15, 2013, from http://www.manager-magazin.de/finanzen/artikel/a-792222.html

Habersack, M., Kalss, S., & Goette, W. (2010). *Münchener Kommentar zum Aktiengesetz (Munich Comment on the German Stock Corporation Law): AktG,* vol. 2, Articles 76–117. Munich: MitbestG, DrittelbG. (German Codetermination Act, German One-Third Employee Participation Act) Beck.

Hlavica, C., Klapproth, U., & Hülsberg, F. M. (2011). *Tax Fraud & Forensic Accounting, Umgang mit Wirtschaftskriminalität (Dealing with White-Collar Crime).* Wiesbaden: Gabler.

Kreft, G., Depré, P., Eickmann, D., Flessner, A., Kayser, G., Keller, U., Kirchhof, H., Kleindiek, D., Landfermann, H., Linck, R., Lohmann, I., Marotzke, W., Ransiek, A., Ries, S., & Stephan, G. (2011). *Insolvenzordnung (Heidelberger Kommentar) (German Insolvency Act (Heidelberge Comment)).* Heidelberg, München, Landsberg, Frechen, Hamburg: C. F. Müller.

Krieger, G., & Schneider, U. H. (2007). *Handbuch Managerhaftung: Risikobereiche und Haftungsfolgen für Vorstand, Geschäftsführer, Aufsichtsrat (Handbook on Manager Liability: Risk Areas and Liability Exposure for Management Boards, Managing Directors, and Supervisory Boards).* Cologne: Dr. Otto Schmidt.

Malik, F. (2008). Herr der Komplexität (Master of Complexity). *Handelsblatt*, Printed Issue from May 2, 2008. Accessed June 24, 2013, from http://www.handelsblatt.com/karriere/mba-news/denkfutter-herr-der-komplexitaet/2956046.html

Moosmayer, K. (2012). *Compliance, Praxisleitfaden für Unternehmen (Compliance, Practical Guidelines for Companies).* Munich: Beck.

Official Journal of the European Union. (2006). *Directive 2006/43/EC of the European Parliament and of the Council* (May 17, 2006 Official Journal of the European Union). Accessed June 24, 2013, from http://eurlex.europa.eu/LexUri-Serv/LexUriServ.do?uri=OJ:L:2006:157:0087:0087:DE:PDF

Ott, K. (2011). *MAN-Korruptionsaffäre, Meutern gegen das alte Management (The MAN Corruption Affair, Mutiny against the Old Management).* 2013. Süddeutsche.de. Accessed June 24, 2013, from http://www.sueddeutsche.de/wirtschaft/man-korruptionsaffaere-pich-gnadenlos-1.1047302-2

Paetzmann, K. (2008). *Corporate Governance, Strategische Marktrisiken, Controlling, Überwachung (Corporate Governance, Strategic Market Risks, Controlling, Monitoring).* Heidelberg: Springer.

Richard, L., & Ripley, A. (2002). Persons of the Year 2002: The Whistleblowers. *TIMES Magazine*. Accessed June 24, 2013, from http://www.time.com/time/specials/packages/0,28757,2022164,00.html

The Stationery Office. (2011). *Serious fraud office annual report and accounts 2010–11*. The stationery office. Accessed June 24, 2013, from http://www.sfo.gov.uk/media/175084/resource-accounts-2010-11.pdf

Werle, K. (2006). Managerhaftung, "Daumenschrauben angezogen" (Manager Liability, "The Thumbscrews Are Being Tightened"). *Manager Magazine Online*. Accessed June 24, 2013, from http://www.manager-magazin.de/unternehmen/karriere/a-421240.html

Perpetrators and Offenses

2

The Origins, Players, and Consequences of White-Collar Crime

"I need a miracle." This was the last Facebook status update sent to date by Kweku Adoboli to his 400 friends on September 13, 2011. The following night at 3:30 a.m. the handcuffs clicked shut around his wrists. The photo of the star banker with his boyish good looks in a lavender-colored pullover, which was handed over to the police in London by UBS, was seen around the world. The 31-year-old investment banker would be responsible at the final reckoning for losses of around US$2 billion at the major Swiss bank.

Yet it all started on a relatively small scale—at least by the standards of an investment bank. Adoboli, who had always dreamed of pursuing a successful investment banking career in the most glamorous financial centers of the world, suffered a US$400,000 trading loss in October 2008. He decided not to register the loss so as not to endanger his meteoric rise at UBS. Instead, he extended the settlement dates for his failed trading activities and thus managed to manipulate his own accounting department and internal controls—in order to buy himself time to cover the loss through other business transactions. His employers were under the impression that Adoboli was bringing in millions of dollars of profit, yet in reality he continued to incur heavy losses. His business transactions became increasingly reckless and more costly, while the illusion he created to try to conceal his manipulation became ever more complex and adventurous. That is until everything fell apart with a bang! It was all uncovered by an unrelenting accountant in the back office, as Adoboli got himself embroiled deeper and deeper in a series of contradictions. The miracle Adoboli so yearned for never materialized and he was found guilty of fraud and sentenced to 7 years in prison in November 2012.

The Adoboli case reveals—in a very vivid and topical manner—a great deal about the nature of white-collar crime, its players, and its consequences, all of which will be presented and reflected upon in this chapter. It is not uncommon for major scandals to start off with small offenses, in whose genesis the personality profile of the perpetrator and his/her motives play a decisive role. Understanding this role and being able to apply the knowledge to the investigation of fraud cases,

S. Heissner, *Managing Business Integrity*, Management for Professionals,
DOI 10.1007/978-3-319-12721-7_2

as well as to all preventative measures, is a fundamental skill required by all those dealing with white-collar crime.

2.1 White-Collar Crime: A Practical Definition

What do we mean precisely when we talk of white-collar crime? The specialist literature and those practically involved in this area are very divided on the matter. The definitions and key features of this term become blurred depending on the relevant academic discipline or the jurisdiction of the relevant authority. Therefore, there is no generally accepted definition upon which all those involved in social science, political science, criminology, and law enforcement can agree (see Heissner 2001, p. 236 ff.). Does white-collar crime mean crime committed in the economy, crime committed by the economy, or crime committed against the economy? And does white-collar crime only deal with actions that can be penalized according to the statute book, or also with other socially damaging behavior?

The sheer complexity of this phenomenon (see Göppinger 1997, p. 541) and the broad range of possible offenses make it difficult to generalize on this subject. Because even if the term white-collar crime itself were clearly defined, there is still no clear differentiation between this term and equally relevant phenomena, such as corruption and antitrust crimes, that—at least in a judicial sense—form their own individual categories.

For the sake of clarity and practical application, this book will refrain from providing an overly theoretical derivation of the term at this point.[1] Instead, a practical working definition will be derived and explained, which will cover everything that managers in the world of business and, by implication, a forensic audit and crime enforcement authorities come across in their work. This method will help to develop a holistic overview of the subject.

2.1.1 Different Aspects for a Comprehensive Understanding of White-Collar Crime

The term white-collar crime can be highly misleading. This is simply because it is so complex and is not uniformly applied as previously mentioned above. The term is eagerly used to describe all manner of different things, from one context to the next, all of which could be encapsulated by the phrase "actions damaging to business." To be sufficiently prepared to tackle liability issues and the debate surrounding them, it makes good sense to delve a little deeper into the material in order to gain an overview of which "actions damaging to business" are designated as legal offenses by lawyers, auditors, district attorneys, and the police, and what is actually meant when it comes to white-collar crime or corruption.

[1] Subject covered by, among others, Heissner (2001, p. 25–31) and Hlavica et al. (2011, p. 84 ff).

It is difficult to develop a comprehensive understanding of the phenomenon of white-collar crime due to the existence of such an enormous range of different offenses—all with countless gradations and variations. Depending on the definition, this can start with interns stealing pens and printer paper out of the office supplies cupboard and definitively ends with complex manipulation of balance sheets and unauthorized market speculation as in the cases of Adoboli and Kerviel. It already becomes clear at this point that some offenses are committed at a superficial level for the company—meaning they initially benefit the company—for example, in some cases of corruption. On the other hand, there are also white-collar crimes that are clearly directed against the company, such as breaches of trust or embezzlement. Because there is no legal definition for the term white-collar crime in Germany, the Federal Criminal Police Office (Bundeskriminalamt—BKA) refers to the purely criminal definition of white-collar crime found in Article 74c of the German Code on Court Constitution (Gerichtsverfassungsgesetz—GVG).[2] This stipulates which court is responsible for handling which offenses and defines practically everything that crime enforcement authorities understand to be white-collar crime in concrete terms. This includes criminal offenses:

1. According to the Patent Act (Patentgesetz), the Industrial Design Act (Gebrauchsmustergesetz), the Semiconductor Protection Act (Halbleiterschutzgesetz), the Plant Variety Protection Law (Sortenschutzgesetz), the Trade Mark law (Markengesetz—MarkenG), the Design Act (Geschmacksmustergesetz), the Copyright Act (Urheberrechtsgesetz—UrhG), the Law Against Unfair Competition (Gesetz gegen den unlauteren Wettbewerb—UWG), the Stock Corporation Law (Aktiengesetz—AktG), the Company Disclosure Law (Gesetz über die Rechnungslegung von bestimmten Unternehmen und Konzernen), Limited Liability Companies Act (Gesetz, betreffend die Gesellschaften mit beschränkter Haftung), the German Commercial Code (Handelsgesetzbuch—HGB), the Law for the Implementation of the EEC Regulation on the European Economic Interest Grouping (Gesetz zur Ausführung der EWG-Verordnung über die Europäische wirtschaftliche Interessenvereinigung), the German Cooperatives Act (Genossenschaftsgesetz), and the Reorganization of Companies Act (Umwandlungsgesetz).
2. According to the laws dealing with the banking, securities, stock market, and credit systems, as well as those according to the Insurance Supervision Act (Versicherungsaufsichtsgesetz) and the German Securities Trading Act (Wertpapierhandelsgesetz—WpHG).
3. According to the Economic Offenses Act (Wirtschaftsstrafgesetz) 1954, the Foreign Trade Act (Außenwirtschaftsgesetz), the Foreign Exchange Control Laws (Devisenbewirtschaftungsgesetzen) and fiscal monopoly, tax, and customs law, even insofar as such penal provisions according to other laws are applicable; this is not true if the same action represents a criminal offense according to

[2] Web link: http://www.gesetze-im-internet.de/gvg/__74c.html. Accessed: June 26, 2013.

the Narcotics Act (Betäubungsmittelgesetz), nor a tax offense related to motor vehicle tax.
4. According to the German Wine Act (Weingesetz) and food law.
5. Classified as computer fraud, subsidy fraud, investment fraud, credit fraud, bankruptcy offenses, fraudulent preference and fraudulent preference of a debtor, and anticompetitive agreements for invitations to tender, as well as corruption and bribery in business transactions.
6. Classified as fraud, a breach of trust, profiteering, the granting of an undue advantage, and bribery, insofar as special knowledge of economic life is required to assess the case (Article 74c GVG, see Heissner 2001, p. 28 ff.).

Statistics on offenses and responsibilities of each court as defined in Article 74c of GVG are published, for example, in the Police Crime Statistics (Polizeilichen Kriminalstatistik—PKS) and yearly in the Situation Report on White-Collar Crime ("Bundeslagebild Wirtschaftskriminalität") by the BKA. The fact that the descriptions of these offenses, as well as the case numbers, should be treated with caution from a practical point of view will be dealt with briefly when we come to examine the actual damage caused by white-collar crime later.

A critical examination soon reveals that the term white-collar crime as it is formally used in Germany is not all-encompassing. Anybody who only counts those offenses that are listed from a legal standpoint under the heading of "white-collar crime" will then be likely to overlook the manipulation of balance sheets, corruption of officials, industrial espionage, or money laundering.

To form a practical overview of all relevant offenses, it is necessary to broaden our view. Therefore, this chapter will initially define in detail what corporate leaders, management boards, managers, and supervisory boards should understand under the term white-collar crime when it is discussed in this book. This means that the following sections will examine offenses that cause damage in companies and destroy assets—and for which company executives are responsible, or even liable, for detecting, solving, and preventing.

This will then be supplemented by offenses in the areas of competition and antitrust law, which are being more strictly regulated on an international and supranational scale, plus the whole area of corruption: from illegally accepting an advantage through bribery payments to the manipulation of invitations to tender and price fixing. Although these are also included, to some extent, in Article 74c of GVG, they almost form their own type of offense due to the large number of legal aspects included in international regulations. This is also valid, to a similar extent, for the areas of IT security, data protection, industrial espionage, and so-called "cybercrime."

The term white-collar crime takes on another dimension when we examine what is today called "noncompliance"—even if this area already implicitly includes special offenses related to corruption.

A really clear distinction between white-collar crime in its strictest sense and noncompliance is, however, essential to be able to form a comprehensive understanding. White-collar crimes such as fraud or manipulation are, in general, directly committed against the company. A bookkeeper who sets up imaginary employees in order to transfer salaries to a private bank account is directly costing the company money because capital is being drained away.

In contrast, many cases of noncompliance appear at first glance to be beneficial to the company. For example, if a company gains a competitive advantage by bribing officials or decision-makers in relation to invitations to tender, then it is certainly not detrimental to the company's short-term success—quite the opposite. In fact, it is possible to trace the success stories of whole companies back to a corruption or antitrust offense. Even the types of offenses that do not directly cause damage within the company need to be taken into account to prevent value destruction in the long term.

The Siemens case is likely to mark a significant turning point when it comes to international law enforcement in the area of corruption. The times of openly practiced and silently tolerated corruption are now truly a thing of the past. These types of antitrust offenses are now consistently and professionally investigated and represent a threat to the very existence of even larger companies if the criminal investigations are carried out in a correspondingly committed manner. For example, if profits are disgorged or the offenses result in sanctions such as companies being blacklisted.

2.1.2 Alternative Term: "Deviant Behavior"

Experience working both as a police detective and in forensic auditing has shown that it is, however, necessary to critically evaluate the use of the umbrella term white-collar crime to describe all of the listed offenses. This is because it is not always appropriate nor does it properly reflect reality. The term white-collar crime is also simply too harsh in many cases at a purely human level. Those who seek to understand this phenomenon and its manifestations must be capable of recognizing the people behind the phenomenon and understanding their motives. It is certainly understandable that people need to tell it like it is in order to discourage this type of behavior and to develop awareness of the problem. These crimes are not trivial offenses but in many cases criminal acts—even if the perpetrators aren't wearing balaclavas.

Yet there is also a danger here of overgeneralizing. Again and again we see cases where employees wind up in difficult situations due to personal pressures, the criminal involvement of third parties, or simply due to ignorance—only to then be punished as criminals. Even in the Adoboli case described earlier, it would be a mistake to view the perpetrator as a lone operator driven simply by greed. From a criminalistics point of view, perpetrators are more often products of their environment than we or our own prejudices would like to admit.

An alternative, which could certainly be used as a synonym in this book, is offered by the term "deviant behavior"—a more encompassing description of white-collar crime, corruption, fraud, and all other imaginable cases of infringements against the existing regulations in the sense of noncompliance. The phrase "deviant behavior" originally stems from the field of sociology and has gradually found its way into the area of criminology (see Dollinger and Raithel 2006, as well as Göppinger and von Bock 2008). In principle, the term describes everything that is not considered adequate or desirable from a business or social standpoint. This does not necessarily mean, however, that they are criminal offenses.

In summary, the term "deviant behavior" is used in this book to describe everything that causes damage from a company perspective—behavior that a forensic audit is designed to detect and prevent. In many cases, this is connected to the liability of supervisory persons in terms of their obligation to protect against and detect this behavior in accordance with German and international legislation, as already explained in Chap. 1.

2.1.3 Overview of the Relevant Offenses Included Under "Deviant Behavior"

Any attempt to systemize "deviant behavior" is thus difficult due to the many different forms in which it manifests itself. Nevertheless, a number of different approaches can be found in relevant literature that are dedicated to precisely this task. This book will initially focus on a commonly used approach found in the Anglo-American world for the classification of white-collar crime: the so-called "Fraud Tree" (see ACFE online, for example http://www.acfe.com/fraud-tree.aspx) from the Association of Certified Fraud Examiners (ACFE 2013). It divides "deviant behavior" into three main categories from an economic perspective, representing them and their relationship to one another in the form of a family tree. The main categories in the Fraud Tree are Misappropriation of Assets, Financial Statement Fraud, and Corruption. This approach already deviates from the strictly judicial definition of white-collar crime to view the subject much more from an economic perspective.

2.1.3.1 Elements of the Fraud Tree: Misappropriation of Assets

The assets of a company can generally be damaged in two different ways. One way is as a result of theft or misuse of material goods: such as a warehouse manager who falsifies stocktaking sheets in order to sell goods to criminals on the black market. However, it could also be a manager using the company car to drive to Portugal for a family holiday. What is true for "physical" assets is naturally also true for liquid assets.

In its simplest form, this involves the theft of cash. However, money can also be skimmed off through the manipulation of sales revenues, receivables, or credit notes. In addition, the misappropriation of assets through liquid means can also be achieved in the form of fabricated expenditure. For example, this could be the payment of a fictitious employee, or alternatively, fake incoming invoices, false refunds, or forged checks (Fig. 2.1).

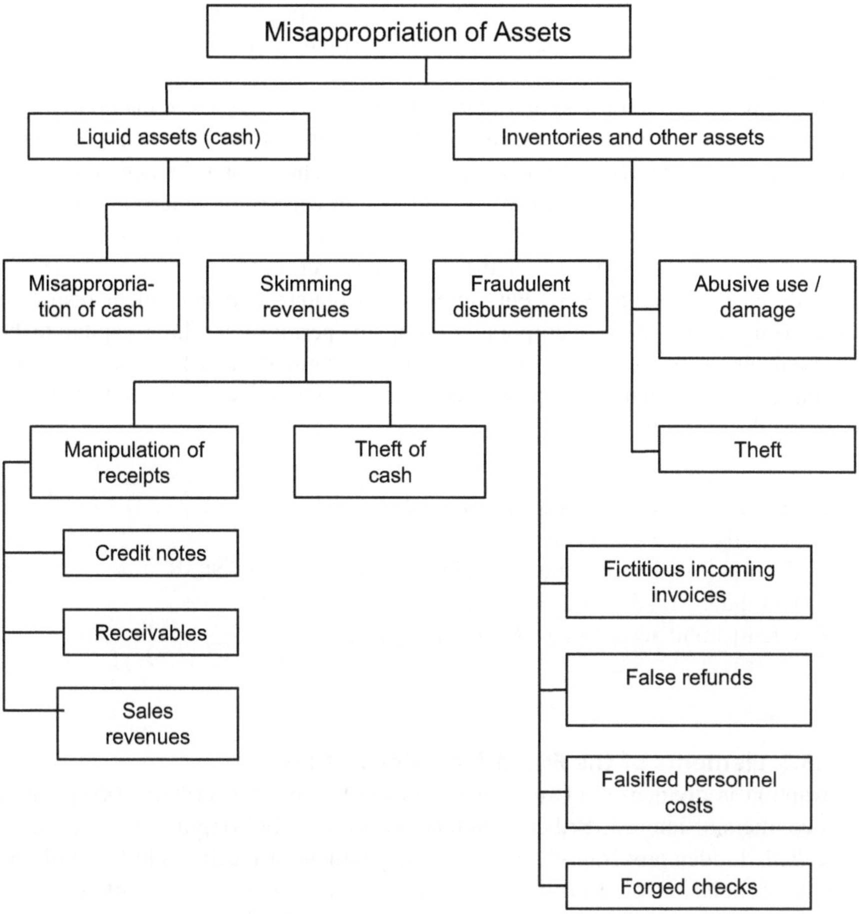

Fig. 2.1 The ACFE fraud tree: misappropriation of assets

2.1.3.2 Elements of the Fraud Tree: Financial Statement Fraud

Financial statement fraud is a special form of the misappropriation of assets and covers six different types of crime. These include misleading statements such as invoicing excessive amounts, crimes in the area of company valuations such as the overstatement of assets or the understatement of liabilities, incorrect reporting period accrual such as booking profits before they are realized, the concealment of expenses and liabilities, and the booking of fictitious revenues, for example, from fake customers or bogus companies (see Hofmann 2008, p. 79 ff.).

From the perspective of criminal law, most of the crimes involved in the misappropriation of assets and financial statement fraud are simply classified as fraud. Fraud in accordance with the definition in Article 263 of the German Criminal Code (Strafgesetzbuch—StGB) always includes deception or fraudulent representation—completely characteristic elements of white-collar crime. This is also the reason why fraud makes up the largest proportion of cases dealing with white-collar crime (see Bundeskriminalamt, Situation Report on White-Collar Crime 2010).

While the perpetrator who plays the active role in these types of manipulation is generally charged with fraud, the responsible supervisory persons such as management boards or supervisory boards must answer the charge of a "breach of trust." In accordance with Article 266 of StGB, a breach of trust is classified as a so-called "special crime" that only affects those people that have a "fiduciary duty to protect third-party financial interests" at the time of the crime (see BGHSt 24, 387 in Hlavica et al. 2011, p. 303). Put simply, if a manager, management board, or supervisory board at an incorporated company permits the share capital to be diverted, endangered, wiped out, or used for criminal activities then they are committing a criminal act. A prison sentence of up to 10 years can be handed out in particularly serious cases (Fig. 2.2).

Specialist Information: Special Elements of Fraud[3]

- Subsidy fraud according to Article 264 of StGB
- Capital investment fraud according to Article 264a of StGB
- Computer fraud according to Article 263a of StGB
- Credit fraud according to Article 265 of StGB[4]

2.1.3.3 Elements of the Fraud Tree: Corruption

Corruption is divided into two branches in the Fraud Tree: bribery/corruptibility and conflicts of interest. Bribery can take the form of bid rigging or kickbacks—so-called "hidden provisions"—meaning the payment or receipt of bribes. Following the conclusion of a business transaction, this involves a proportion of the amount paid being refunded to one of the parties involved in the transaction.

A conflict of interests can develop quicker than one would initially think. If the purchaser at one company, for example, has a good acquaintance in the sales department at another company and they confide in their acquaintance that they depend on the conclusion of the transaction for personal financial reasons, the purchaser already has a conflict of interest, which could possibly lead to the purchase of raw materials or other products at overinflated prices. In this way, a conflict of interest can thus develop in both purchasing and sales.

Just as with the term white-collar crime, there is also no legal definition for the term "corruption" in German criminal law. Depending on who is bribing whom or

[3] The German Criminal Code (Strafgesetzbuch) defines a lot of other special elements in the area of fraud, which go above and beyond the basic definition of the offense according to Article 263 of StGB, in order to close any loopholes in the criminal legislation.

[4] For detailed descriptions see Hlavica et al. (2011, p. 301 ff).

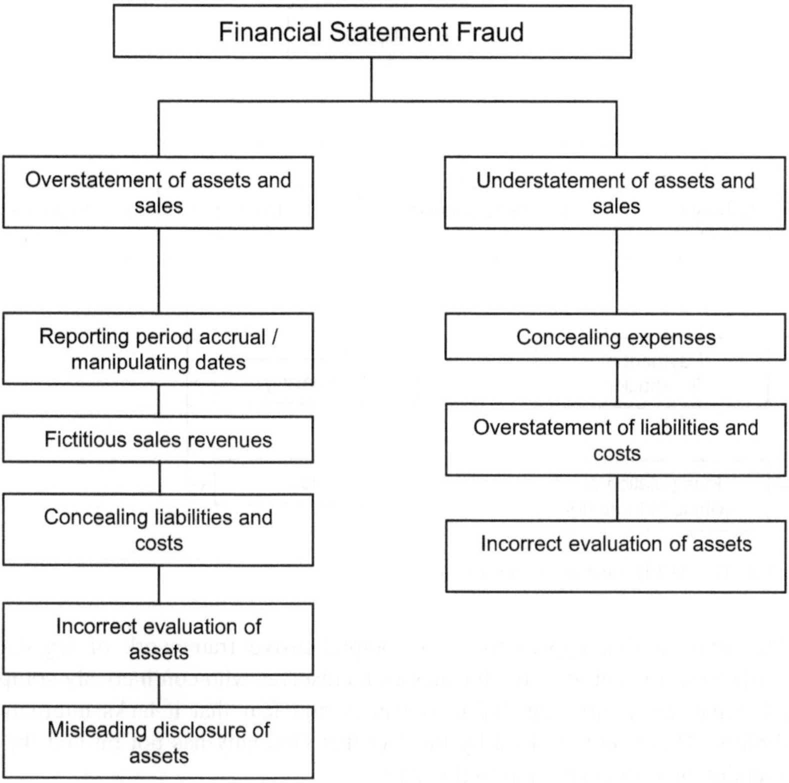

Fig. 2.2 The ACFE fraud tree: financial statement fraud

who is providing whom with what advantage, different paragraphs of criminal law are valid (Fig. 2.3).

Specialist Information: Elements of Corruption

- Bribery of voters or members of parliament according to Articles 108b and 108e of StGB
- Commercial bribery according to Articles 299 to 302 of StGB
- Bribery of public officials according to Articles 331 to 335 of StGB
- Other relevant legislation includes the Law on Combating International Corruption (Gesetz zur Bekämpfung der internationalen Bestechung—IntBestG), the EU Bribery Act (EUBestG), and, depending on the nature of the business, the UK Bribery Act and the Foreign Corruption Practices Act (USA).

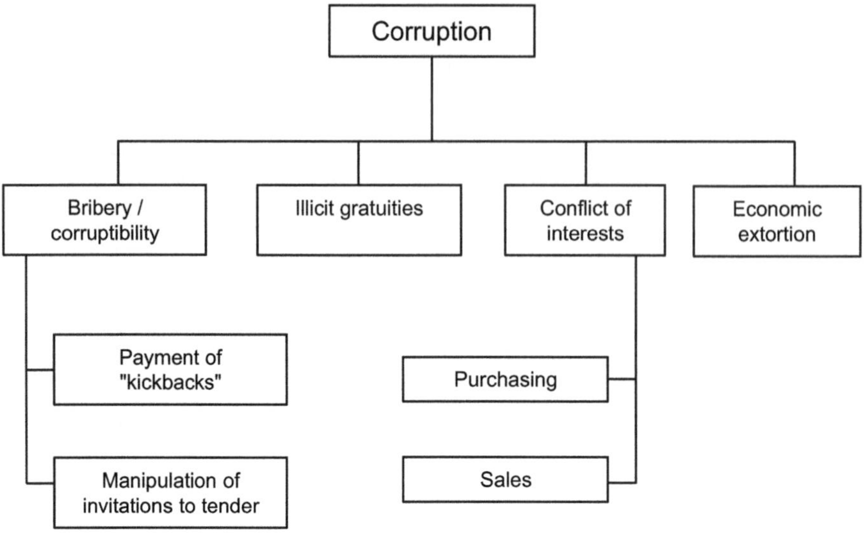

Fig. 2.3 The ACFE fraud tree: corruption

This may at first appear to be a comprehensive framework of legislation. Nevertheless, it is not least the businesses themselves who continuously complain that German corruption legislation is patchy and fear that it lacks international credibility. This is emphasized by the fact that Germany has not ratified the UN Convention against corruption to this day.

The bone of contention in the past was the repeated bribery of public officials, which in practice is only punishable in advance of parliamentary elections. Many other forms of corruption are thus not covered: for example, exerting influence on the issuing of public contracts and corresponding "remuneration" in the form of favors or gifts; or one classic form of corruption: the offer of a free vacation on a Spanish finca.

The three main categories of the Fraud Tree from the ACFE are concentrated on corruption and fraud in the area of assets and financial statements. Alongside these crimes there are, however, other special forms of white-collar crime that management boards and supervisory boards need to take into account. Due to their topical nature and liability-related relevance, the following sections will take a particularly detailed look at money laundering and tax and balance sheet fraud—before the list of crimes is complete.

2.1.3.4 Money Laundering

Money laundering is a term that should be familiar to everyone from Mafia films. In general, gangsters have the problem of channeling their illegally acquired money into the general economic cycle while attracting as little attention as possible. Any other solution would be too suspicious and merely provide authorities with needless opportunities for criminal investigations. Therefore, money laundering describes nothing more than the process of integrating illegally acquired money into the legal financial system under some sort of pretense.

This might sound a little far-fetched at first, but banks in particular can experience massive problems with money laundering as a result of their extremely complicated and convoluted financial transaction systems. These mean it is not always clear at first glance which money is illegal and must be laundered. However, the consequences of overly lax controls can prove disastrous: In December 2012, the major British bank HSBC paid a US$1.9 billion fine because they had been found guilty of facilitating money laundering through dubious transactions.

Naturally, there are not many bankers whose intention at the very beginning is to break arms embargos, launder drug money, or finance terrorism through their transactions. Yet the banker and his superiors must nevertheless fulfill comprehensive international monitoring and reporting obligations using so-called "legitimization and identification checks."

In Germany, money laundering is a crime according to Article 261 of StGB, while it is regulated on an international stage by a diverse range of laws, regulations, and directives from the EU, UN, OECD, and OSCE.

2.1.3.5 Tax and Balance Sheet Fraud

Tax offenses and corresponding balance sheet fraud are extremely typical examples of white-collar crime that remain hidden for a long time yet cause huge damage over the years.

However, as soon as they are discovered, they quickly attract massive public attention and result in draconian punishments. One reason for this is that both tax fraud investigators and criminal investigators are becoming ever-more specialized and now relentlessly pursue these types of crime.

One recent example saw the business premises of the Deutsche Bank turned upside down by 500 (!) police officers, officials from the tax fraud investigation office, and the BKA during a raid that resulted in the arrest of five employees in the middle of December 2012. Their suspicion was sales tax fraud, tax evasion, money laundering, and obstruction of justice relating to the trade of CO_2 emission certificates. The bank was accused of utilizing the so-called sales tax merry-go-round method in which tax was refunded by the state in advance to bogus companies but never paid back.

In a legal sense, German balance sheet and tax law is probably the most complex in the world. Related crimes are listed according to Articles 369 to 384 of the General Fiscal Code (Abgabenordnung—AO) between tax offenses and tax infringements.

Specialist Information: Elements of Balance Sheet and Tax Law (Excerpt)

- Tax evasion according to Article 370 of AO
- Infringement of the tariff laws (professional, violent, and gang-based smuggling) according to Article 372 of AO
- Illegal import or export of objects subject to duty according to Article 373 of AO
- Handling the profits of tax evasion according to Article 374 of AO
- Counterfeiting of money or tokens according to Articles 148 to 149 of StGB

Incorrect or incomplete statements according to Article 370 of AO can relate to tax declarations for income tax and sales tax, but also to notifications and corrections according to Article 153 of AO, or tax benefits such as deferments according to Article 222 of AO (see Harz et al. 2013, p. 83).

Tax infringements usually result in fines in accordance with Article 377 of AO.

These infringements include frivolous tax evasion (Article 378 of AO), minor tax fraud (Article 379 of AO), and illegally obtaining entitlements to tax refunds or tax rebates (Article 383 of AO).

Balance sheet crimes are covered by Article 331 No. 1 of HGB, which sanctions false statements in interim reports, annual reports, statements of affairs, or opening balance sheets with fines and terms of imprisonment of up to 3 years—all members of the corporate bodies authorized to represent the company who were aware of the incorrect statements or approved them are held criminally responsible.

2.1.3.6 Other Relevant Offenses and How They Are Dealt with Under Criminal Law

Even if the already described offenses of fraud, corruption, and manipulation make up the majority of white-collar crimes in Germany, it is important not to forget other relevant offenses and how they are dealt with under criminal law. Depending on the industry sector or the focus of the company, these offenses should be included in the risk analysis to a greater or lesser extent.

This includes, for example, offenses dealing with insolvency. The hectic and emotional nature of an insolvency process provides fertile ground for practically every form of white-collar crime. This ranges from straightforward fraudulent actions in accordance with Article 262 of StGB through to serious crime.

Specialist Information: Elements of Insolvency Offenses (Excerpt)

- Withholding social security payments according to Article 267 of StGB
- Forging documents according to Article 266a of StGB
- Delaying insolvency proceedings according to Article 15a of the German Insolvency Act (Insolvenzordnung—InsO)
- Bankruptcy according to Article 283 of StGB

Naturally, it is not necessarily illegal per se for a company to "go bust" as a result of commercial factors. However, bankruptcy becomes a crime if the company's inability to pay is brought about either through negligence or intentional actions.

A comparatively new discipline in the area of white-collar crime is Internet and computer crime, which the BKA futuristically names "cybercrime" in its overview of the subject. This includes, for example, forming fraudulent networks or "phishing" sites on the Internet, and manipulating or sabotaging computers, which is still covered under the crime of willful damage to property (Article 303 of StGB). As a reaction to the increasing danger posed by computer crime, the legislators have supplemented the legal regulations with Article 303a of StGB "Data manipulation" and Article 303b of StGB "Computer sabotage" (see Schönke et al. 2010, StGB, Article 303a in Harz et al. 2013, p. 168).

The situation becomes even more fascinating when it comes to product piracy and the infringement of intellectual property (Articles 106, 107, and 108 of UrhG, as well as the threat of punishment in accordance with Article 143 of MarkenG) in the unauthorized disclosure and interception of data.

Today, the digital nature of companies and their data has inevitably heralded a new chapter in the history of economic and industrial espionage, the defense against which falls increasingly under the responsibility of top managers—regulated in Germany in antitrust law according to Articles 17 ff. of UWG and supplemented since 1997 in Articles 298 ff. of StGB.

As a result of the major loss of assets in the cases surrounding Jerome Kerviel, Nick Leeson, or Kweku Adoboli, attention has now been focused even more on unauthorized trading and insider trading. While insider trading is defined in Germany according to various articles of WpHG and is punishable with a prison sentence of up to 5 years, the area of market speculation is stuck in a grey zone with respect to criminal law. American legislators and judicature handle insider trading, in particular, much more rigidly: in October 2011, an American federal court sentenced Raj Rajaratnam, head of the unfailingly and mysteriously well-performing hedge fund Galleon, to an 11 year jail sentence and a fine of over US$60 million for insider trading and conspiracy. It turned out that the stock market guru was extremely well connected among the high circles of the American economy—even receiving exclusive information seconds after the conclusion of important supervisory board or management board meetings. In a subsequent civil process, the SEC issued Rajaratnam with a claim for damages amounting to US$93 million.[5]

In the area of unauthorized speculation, it is less the criminal dimension and more the liability issues that face management boards and supervisory boards, together with the very high damages awarded on average in these cases, which has created the sense of urgency for preventing unauthorized speculations in

[5] This sentence is the severest ever issued to date for insider dealing—despite the fact that the social engagement of the perpetrator was already taken into account as a mitigating circumstance.

advance. The technical and forensic capabilities for preventing this behavior will be specifically examined in Chap. 4.

2.2 The Development of White-Collar Crime

A holistic examination of white-collar crime needs to focus of course on more than just the offenses themselves and their liability implications. Therefore, this section will look in more depth at how and why criminality as a whole and white-collar crime in particular develops. What theoretical models exist that can help us to understand this phenomenon? These models already encompass basic features of criminology that need to be taken into account in the design of compliance management systems, even though the development of white-collar crime or "deviant behavior" is too complex and too dependent on individual factors to be represented using a general formula.

2.2.1 White-Collar Crime: A Necessary Evil of the Market Economy?

Humans are thoroughly rational animals. Yet the things that make them tick are relatively simple according to the findings of an economic analysis of human actions (see Heissner 2001, p. 282 ff.)—which found they basically strive for self-improvement and optimization. It is thus no coincidence that humans have developed a framework in the form of the market economy that promotes the credo of self-improvement as its highest guiding principle.

If we study cases of white-collar crime long enough, it becomes clear that self-interest—the driving force for social prosperity—also acts as an incentive to step outside the boundaries of what is allowed. The positive energy that our economic system draws from the human drive for improvement is, to a greater or lesser extent, in natural conflict with standards such as laws. After all, not everybody is simply allowed take what they want, even if the basic mechanisms of the market economy ensure that in reality this remains the golden rule.

Therefore, it is safe to say that white-collar crime is a necessary evil of the market economy and will never really disappear from it. As long as people seek their own personal advantage in a competitive setting, they will also defraud and deceive others. An important element contributing to the very existence of white-collar crime is an intrinsic level of uncertainty when it comes to the quality of goods. This basically describes nothing more than a permanent lack of information. If everybody always knew everything about everything, then fraud would be impossible; it would prove futile to offer goods and services at excessive prices, falsify balance sheets, or break promises. The same applies to scarcity: If there were always sufficient contracts for all of the construction companies then nobody would need to seek an advantage through the payment of bribes.

As a result of its inherent characteristics, the market economy thus promotes this type of criminality to a large extent. But anybody who thinks that less competitively driven economic systems, such as communism, escape white-collar crime and corruption is of course equally mistaken. It was not even possible to ask for directions in Russia in the 1980s without having money or cartons of cigarettes at the ready to offer as bribes. Therefore, the fact that white-collar crime occurs cannot only be due to the systems and their rules. A major role must also be played by humans themselves, who are, in reality, not always the completely rational animals they are portrayed to be, nor are they only driven by self-interest.

At the end of the day, white-collar crime is not a purely economic issue. It is actually reassuring that white-collar crime is just as foreseeable and "normal" inside the factory gates as it is outside of them. Because, when viewed in light of the concept of "deviant behavior," fraud and corruption are and shall remain nothing more than cultural, sociological phenomena that occur in every situation where people have to manage scarce resources. When white-collar crime can be understood with these points in mind, it becomes a great deal more predictable. This makes it easier to prevent in a systematic way than, for example, capital crimes. Murder and manslaughter are much more frequently governed by emotion than white-collar crime, which is much more carefully planned on the whole.

2.2.2 Sociological Aspects in the Development of White-Collar Crime

What is "deviant behavior"? And what is criminal behavior? In response to these fundamentally philosophical questions, the "traditional" criminologist proposes the following theory: In all its various facets, criminality has always been the result of standardization processes (see Heissner 2001, p. 171). It is irrelevant whether we are dealing with Neanderthals, South Sea pirates, or managers, every society develops its own standards and ground rules over time, irrespective of whether these "social factors" (see Merton 1968) are later introduced into legislation and become subject to social control or not. Therefore, anything outside of the norm can be classified as "criminal." In simple terms, there is good, and there is evil.

According to the "Labelling Approach" (see Heissner 1996, Sect. 4.2.2), this social control is, however, not only a consequence of criminality but also contributes to criminality at the same time. "The young delinquent becomes bad, because he is defined as bad" (see Tannenbaum 1938, p. 17) is a particularly meaningful quote in this context. It ultimately calls for us to rethink the way in which criminality is explained—to focus not just on the concepts of "outside the norm" or "inside the norm," but to incorporate much more powerful sociological aspects into any explanation of (white-collar) crime.

Those who look deeper will find that social factors influencing the development of white-collar crime in particular are just as complex and multifaceted as those found in the area of capital crime—and despite common assumptions, they are not always based around money.

This is also the reason why controls and documentation are only the first step in protecting oneself against white-collar crime. At the very heart of every deviant act lies the person—the person themselves, and the environment in which they live and with which they interact. The following considerations will focus on precisely this point and use the practical knowledge acquired while fighting white-collar crime to help understand, recognize, and, in the next step, prevent "deviant behavior."

2.2.3 The Fraud Triangle: A Standard Instrument for Explaining White-Collar Crime

It is useful to firstly make an important observation. Economists and management consultants constantly try to outdo themselves by producing ever-more wondrous geometric structures to explain white-collar crime in its proper context—using triangles, squares, sparkling diamonds, or rotating cylinders. However, the process of meaningfully simplifying complex phenomena and illustrating them with some geometric form is not easy and often ends in failure.

Nevertheless, it is useful to briefly introduce the so-called "Fraud Triangle" as a standard instrument for the explanation of white-collar crime. This is because it illustrates some important patterns that can act as stimuli for white-collar crime and corruption, which should be considered during the development of a compliance management system. The triangle can be traced back to the 1940s, when it was developed by Donald R. Cressey[6] as part of his dissertation (see Hofmann 2008, p. 204).

The three corners of the triangle symbolize the conditions required for the development of white-collar crime, namely "Motivation," "Opportunity," and "Rationalization," According to the Fraud Triangle, offenders must experience some form of motivation to deceive, find themselves in an organizational structure that provides the opportunity to commit the crime, and also be able to rationalize the consequences of their actions within their own sense of wrongdoing. Only then will employees become perpetrators—this is the fundamental theory behind the triangle. The Fraud Triangle has long been the source of some dispute among criminologists. The reason is that it encourages us to simplify the extremely complex personal, sociological, or cultural factors that influence a person before and during every action. In addition, this triangle could in turn be used to explain almost every form of crime. The fact is that every single crime creates its own small Fraud Triangle.

Nevertheless, anybody who is keen to understand and fight white-collar crime in their company over the long term can use the different corners of the triangle as points of orientation. In the interests of completing the picture, the three corners of the triangle should be briefly described. This is done from a managerial viewpoint and with the some key points depending on the crime (Fig. 2.4).

---

[6] Incidentally, Cressey was a student of the notable criminologist Edwin H. Sutherland, who introduced the term "white-collar crime" to the field of criminalistics and put an end to the perception of criminality as a "phenomenon of the underclasses."

Fig. 2.4 The fraud triangle

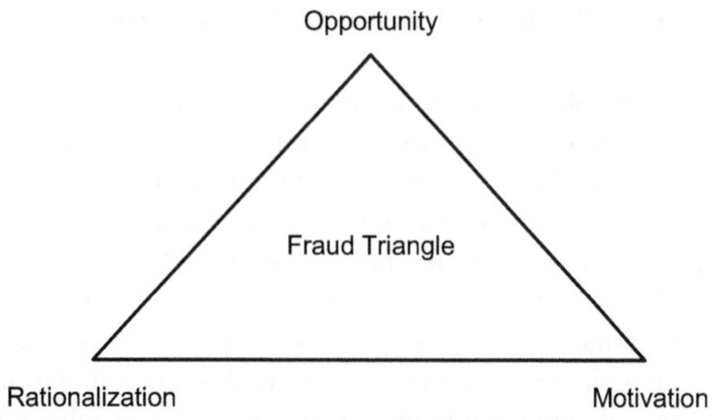

2.2.3.1 Opportunity

The corner of the Fraud Triangle named "Opportunity" is certainly the easiest to control from a management perspective. This is because every opportunity to commit fraud or corruption is synonymous with a weakness in the internal control system. It is necessary for this system to fail before criminal actions become possible at all, and are then allowed to mature in secret. The perfect anti-fraud or compliance management system would remove all opportunity for fraud and thus eliminate white-collar crime at its very roots.

This means that every company, depending on its organization and management, creates the opportunities for its employees to commit fraud itself. Overly complex processes and systems provide perpetrators with an open invitation to conceal and disguise these sorts of crimes.

2.2.3.2 Rationalization

There is hardly any other criminal discipline outside of white-collar crime where future perpetrators are inclined to view themselves as the victim to such an extent. Justifications such as "but everybody does it" are often heard, while this attitude is often combined in many cases with a sudden and clear desire for fair treatment. However, it is also possible to manage these reactions in advance. People do not ultimately feel misused or unfairly handled and simply take the idea of "fairness" into their own hands without reason.

2.2.3.3 Motivation

The third corner of the triangle is "Motivation." According to Cressey, this is usually a financial problem that cannot be shared or transferred to somebody else (see Cressey 1973, p. 30 ff.). Particularly when examining white-collar crime, "motive" as a key criminalistics term deserves closer examination, and will thus be discussed in greater detail in the next section of this chapter. Especially because, in contrast to Cressey, practical experience has shown that the various motives that influence the behavior of individual people are considerably more multifaceted than just those that fall into the financial category.

2.3 Motives for White-Collar Crime

In principle, the motives behind white-collar crime differ hugely from person to person and from culture to culture. The difference between Western industrial nations and the economic systems in Southeast Asia is particularly notable. What are the reasons behind this different mentality when it comes to the development and rationalization of white-collar crime?

In the last few decades, the Western world has evolved to become much more individualistic and anonymous. In Germany, this can be seen especially in the demographic disintegration of multi-generational households. Wherever these types of social communities along with their inherent value systems are missing, the concept of individualism gains in importance. And wherever "everybody is looking out for number one," the motives for (white-collar) crime almost inevitably develop—and are expressed—in a wide variety of forms. The decisive question here is: What needs to happen in a person's head for them to decide to break with their own norms, take unusual risks, and permanently create an illusory world around themselves that needs to be maintained? In general, we are dealing ultimately with people who have received a sound base of values and norms on their journey through life—not with those who have grown up in an environment of complete lawlessness. Every future perpetrator ("deviant") experiences a shorter or longer period of metamorphosis and ultimately leaves their familiar value system behind. This can be due to a number of reasons.

In the following section, the most common motives encountered by fraud and corruption investigators will be briefly mentioned and explained. This section does not claim to be complete from an academic point of view, but rather it serves to offer a practical understanding of the subject matter.

2.3.1 Motive: Pursuit of Social Status

Everybody wants to be successful. Everybody wants to maintain or improve their quality of life and conform to the ideal image of the dynamic, successful social climber promoted by the world of advertising and the media. Therefore, this means that rationalization in America and Europe is primarily about one thing: myself. This is then combined with the pursuit of social status and recognition.

It is especially true that in those sectors of the economy where remuneration is given in the form of bonuses, such as the banking and insurance sectors, employees often find themselves in a situation where they can obtain business transactions through manipulation. Nevertheless, experience has shown that it is not simply "greedy" individuals who are behind fraud cases in reality.

In particular, the intention to achieve "personal gain" is a motive that is heavily dependent on the social environment of the individual. Therefore, the much-quoted concept of "greed" is only a subcomponent of people's pursuit of social status. And, every now and then, it is possible to identify cases where this clearly plays no role at all.

2.3.2 Motive: Feeling of Obligation and Emergency Situations

In Southeast Asia, motives are often completely different, for example. In the much more hierarchical state and economic systems in countries such as China, Japan, or Korea, it is often the case that families or superiors enjoy unreserved loyalty from an individual that will often supersede their own moral conscience. For example, if a manager in China puts money aside to support his or her family, he or she in many cases will not consider it to be unjust—and will certainly not consider it a crime. Instead, it is a service for the benefit of his or her family and thus an obligation.

Outside of Asia, it is also of course possible that personal and family crises become a motive for white-collar crime. These motives can range from a family dog who needs an operation right through to the provision of expensive medication for parents, grandparents, a spouse, or children when this treatment is not covered by their health insurance—if there actually is such a thing as a health system in that country.

2.3.3 Motive: Obedience to Authority

Obedience to authority can also be a motive for acting in a deviant manner. If all instructions issued by superiors are carried out unconditionally—as is the culture in many corporations—the risk of corruption and fraud also increases. This is because anonymously informing and reporting fraudulent actions, via a whistle-blowing system for example, is not viewed as acting honestly but rather as betrayal. In general, the international fight against crime has shown that this phenomenon is particularly widespread in Asia because Europeans and Americans historically have a different approach to this subject.

2.3.4 Motive: Pragmatism

Economic pragmatism can also become a motive for white-collar crime. For example, take a sales representative in the plant construction sector who has been employed by their company for 30 years or more. In these 30 years, the employee has inevitably developed a certain routine and a "hustling" approach, which has included learning a trick or two. "In some countries it's impossible to do anything without paying a few bribes" or "everybody does it that way" are typical quotes from these types of employee.

It certainly doesn't have to be this exotic though. There have certainly been a few very pragmatic bookkeepers who have ensured that their companies have de facto falsified their balance sheets due to incorrect accounting procedures, advance billing, or prepayments—even if they only wanted to help out their colleagues because "it simply wasn't possible any other way."

2.3.5 Motive: Ignorance

Although ignorance offers no protection against punishment, it is nevertheless necessary to take into account whether a crime was committed intentionally or through negligence when passing judgment on and sanctioning white-collar crime. Anybody who fails to raise the awareness of their employees and inform them about corruption issues increasingly exposes themselves to the danger that offenses will simply be committed due to ignorance. Employees that genuinely do not know that bank transfers to offshore accounts on the Cayman Islands should, at the very least, be critically scrutinized will subsequently become accessories to the act or even criminals themselves.

Legislation in the area of balance sheet and tax law does occasionally change. A company must ensure that its employees understand and can properly apply these changes. Yet they are often quite simply not aware of the reasons for these changes to the legislation. This situation probably occurred when the practice of offsetting tax for so-called "necessary expenditure" was disallowed. There were inevitably one or two employees that were under the impression that these types of payment just had to be accounted for in a different way. Spreadsheets with the standard field "N. E." (necessary expenditure) simply continued to be used.

2.3.6 Motive: Career Ambitions

In America and Europe—but also to an increasing extent in emerging countries—an individual's own career ambitions can clearly become a motive for white-collar crime. Anybody who wants to climb the career ladder at any price will almost inevitably find themselves in a situation where they end up manipulating balance sheets or project results, or intentionally concealing risks in order to look good on their references, work assessments, and CVs.

2.3.7 Motive: Boredom

It may sound banal, but boredom can also be a motive for fraudulent actions. The appeal of testing and pushing the boundaries is deeply anchored in the human psyche and should not be underestimated. Why shouldn't somebody spice up their gray daily routine in the finance department of a medium-sized company by taking their lead from the pages of a John Grisham novel?

It may even sound a little far-fetched, but boredom is a much more common motive for white-collar crime than one would at first imagine.

2.3.8 Motive: Pressure to Perform

A traditional factor in the development of corruption is the pressure that is placed on employees to perform. In many cases, management personnel underestimate the level of pressure experienced by their employees. If targets are too ambitious or simply impossible to achieve, manipulation and falsification are often the only way forward.

2.3.9 Motive: Revenge

Admittedly, revenge is a much more frequent motive for committing capital crimes than it is for economic crimes. Nevertheless, employees are increasingly placed in situations where they feel humiliated or personally attacked. The credo "I'll show them" is almost inevitably a factor in crimes such as "pimping" your own balance sheets, through to internal smear campaigns against other employees. The disquiet resulting from these actions can damage the company and ruin whole careers in one fell swoop.

Another dimension of revenge is defiance: "Others are constantly filling their pockets and I'm being left by the wayside? Not a chance!" is a typical excuse for white-collar crime when factors such as defiance and resignation come into play. This motive can occur particularly frequently if an organization has already experienced a certain "level of corruption" and this fact is also known—at least to a latent extent—throughout the company.

2.3.10 Motive: Social Recognition

As mentioned earlier, those who want to properly understand white-collar crime must wave goodbye to the concept that it develops exclusively from monetary motives. Employees in sales and marketing departments are often just yearning for recognition and a pat on the back, or even just to hear two little sentences such as: "Good news that you closed the deal. Well done." Occasional praise and true appreciation, as well as managers actively listening to their employees, could be enough to prevent some crimes in advance. Praise could also be given in another form: "Good that you didn't act on their demand for a bribe. It isn't worth it. We'll just pull out of the business transaction!"

2.3.11 Motive: Peer Pressure

"Either you are with us or against us." "This is how it works here." These are sentences that you are particularly likely to hear in isolated company departments like purchasing or among field staff. The fact that white-collar crime also occurs everywhere where intense group dynamics come into play is due to two human mindsets: fear of being outcast from the group and the misapprehension that decisions are better when they are made by a group—the so-called "Bay of Pigs Phenomenon" (see Dobelli 2011, p. 17 ff., "Social Proof").

Conclusion About Motives: White-Collar Crime Is a Personal Management Issue that Develops on Three Levels The sheer spectrum of possible motives for "deviant behavior" already demonstrates that the phenomenon of white-collar crime is unbelievably multifaceted, while motivation comes from a much broader background than simply a desire for personal enrichment. Social factors also play an important role. The consequence is that rigid controls do not offer any impenetrable protection against damage because the dynamics behind "deviant behavior" almost always transcend mechanical control systems. There is no question that internal control systems (ICS) are a good idea and important. However, if we take into account the serious sociological and psychological factors at play in the heads of each individual perpetrator then we can come to only one conclusion. The development and prevention of white-collar crime is ultimately a personal management issue involving "soft skills."

As long as the fight against corruption and fraud remains stuck at the middle management levels of an organization, the corresponding measures will remain reactionary and limited to mechanical controls that do not do justice to the complex sociological phenomenon that is white-collar crime. Practical experience gained from working around the world for one of the big four auditing firms shows that many crimes—or deviant actions—that later result in tangible public scandals could have been prevented if "deviant behavior" had been taken seriously as an element of personal management. This sometimes includes unbelievably banal aspects such as praise for frustrated employees, a firm commitment made to the sales team on clean business practices, or merely having a sympathetic ear for employees and understanding their moods. Indispensable in these situations are the manager's own belief in what he or she is saying and being able to communicate this clearly.

Personal impressions gained from discussions with colleagues and employees are—with a bit of previous knowledge about criminal psychology and a little practice—probably the most effective method for developing a feeling for the current risks with relation to fraud and corruption. If the company management are disinterested, too proud, or simply not around to talk openly and honestly with their employees every now and then, it is still possible to develop sophisticated control systems. Yet the danger of offenses being committed remains, however, many times greater than if relevant awareness raising and training measures are implemented.

If damaging cases have already occurred or need to be resolved in the company, the process of anchoring awareness for the issue within the personnel management is the decisive factor for success. If the situation involved fraud or corruption, and in the next step compliance, it is fatal if superiors are not really aware of what has happened—meaning how the manipulation was being carried out and how the offense can be prevented in future. It is also dangerous if attentive employees or whistleblowers are not taken seriously because management boards or managing directors ignore the matter.

Fraud and corruption cases over the last few years have clearly demonstrated that the following is true. Every time there is a lack of commitment to compliance and clean business practices, it is an unspoken invitation for people to carry out criminal acts. This starts at the level of the management board and impacts on all management levels across the whole organization. It may initially sound extremely drastic but all companies are, to a large extent, responsible themselves for the level of awareness they generate on "deviant behavior" via corporate policy and corporate management. In summary, it is possible, when examining how white-collar crime arises in companies and organizations, to define three levels where conditions can be decisive for enabling white-collar crime to develop, thrive, or be prevented.

1. **Awareness of the problem among the management of the company** How does the management of the company deal with the issue of white-collar crime? What do management boards and top-level managers say about the subject? What incentives have really been introduced? The importance of developing an overarching level of awareness for the problem of "deviant behavior" in a commercial enterprise cannot be overstated.

   Companies with management teams that either do not take the subject seriously enough or even deliberately look the other way—i.e., create no awareness within the corporate culture—are condemned to somehow come to terms with the loss of assets due to white-collar crime and the threat of damaging penalties and profit disgorgement settlements, as well as personal liability risks. Corrupt leaders will never control a clean company.
2. **Selection and recruitment of personnel** The selection of staff and the recruitment of management personnel has a direct influence on the management culture and the level of compliance. The company once again finds itself at a critical junction that will decisively define how the issue of white-collar crime is confronted in the future. The situation is relatively clear: if I fill my sales team with extrovert, high achievers and issue directives from a management level such as "closing the business transaction is the absolute priority," no one should be surprised if employees start to pay bribes. Or if I recruit "gamblers" into my investment banking division then I have to accept that risks will be taken. Anybody who thinks that seasoned managers can be taught to act differently is deluding themselves.

   The selection of personnel is already a pivotal factor in deciding whether there will be compliance or noncompliance in the company.
3. **Design of the business processes themselves** Ultimately, it is also the business processes that prevent, enable, or even promote white-collar crime because every lack of transparency and every form of complexity facilitates manipulation.

   Companies all too often sign up to the "four-eye principle." Yet once business processes and the basis for making decisions becomes so complicated that the company management are practically no longer able to take decisions, it is only a

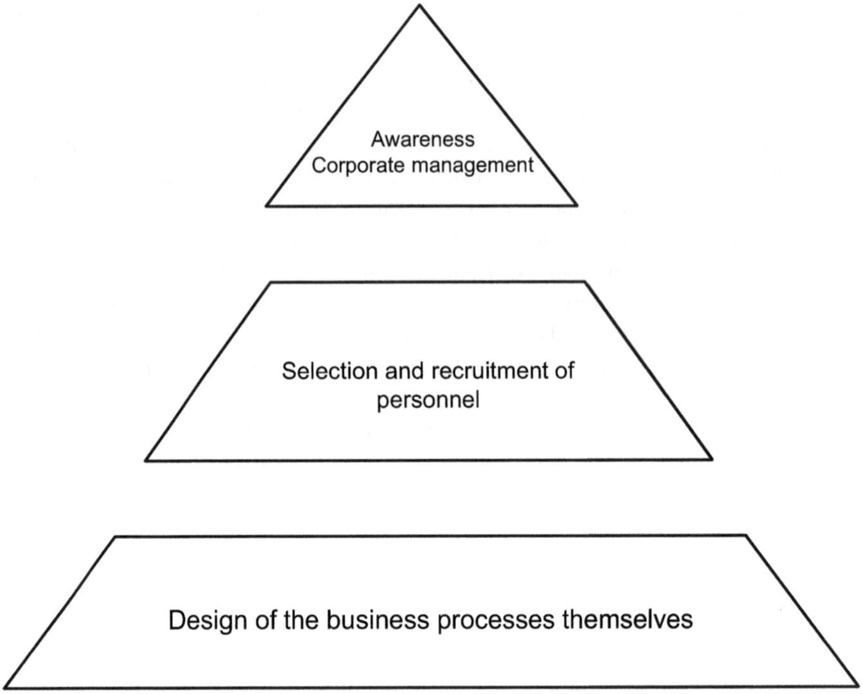

Fig. 2.5 Three levels for the development of white-collar crime

question of time until somebody exploits this complexity to intentionally conceal risks, or to deliberately mislead supervisory bodies. The supervisory boards hold a position of responsibility in this area. It is all too rare for them to actively demand clearly understandable and transparent decision-making criteria—or for them to actually read them.

Something that is complicated can never be completely free of risk (Fig. 2.5).

2.4 Perpetrator Typologies in the Area of White-Collar Crime

If you are not careful when attempting to explain white-collar crime and identify "typical perpetrators," you will quickly end up with the same old stereotypes and clichés. The fascinating attraction of this subject, fortified by memorable images of these sorts of crimes on film and television, encourages people to overdramatize the situation. Incidentally, journalists are particularly prone to repeatedly fall into this trap.

Attention is thus quickly focused on ambitious employees striving to climb the career ladder: university graduates in their mid-thirties, with an above-average income, and a penchant for expensive suits, fast cars, and beautiful women. A description of suave, sophisticated types in the 007 mold. Next down the line of course will always be the quiet, introverted financial accountant who secretly sneaks into the office at the weekend to devote himself to his secret passion: crime. And finally, there is the diligent workaholic, always the last to leave the office and then later, during the court proceedings, everyone will say of him: "It came as no surprise. He was a ticking time bomb."

And these characters are all naturally linked by their seemingly insatiable lust for money.

Anybody who focuses on these types of fantasies is clearly on the wrong track. In the previous section discussing the motives driving people to commit these types of offenses, it was already possible to demonstrate that white-collar crime is a highly adaptable phenomenon that cannot be adequately described using generalizations. The situation is exactly the same when it comes to perpetrators and their typologies. After two decades working in the fields of criminal investigation and forensic auditing, it has naturally been possible to identify reoccurring criminal profiles. Nevertheless, it would be foolish to claim that there could ever be a universally valid categorization of white-collar criminals—there is quite simply no typical white-collar criminal, just as there will never be typical murderers, drug dealers, or traffic violators. No fraud or corruption investigator or their respective employer should make the mistake at the very onset of focusing on a specific criminal profile, whether this is identifying a "perpetrator of choice" at a certain hierarchical level, or associating the crimes with a particular social class. The world of crime—as has often been shown through experience—is always good for a surprise or two.

2.4.1 An Overview of the Perpetrator Typologies

What turns an employee into a perpetrator? On the one hand, it is of course the right motivation. However, if the colorful assortment of offenses classified as white-collar crime are examined for long enough, patterns start to emerge in which certain types of personality appear particularly frequently. Nevertheless, there are exceptions to this rule.

The following typologies are based on experience gained from fighting corruption and fraud. It does not claim to be universally or seamlessly applicable. However, it is designed to facilitate a better understanding of the origins of white-collar crime—and to help discover corresponding approaches for detecting and protecting against it. By taking a broader view on the subject, a model can be developed that combines the criminological perspective of crime together with the more sociological view of perpetrators. In the fight against fraud and corruption, this then forms a basis from which employees can start to understand risk in their company, or to retrace the development of offenses—thus providing the basic knowledge required for the following chapter on "forensics."

2.4.1.1 The Crooks: Criminals Through and Through

In already existing criminal typologies, it is amazing that one type of person is almost consistently missing: the crooks. These are people who have simply done nothing else their whole lives except lie, cheat, and manipulate. Not only are they to be found out on the street but also in the office. It is both surprising and alarming at the same time to realize how many people in top management positions at successful companies are quite simply criminals through and through.

This category of perpetrator routinely commits offenses as a matter of course. And with each success they become more self-confident and their inhibitions are lowered. Criminals become really dangerous for an organization when their supposed success in business creates an appearance of genius—and any critical investigation would be viewed almost as heresy. This success usually continues until their self-confidence turns into carelessness and these crooks commit offenses that cannot be overlooked even by loyal subordinates or supervisory boards, or their web of lies simply collapses in on itself.

2.4.1.2 The Gamblers: Untouchable

People who commit white-collar crime are naturally not all bad by definition, nor criminal. A tendency for risk taking combined with corresponding pressure to perform is often sufficient. A good example are gamblers: extrovert, success-orientated, and confident of victory at all times. Americans would call these types of people "overconfident."

The gambler remains untouchable and unaware of any wrongdoing right up until they are convicted—and in some cases even afterwards. They believe that they are the only ones who understand the world and nobody else has any idea how "business actually works." The fact that gamblers are employed almost by nature in exposed areas of the company like fieldwork, sales, or distribution should not come as much of a surprise to anybody.

2.4.1.3 Free Riders: Particularly Clever

Free riders are less self-confident than gamblers or outright crooks. They appear everywhere where the actual perpetrators are not able to keep their crimes hidden—or the real perpetrator requires somebody else to cover up their actions. For example, an accountant or controller who covers up kickbacks—or the payment of bribes.

In these cases, "particularly clever" free riders decide not to report this irregularity. Instead, they decide to make a little something for themselves on the side—after all, if everybody else is a criminal why should they forgo their own share? They believe that "it's going to happen anyway so why not." It sounds quite practical: Earn a little more on the side without getting your own hands dirty.

Free riders tend to accumulate more frequently in those organizations in which corruption and white-collar crime become almost a natural part of everyday business. As part of the discussion about setting up compliance management systems in Chap. 4, we will once again see how important it is to create the right whistle-blowing system to turn potential mutual beneficiaries into important informants.

2.4.1.4 The Neglected: Being the Hero Just Once

Another type of perpetrator that is also frequently overlooked are those neglected personalities in the company. In the case of the neglected, their offenses are almost never committed for the purpose of earning more money—at least not in the first instance. These people are much more interested in being the hero for once or receiving some recognition within the company.

Therefore, when the neglected decide to manipulate an invitation to tender for their own benefit, conceal costs, or acquire projects by bribing decision-makers, they are only really interested in one moment: the moment they turn up at the office the next day, somebody pats them on the shoulder and says: "Super, well done." It sounds trivial but a large proportion of the crimes committed by this group of perpetrators could be prevented in advance by fairer employee management or the actual presence of management personnel.

If management personnel are drowning in their daily flood of e-mails and rushing from appointment to appointment while losing any chance of personal contact with their employees, the chances increase that the neglected will try to obtain attention and recognition in their own way.

2.4.1.5 The Unsuspecting: Good Employees

White-collar crime does not necessarily have to be combined with criminal energy or particularly devious intentions—at least not at the level it is actually performed. The class of perpetrators described under the banner of the "unsuspecting" demonstrate that it is often ignorance that leads to substantial offenses.

The unsuspecting are actually "good employees" who follow instructions and refrain from questioning the situation. Let us look at the example of a sales manager who wants to generate illegal earnings and asks one of his employees to accept an invoice for consultancy services that never in fact took place—the fee for which should be paid into a dummy account.

If the required awareness about white-collar crime is lacking, the good employee does as they are told and accept what is going on without enquiring any further. They fail to check the services stated on the invoice, and do not seek any reassurances from other parties that they were ever provided. As already mentioned, they are simply doing their job—and making themselves guilty of (or complicit in) serious manipulation.

This situation can also arise when laws change and business practices that were previously permitted are now forbidden. A lack of awareness and training almost inevitably leads to offenses being committed. District attorneys and corruption investigators are not particularly interested whether crimes are committed out of ignorance. A crime remains a crime.

This makes handling convicted "perpetrators" who have in reality "only done their job" even more difficult. In many cases, the unsuspecting simply do not accept that they have done anything wrong. Their justification is ultimately that "we have always done it that way." In practice, these employees are quickly dropped like hot potatoes without the employer following up the case with the person involved and examining the background to the crime. Investigating these types of cases often reveals fatal errors in the system.

2.4.1.6 The Lost: Feeling Wretched

A final class of perpetrators—also often forgotten from the perspective of theoretical sociology—are the lost. This comprises those people who have already become drawn into white-collar crime and corruption and who over time probably cause the greatest damage to companies if management personnel do not identify the situation and offer them a possible exit strategy.

While not meaning to trivialize their actions in any way, a significant number of white-collar criminals find themselves simply "drifting" into crime through peer pressure, the pressure to perform, or for personal motives—and feel wretched about the situation every single day.

The lost generally can't find a way out of the situation themselves. This is because confessing to their actions would expose them, brand them perhaps forever as fraudsters, lead to the loss of their jobs, and possibly ruin their painstakingly constructed social lives. A feeling of solidarity with, or even fear of, their accomplices can also play an important role. It is not uncommon for those who wish to abandon white-collar crime to fear the consequences of their decision. The results can range from social condemnation and dismissal through to threats and violence.

In this context, there is an increasing demand within organizations for management personnel to develop a feeling of intuition for distinguishing in each case between real manipulators or remorseful perpetrators who are really searching for a way out of a bad situation.

2.5 The Consequences of White-Collar Crime

There are two approaches for examining the consequences of white-collar crime. One is more focused and direct, and takes the viewpoint of the company. The other provides an overarching, global view from the perspective of the economy in general. For the sake of simplicity, this chapter will only describe the direct consequences for companies and organizations of both major and minor white-collar crimes. The consequences of white-collar crime and corruption as viewed from the perspective of the economy and society as a whole will be subsequently examined in the final chapter of this book.

It is necessary to initially attempt at this point to quantify the actual level of damage caused to the German economy by white-collar crime. However, it soon becomes clear by examining the Situation Report on White-Collar Crime from the BKA that it is almost impossible to reliably assess this damage, which makes any attempts to quantify the actual consequences of white-collar crime extremely difficult.

It is certainly the case that the damage caused by white-collar crime is greater than is often thought, or reports issued by the press or the authorities would lead us to believe. For example, the BKA estimated in its Bundeskriminalamt, Situation Report on White-Collar Crime (2010)[7] that the damage caused by white-collar crime amounted to 4.7 billion euros. The fact that this at first seemingly gigantic sum only represents a tiny proportion of the damage actually inflicted by white-collar crime, or rather "deviant behavior," is not clear at all to most.

It is interesting to focus on the statistics issued by the BKA for a moment in order to consider what really lies behind these figures. The Situation Report on White-Collar Crime only actually contains those cases reported to and investigated by the police authorities. Offenses and any associated damage that are detected by internal auditing departments, law firms, or auditing firms, and whose consequences are dealt with internally within the company, are not included in the statistics. The same is also true for cases of corruption, espionage, and other offenses causing damage. All cases of damage resulting from noncompliance that may prove expensive for the company but where the perpetrator is not punishable under criminal law are also missing from the BKA statistics. After all, the police were not required to detect and investigate, and so the crime was not reported.

But that's not all. Even damage caused by criminal acts that are immediately detected by the public prosecutor's offices or the financial authorities without the involvement of the police authorities are also missing from the statistics—for example in the event of subsidy fraud, illegal labor, or tax evasion.

The virtual damage caused by white-collar crime—in comparison to the figures taken from the BKA Situation Report—is now sure to have grown considerably.

There are only two other things that we need to add to properly understand the actual situation. If we take all of the crimes that are actually detected and investigated with police involvement, only those cases that resulted in a conviction before the courts would, by definition, make it into the statistics. Should it emerge in a fraud case that the accused was in reality a victim of an evil plot and is acquitted, the court costs, legal fees, and expenditure for solving the case are not entered into the statistics as damage caused by white-collar crime—even when they originated de facto within the company.

And last but not least, white-collar crime continues to be a phenomenon in which an above-average number of crimes fail to be reported and thus never appear in any criminal statistics around the world. Therefore, the damage caused by these crimes remains hidden in the rows of files stored at law firms or in the company archives. What is the reason for this? It is certainly dependent on the individual case and the person involved in the crime. However, it is rarer than one thinks that the failure to report these crimes is due to the completely corrupt nature of the organization, the clandestine celebration of criminality in dark conference rooms, or a lack of awareness for wrongdoing. From a purely practical perspective, supervisory boards, management boards, or managing directors often refrain from reporting these crimes in many cases in order to limit damage, or to protect the company from

[7] These were the most current reports (Bundeslagebilder) available up to February 2013.

the sorts of damage that can prove even worse. Some of these types of damage will now be presented here.

Therefore, we hold to the premise that quantifying the damage caused by white-collar crime is almost impossible for the simple reason that many cases remain undetected, unsolved, uninvestigated, or not even reported. Official criminal statistics such as those provided in the Situation Report on White-Collar Crime from the BKA, and their assessments of the damage caused, thus need to be treated with caution. They only deal with a very small proportion of the total scale of destruction to company assets caused by fraud and corruption[8]—which goes far beyond a purely material perspective.

This almost inevitably brings us to the following question: Which areas of companies and organizations are most damaged by white-collar crime, and to what extent?

2.5.1 Extent of the Damage Caused by White-Collar Crime

White-collar crime never solely results in just material damage alone. In order to fully appreciate the immense difference that can be made today by protecting against fraud and corruption, no one can avoid taking a holistic view of all of the possible types of damage. It is a good idea in this process to move away from merely focusing on figures and to look into the deeper consequences and damage that could be caused by white-collar crime in your own company. Just because it is impossible to express some types of damage in numbers does not mean that they should not be taken seriously. The recent history of fraud and corruption scandals has demonstrated that directly observable financial losses are generally the most harmless type of damage that a company sustains due to white-collar crime. Nevertheless, we will examine this type of damage first, which is purely material in nature and directly affects company assets.

2.5.1.1 Damage to Company Assets

When white-collar crime is experienced in a company, somebody is certain to ask at the end of the day: "What did it all cost us?" In this context, all of the cash-value assets that were directly lost due to the fraudulent or criminal actions must be calculated. As soon as the first suspicions of fraud or corruption arise, it is important to keep account of the damage and costs involved in clearing up the crimes. This is because the company may have insurance against this sort of damage, or the damages may be legally recoverable from those people involved in the crime in the form of compensation.

This includes all company assets that disappear from the company without the provision of anything in return. Irrespective of whether it is through theft, forgery,

[8] It is likely that this accounts for a figure in the tens of billions per year; it is not really possible to carry out a valid assessment of this figure for the reasons stated.

or fraud—which occur to varying extents depending on the individual case. The company is thus directly damaged. This can occur in an "explosive" way and be immediately visible or develop slowly over a long period of time in a more concealed manner.

A Blessing in Disguise: Promptly Identified Damage

The first example should be familiar to everybody: money is embezzled or misappropriated and assets are stolen or destroyed. This mostly involves a "one-time perpetrator" who just wanted to land a "major coup"—and failed. The larger the fraud and the greater the damage that has to be concealed, the more conspicuous it is likely to be and the easier it is for a trained investigator to uncover it. Companies that are hit by these types of immediate damage can actually view it as a blessing in disguise. Although the company has to pay for the damage until compensation can be claimed from the perpetrators, or the insurance pays out, the losses are more or less immediately known and have, for example, been quantified and traced by an independent auditing firm. In addition, they do not represent a major threat to the existence of most companies.

Every Minute Is Critical: A Creeping Exponential Loss of Value

The situation becomes more serious when these crimes remain hidden over a long period of time and control mechanisms have either failed, were not available, or have been undermined. If the damage is not directly noticed and the fraudulent activities are too ingenious or complex for the existing prevention systems, the result will be the creeping destruction of company assets.

Even if this "only" results in material damage in the end, the longer the period of time in which a crime remains undetected, the more fundamental the damage will be. This damage can very quickly reach critical dimensions for companies of all sizes. The UBS case surrounding Kweku Adoboli demonstrates this clearly. If you were to plot a curve to illustrate the typical damage caused in these cases, you would find time and time again from a certain point on that the resulting damage no longer increases in a linear fashion but instead shoots exponentially upwards. Why is this the case? Fraud, trafficking, and manipulation are always based on the pretense of reality—thus the more complex a fraudulent act becomes, the greater the investment that has to be made by the fraudster to keep this pretense of reality alive. Money has to be relocated, an increasing number of documents falsified, and an ever-greater number of people bribed to avoid exposure. This is the point at which the truly major damage occurs—when this spiral effect has been set in motion and the internal control systems fail.

2.5.1.2 Damage Due to Fines and Sanctions

Technically speaking, fines and sanctions could also be classified as material damage, but they need to be viewed much more critically than basic "damage to assets" and thus represent another type of damage caused by white-collar crime. This is especially true in cases of corruption and antitrust crimes. We are primarily talking here about penalties issued in response to manipulation, or fraud crimes according to StGB, or fines issued in accordance with OWiG for violations of the duty of supervision. These fines can be issued and enforced by courts or crime enforcement authorities. In Germany, the maximum fine that can be issued to managers for violating their duty of supervision according to Article 130 of OWiG is limited to 1 million euros—which does not really represent a deterrent if you compare it to the average wage earned by top managers. Politicians are currently discussing whether to increase this figure from 1 to 10 million euros in order to—in the truest sense of the word—take account of the potential riches to be made from white-collar crime and the bulging wallets of managers.

If we go one step further, we encounter a much more significant type of damage for companies in the area of fines and sanctions—namely internationally enforceable fines, profit disgorgement settlements, and market restrictions that are imposed, for example, under EU law. This naturally deals in the first instance with crimes of corruption such as cartelization, price fixing, and the abuse or granting of privileges in invitations to tender. The international antitrust authorities in the EU and the American Federal Trade Commission have, in particular, not been squeamish when it comes to issuing fines for antitrust crimes. For example, the energy company e.on was ordered to pay 38 million euros for damaging a seal on a room in which EU competition investigators had secured files. e.on already had first-hand experience of the extent of the damage that can arise due to antitrust fines from back in 2009. As a result of price fixing on the gas market, e.on and the French gas importer Gaz de France Suez were each fined 553 million euros. The record EU fine was issued at the end of 2012 to the so-called "TV and computer screen cartel." The total amount came to 1.47 billion euros.

Although they do not result in quite so spectacular sums of money, international sanctions such as exclusion from certain markets can have even more drastic consequences. Something that may only "hurt" a global player could quickly mean the end of a medium-sized company. In contrast to profit disgorgement settlements for antitrust crimes, it is simply sufficient in these cases to have reasonable suspicion or evidence of a single incident in order for licenses to be revoked and for companies to be excluded from certain markets for long periods. The FCPA represents the legal basis in this area, for example, in the USA. After all, the regulatory authorities in each country decide themselves with whom they want or don't want to do business.

2.5.1.3 Damage to Innovation and Competitiveness

Corruption in the form of antitrust crime can result in sustainable damage that stretches far beyond the level of any fines issued to companies, affiliated groups, and even whole economic sectors. We are now dealing with truly self-inflicted damage that—once established—can only be put right through a great deal of effort or radical intervention. We are talking here about operating "outside the competition," when companies simply purchase their sales success through bribery, cartelization, price fixing, or the manipulation of invitations to tender. And then use these methods, at least for a period of time, to simply bypass the competition.

Why is this dangerous and why does it damage companies? The answer is that it prevents the sustainable development of the company because at some point corruption becomes routine. And freeing yourself from this routine is difficult because, on paper at least, the company is performing really well so why should it change anything? But there will never be any real innovation in the company's products and services because their money is invested in bribes instead of in corporate or product development. This is a system that is doomed to failure, particularly in the fast-moving cycles of a global economy. Because the poorer the products become in comparison to the ever-evolving competition, the more bribes need to be paid in order to generate turnover. When it is finally discovered that a huge problem exists in the area of innovation, competitiveness, and product quality, the impact is usually unbearably harsh and extremely damaging.

2.5.1.4 Damage to Public Reputation

In the wake of, and in reality also often simultaneously to, the fines and the corruption investigations, companies do not only face business-related damage due to white-collar crime. Damage to reputation pushes the effects of white-collar crime into larger and almost impossible to quantify dimensions. This is because the stakeholder relationships with suppliers, investors, customers, politicians, and business partners become strained, or are directly destroyed by publicized cases of white-collar crime.

Trust that has been painstakingly built up, a carefully managed market image, or credibility developed over years can all be blown away in seconds. The consequences can be extremely varied in nature and go far beyond the idea that "now people think badly of us," to include falling sales, customer and supplier boycotts, impeded access to the capital markets, loss or exclusion from public contracts, and an exodus of employees. These are all short-term or long-term consequences of white-collar crime and corruption. There are then also those companies or NGOs whose public reputation is decisive for their very success or failure. This was the situation at UNICEF (see Leyendecker 2010), where it was revealed in 2008 that money had been systematically embezzled at the organization—the consequence was a massive fall in donations and, for a brief moment, it looked like UNICEF had completely lost its right to exist.

2.5.1.5 Damage to Employees and the Corporate Culture

At least as serious as the external effects of fraud and corruption scandals on a company are the direct consequences on internal life at a company. These consequences are felt at a number of different levels: heads generally roll when white-collar crimes are suspected, investigated and punished. This naturally involves the perpetrators themselves but also subsequently includes uninvolved persons with supervisory responsibility and, in the final reckoning, the management boards. A company needs really good reasons not to dismiss a manager or management board implicated in the scandal once it has become public. The public pressure is quite often simply so great that a company—then represented in the form of the supervisory board—will also remove high-ranking and otherwise irreproachable managers from their offices to enable a clean start, or simply to signal that the company is taking the fight against fraud and corruption seriously.

Therefore, companies are almost inevitably forced into the situation where they have to dismiss employees—the type of perpetrator involved or the motives behind the action are relatively academic. In this chapter, we have already seen that we are not only dealing with hardened criminals. The loss of employees results in really serious damage if competition-related expertise leaves the company or strategically important company departments need to be newly staffed.

Something that is also hardly taken into account in Europe when calculating the level of damage is management attention. This means the time required by the highest management levels in the company to deal with these events. It is only logical that while the CEO and supervisory board are busy with white-collar crime and its consequences, they lack the time to devote to their real task—managing the company.

But what happens if there are no personnel-related consequences and top performers are retained at all cost? And what if the company fails to express a clear commitment to transparency, the resolution of the problem, and the implementation of future provisions to the public and the workforce? Experience has shown that everything will then only become much worse because there is nothing that is more damaging to a company's corporate culture in the long term than the feeling that fraud and corruption has not been fairly dealt with. Any company that acts in line with the motto "punish the little guy but let the big guns walk away" is at risk of sustainably undermining their corporate culture. What are the results in these cases? Mistrust, defiance, frustration, rage—practically everything that stands in the way of smooth cooperation and thus healthy value creation in the company—while at the same time laying the foundations and motivation for further white-collar crime.

Major Damage Develops in Secret This examination of the different types of damage has shown that the really major damage caused by white-collar crime and corruption in a company develops under the surface. Namely, when misconduct or criminal actions are not immediately identified and dealt with. There are an increasing number of cases in which the original cause of massive damage in a company were trifling matters that gradually grew in scope until they became serious issues.

Purely financial damage is still the least important evil from the perspective of the company management. Those companies who have already suffered significant damage to their public reputation, general competitiveness, or corporate culture are hit much harder.

This makes providing executives and managers with a holistic awareness of this subject even more important because the earlier misconduct is detected, the lower the chance that the damage quietly accumulates under the surface until it finally erupts.

2.6 Conclusion: Management Bears the Responsibility

It can thus be observed from an examination of the perpetrators and offenses related to "deviant behavior" that this subject is much more multifaceted and a great deal more abstruse than one would at first think. Anybody who wants to effectively fight white-collar crime and corruption needs to delve deep into the corporate culture and the personal motivations driving their employees.

In the sense in which it has been defined here, "deviant behavior" is primarily a sociological phenomenon that, although there remains an element of surprise, it is possible to anticipate with the appropriate preparation.

Those who understand how white-collar crime and corruption develop in this context cannot fail to be aware of the position of responsibility held by management when it comes to preventing misconduct before it occurs. In many cases, this is possible simply by ensuring clear communication and having a sympathetic ear for employees.

After this examination of the criminalistics and socioeconomic foundations, the next chapter will focus on the concrete steps that need to be followed when it comes to investigating suspected cases of fraud and corruption. What problematic situations are caused by perpetrators and offenses? What are the typical measures used to conceal crime in critical company departments? And what technical and criminalistics methods can be used today within a company in the field of forensics?

Literature

Association of Certified Fraud Examiners (ACFE). (2013). *Fraud tree*. ACFE. Accessed June, 12, 2013 from http://www.acfe.com/fraud-tree.aspx

Bundeskriminalamt (Federal Criminal Police Office). (2010). Wirtschaftskriminalität, Bundeslagebild 2010 (Situation Report on White-Collar Crime 2010). Bundeskriminalamt (Federal Criminal Police Office). Accessed June 26, 2013, from http://www.bka.de/nn_193360/DE/Publikationen/JahresberichteUndLagebilder/Wirtschaftskriminalitaet/wirtschaftskriminalitaet__node.html?__nnn=true

Bundesministerium, der Justiz (Federal Ministry of Justice): *Article 74c Federal Ministry of Justice*. Accessed June 26, 2013, from http://www.gesetze-im-internet.de/gvg/__74c.html

Cressey, D. R. (1973). *Other people's money: Study in the social psychology of embezzlement*. Montclair: Patterson Smith.

Dobelli, R. (2011). *Die Kunst des klaren Denkens, 52 Denkfehler, die Sie besser anderen überlassen (The Art of Thinking Clearly, 52 Errors of Judgment that are Better Left for Others)*. Munich: Carl Hanser Verlag.

Dollinger, B., & Raithel, J. (2006). *Einführung in Theorien abweichenden Verhaltens: Perspektiven, Erklärungen und Interventionen (Introduction to the Theory of Deviant Behavior: Perspectives, Explanations and Interventions)*. Weinheim: Beltz.

Göppinger, H. (1997). *Kriminologie (Criminology)* (5th ed.) (completely revised and expanded edition of the work started and continued by Hans Göppinger up to the 4th edition). Munich: Beck

Göppinger, H., & von Bock, M. (2008). *Kriminologie (Criminology)*. Munich: Beck.

Harz, M., Weyand, R., Reiter, J. F., Methner, O., & Noa, D. (2013). *Mit Compliance Wirtschaftskriminalität vermeiden, Risikoprävention, Früherkennung, Fallbeispiele (Avoid*

White-Collar Crime with Compliance, Risk Prevention, Early Detection, Example Cases). Stuttgart: Schäffer-Poeschel Publishing House for Economics.

Heissner, P. (1996). *Ökonomische und verhaltenstheoretische Aspekte von Korruption (Economic and Behavioral Aspects of Corruption)*. Diploma project II, University of Kassel

Heissner, S. (2001). *Die Bekämpfung von Wirtschaftskriminalität, Eine ökonomische Analyse unternehmerischer Handlungsoptionen (The Fight Against White-Collar Crime, An Economic Analysis of Options for Corporate Action)*. Berlin: Publishing House for Corporate Communication.

Hlavica, C., Klapproth, U., & Hülsberg, F. M. (2011). *Tax Fraud & Forensic Accounting, Umgang mit Wirtschaftskriminalität (Dealing with White-Collar Crime)*. Wiesbaden: Gabler.

Hofmann, P. (2008). *Handbuch Anti-Fraud-Management, Bilanzbetrug erkennen–vorbeugen–bekämpfen (Manual for Anti-Fraud Management, Detect–Prevent–Fight Balance Sheet Fraud)*. Berlin: Erich Schmidt Verlag GmbH & Co.

Leyendecker, H. (2010). *Skandal bei Unicef, Verspieltes Vertrauen (Scandal at Unicef, A Loss of Trust)*. Süddeutsche.de. Accessed June 26, 2013, from http://www.sueddeutsche.de/panorama/skandal-bei-unicef-verspieltes-vertrauen-1.260511

Merton, R. K. (1968). Sozialstruktur und Anomie. In F. Sack & R. König (Eds.), *Kriminalsoziologie (Social Structure and Anomie. In Criminal Sociology)*. Frankfurt: Academic Publishing Company.

Schönke, A., Schröder, H., Stree, W., & Hecker, B. (2010). *German criminal code: StGB*. Accessed June 26, 2013, from http://www.beck-shop.de/fachbuch/leseprobe/Schoenke-Strafgesetzbuch-StGB-9783406604041_0305201208360809_lp.pdf

Tannenbaum, F. (1938). *Crime and the community*. New York: Columbia University Press.

Forensics

3

Criminal Investigations into Fraud and Corruption

Simon Newcomb made a strange discovery in 1881. The mathematician noticed that the number *one* on used logarithmic tables was much dirtier and worn than for example the number *seven*. A quick explanation is required at this point for those people not familiar with logarithmic tables: Before calculators were invented, huge hand-written numerical tables were used to help solve complicated arithmetic problems.

Newcomb would never have believed at the time that his discovery would ultimately lead to business people going to jail a little over 100 years later. He simply gathered from his observation that certain numbers appeared to be used more frequently than others when the logarithmic tables were being used practically to solve arithmetic problems. This discovery was not too spectacular initially, nor was it particularly relevant for forensic audits of the future.

However, the physician Frank Benford picked up on Newcomb's strange observation again at the end of the 1930s and used it to develop a law. This law used a simple formula to predict the relative frequency at which the numbers one to ten will occur in all those real-life commercial transactions such as orders, invoices, inventory sheets, bank account statements, etc. Benfords's Law states, for example, that the number four will occur significantly more frequently than the number eight. What at first sounds like some sort of numerical witchcraft has actually been proven to be a sort of "quasi natural law" in numerous experiments and studies.[1] It is not really possible for anybody to hide from this "law of numbers."

And at the latest from this point onwards, Newcomb's discovery of the varying degrees of dirt found on logarithmic tables also became of interest in the fight against modern white-collar crime. This is because if the frequency distribution of

[1] The American behavioral scientist Theodore Hill asked many hundreds of people to write down six figure numbers in a column off the top of their heads and was always able to identify a different frequency distribution in comparison to the "natural" distribution of numbers. Hill adapted the Benford Law further to fit manipulations in the "Hill Distribution" (see here Hofmann 2008, p. 552, and Odenthal 2009, p. 124).

S. Heissner, *Managing Business Integrity*, Management for Professionals,
DOI 10.1007/978-3-319-12721-7_3

numbers in "natural" business transactions follows a law, fraudsters and those falsifying balance sheets in the world of business would need to be outstanding mathematical geniuses in order to precisely replicate these laws through their manipulations. And this is precisely how it works in reality: specialist forensic auditing companies now possess computer programs that analyze company data for deviations from the Benford distribution and report any corresponding divergence. From a statistical standpoint, the cause of these deviations can very often be traced back to random numbers manipulated "by hand," which can then be precisely followed back to the source. These types of programs were used, for example, to expose the extremely "creative" accountancy at Enron and convict those behind these manipulations. The Ilmenau University of Technology was able to use these laws of numbers to prove that Greece fiddled its economic data in order to be accepted into the EU—even though it had already been proven (see Editorial of the Thüringer Allgemeine 2011).

This brief excursion into the analysis of numbers related to white-collar crime already shows how technologically advanced and scientifically sound modern forensic auditing has become today. Even if the detection of the fraudulent manipulation of balance sheets only represents a small proportion of the tasks under the scope of "forensics" that are presented in this chapter.

There are a wide variety of reasons to initiate an investigation for detecting white-collar crime—also called a "fraud investigation" in technical jargon. The wide range of offenses that fall under the heading of "deviant behavior" and the different types of white-collar crime were already discussed in Chap. 2. The objectives of an investigation commissioned during a forensic audit are thus, to a large extent, highly variable. Just like the various contexts and situations in which an investigator can find themselves once they have accepted their mandate.

It is necessary for investigators and clients to be aware in advance that fraud investigations of a certain magnitude are one of the toughest experiences that can be faced in the business world. Companies or organizations that commission investigations themselves, or become the subject of this type of investigation, are entering into an extremely exceptional situation. One that entails high levels of emotion and interpersonal tension. Those investigating cases of white-collar crime will inevitably be supported, praised, harassed, despised, deceived, or even threatened during the process. The fact is that only very few people in management positions have ever had to deal with this type of situation. However, the probability that they will be faced with this type of investigation in future is rising.

The term "fraud investigation" is used in this book to describe a purely reactionary measure for gaining knowledge. Therefore, all of these investigations are based on events that occurred in the past, which were either covered up or it is unclear who carried them out. In contrast to the range of different preventative measures, a fraud investigation describes the actual "detective work"—a reconstruction of the sequence of events in the past based on clues. This criminalistics knowledge forms the basis for implementing corresponding preventative measures and also for the remaining chapters of this book. An effective compliance management system always relies on the methodological knowledge gained from an investigation and simply utilizes it for a different purpose.

3.1 Commissioning a Special Investigation

The basic prerequisite for an investigation must always be a tangible initial suspicion or indication of misconduct. No investigation should be carried out without some tangible form of initial suspicion. A feeling of mistrust held by a member of the management board or supervisory board should not be considered sufficient to carry out a concrete investigation,[2] which could have dire consequences for both the organization and individual employees.

But what form does this initial suspicion take? It could of course be something that arises in the company's internal control systems, such as strange bookings at the end of the year, unusual contracts issued to suppliers, or irregularities in the invoicing and payment processes. Nevertheless, any suspicious circumstances that are identified by the company itself or that emerge as part of routine checks must be significant enough to justify the commissioning of an auditing firm or law firm. Experience has shown, however, that a problem lies in the fact that many of the most significant cases of white-collar crime only become so large and result in so much damage to the company because they have been allowed to develop despite the existence of internal control systems. Although well-functioning preventative systems already exist in a great deal of companies, the initial clues that lead to an investigation are often discovered by chance. A considerable proportion of offenses committed in the areas of white-collar crime and corruption are still detected today by accident (see Editorial of Süddeutsche Zeitung 2012). Or they are uncovered because the perpetrators or their accomplices or confidants lose their nerve under the pressure and simply pull the plug on the crime by slipping an anonymous letter under a door, making a full confession on the corporate intranet or—in some cases—even passing on information to the media.

It is particularly important to proceed with caution when suspicions are aroused due to anonymous tip-offs. The recipients of these tip-offs will not do themselves any favors if they immediately alert the whole organization and in doing so cause the entire legal department to prepare for battle. After all, it would not be the first time that a particularly ambitious employee attempted to rid themselves of an annoying competitor or simply wanted to cause unrest. It is thus important that every tip-off is carefully checked. Should the anonymous tip-off really supply tangible indications of a serious case of noncompliance, or even a criminal act, and the first ad hoc inquiries prove fruitful then it is certainly worthwhile pursuing the issue with a more in-depth investigation.

[2] The lack of an initial suspicion means that you are still at the detection stage, an area of compliance management that will be addressed in detail in Chap. 4.

If details of fraudulent activity have already become known in the company—or they pop up as breaking news on your smartphone—then it is high time to take action. Time and again there are cases where details of suspicious activities at a company find their way into the press while those responsible at the company still do not even realize that they have a serious problem. They should have taken action before the police, public prosecutor's office, or tax fraud investigation office make the decisions for them about whether and how an investigation will be carried out.

How and by whom will an investigation be commissioned? The classic scenario is that a call will be made to a service provider who has the relevant expertise—meaning an auditing firm with a department dedicated to fraud investigations or forensic services. The person making the call is usually—depending on what previous cases have been experienced in the company—a furious proprietor, nervous chairman of the board, discreet supervisory board member, or an agitated and stuttering corporate secretary. All will be frantically trying to explain that they require help—and as quickly as possible. The client actually issuing the formal request for an investigation can be from all levels of the company. In general, it is possible and permitted for anyone who has been issued with relevant decision-making powers to commission an investigation. Naturally, this is provided that there is a concrete suspicion or that something has already occurred. The precise nature of the suspicious circumstances are ultimately always decisive in each scenario: if the suspicions implicate the management board, the supervisory board must become involved to resolve the issue, while if the offenses have been committed within the individual business units, it is strictly speaking the responsibility of the management board to take action. The fact that half-heartedly delegating responsibility to compliance and auditing department personnel is not always considered sufficient by crime enforcement authorities when evaluating the liability of the management board has been demonstrated often enough in both recent and older cases. This can have serious consequences. Handling white-collar crime and corruption is the responsibility of top management—always. Depending on how acutely the investigation is needed, a meeting is usually quickly organized in which the current situation, aim of the investigation, and investigative process are discussed.

Another common scenario is for a call to be received from a law firm which has been commissioned to carry out an investigation into a case of fraud or corruption. Only very few law firms employ their own experts for investigating white-collar crime and, once they have received the appropriate mandate, they thus search for suitable partners to carry out the investigation.

It is also not always necessary for the investigation to be directly commissioned by the damaged company. It is equally possible for the authorities to commission an auditing firm themselves to carry out an investigation or to issue appropriate orders to a company to commission an auditing firm for this purpose. For example, if the Federal Financial Supervisory Authority (BaFin) has a bank in its sights and initiates a special investigation in accordance with Article 44 of the German Banking Act (Kreditwesengesetz), it is quite common that one of the big four auditing firms will become involved. This is because—just as with law firms—

only very few government authorities have their own criminal and forensic experts capable of adequately investigating a suspicion of white-collar crime.

This is also true of public prosecutor's offices and police authorities. Only a few public prosecutor's offices in Germany have the required specialist expertise in the area of white-collar crime to be able to reliably carry out investigations into commercial enterprises. There are two factors that are usually missing: qualified personnel and the necessary time before the statute of limitations for these crimes expires. The public prosecutor's office often finds itself in a dilemma. Their own investigators within the police authorities are not familiar enough with business administration in all its many facets to be able, for example, to comprehensively understand complex balance sheet fraud or they simply have too little experience in the area of white-collar crime. Efficiently securing the required evidence for prosecuting and convicting the perpetrators would only be possible with a great deal of time and manpower. The danger is that the statute of limitations on these crimes will expire before they have been properly investigated.

Why do the authorities not simply employ people with the necessary expertise? It sounds banal but wages in the police service or public prosecutor's office cannot hope to keep pace with those paid by law firms and auditing firms. It is thus safe to assume—while taking into account certain exceptions already mentioned—that the expertise and experience required for comprehensively investigating and combating cases of white-collar crime is increasingly and almost exclusively found in the free market. The demand for forensic auditors/accountants is currently booming—EY Fraud Investigation and Dispute Services currently employs 160 consultants in Germany, Austria, and Switzerland alone. This figure reaches over 2,000 worldwide.

One solution to this dilemma that is being increasingly practiced even in Germany is the so-called "American model"—meaning that auditing firms are employed as investigators in cases of white-collar crime. This model will be briefly presented below.

3.1.1 The Trend in Public Prosecutor's Offices: The American Model

As the name already suggests, this is a method that has made the transition from the USA to Germany and Europe, and it is likely that it will be applied more and more frequently in future by public prosecutor's offices. There are some public prosecutor's offices in Germany—most notably the prosecutors in Munich—who already use the American model. The model works in a similar way to the approach described above in the BaFin example, namely by involving professional and independent auditors as partners in the investigation. The Americans are highly pragmatic in this area and basically begin by offering the following options to those less than cooperative companies faced with accusations of fraud and corruption:

Option no. 1: "You can continue to stay silent while we confiscate your computers, search your business premises, and prosecute you using the full force of the law, not to mention the inevitable headlines that may appear in the press."

The problem with this option for the public prosecutor's office is that it can take years until all the information has been gathered, sentences passed, and fines paid—if it is at all possible to investigate these types of complex commercial crimes with the available resources to the extent required for the resulting evidence to enable a successful prosecution.

What companies dislike about this option is clear: The public commotion surrounding the company and the unsightly images of grouchy criminal investigators carrying cartons full of files out of the company headquarters.

Therefore, **option no. 2** appears to be much more sensible for both parties: "We initiate criminal proceedings but offer you the opportunity to cooperate—and thus potentially benefit from a less severe punishment due to mitigating circumstances. In order for the case to be comprehensively investigated, you will commission an independent law firm and an auditing firm, which you will pay for but which will report to us." The Americans call this type of deal "deferred prosecution." A "deferred prosecution agreement" essentially means that the criminal investigators agree to waive part of the fines in exchange for the cooperation of the accused company—as long as the company fulfils certain requirements and cooperates during the investigation of the crimes. This is a process that was used, for example, in the investigation of Siemens by the US Department of Justice.

The benefits to the public prosecutor's office are that they save resources during the actual investigation, the process can be completed more quickly, and fines flow back into their coffers. In the end it is not always exclusively about justice even for a public prosecutor's office—they also need to balance their budgets and resolve the required number of cases.

What companies like about this option is that they are spared the "hassle" of dealing with the public prosecutor's office and also a large part of the public criticism, while they can also portray themselves as the party investigating the offenses and, hence, as a reformed company.

However, there are other things that companies and their lawyers don't like about this option. For example, there is the fact that nobody can guarantee that the investigation will run 100 % efficiently or that the public prosecutor's office will not still initiate supplementary investigations. And depending on the extent of the crimes, the process can quickly become very expensive due to the large number of external parties bustling about the company. There is also the issue that the willingness among employees to cooperate with "third party" lawyers and auditors is generally less than when compared to representatives of the public prosecutor's office—which can endanger the efficiency of the investigation.

The solution when this happens is to develop a high level of integration and efficient coordination between all parties involved in the investigation.

3.1.2 The Public Prosecutor's Office and Companies: Divergent Interests in the Investigation of White-Collar Crime

Anybody entrusted with investigating white-collar crime and corruption in their own company, or anyone who is in a position of liability for misconduct, should be clear about the following: During an investigation, the public prosecutor's office and the police do not have even remotely the same interests as those people in responsible positions at the company. In order to really exclude the risk of liability in the long term, those in responsible positions at companies such as members of the management board, supervisory board, and the head of the audit committee need to delve much deeper than a public prosecutor's office would do.

The investigative process conducted by the police and the public prosecutor's office has no other aim than to enforce the state's right to administer punishment in order to maintain law and order. And this process is carried out almost always in accordance with the principle of procedural economy—which prescribes that criminal proceedings must be carried out and concluded as efficiently as possible. For example, the public prosecutor's office will pass sentence as soon as sufficient proof has been found for a crime, the perpetrators have confessed, or corporate negligence could be established. This will preferably be in the form of fines in accordance with OWiG or by calling to account those persons in positions of responsibility who are deemed liable for the crimes. Once all of the charges have been processed, the case is generally considered closed as far as the public prosecutor's office is concerned.

Yet in certain circumstances it may still be far from clear whether other similar cases have occurred at the company, what the real magnitude of the resulting damage is, or what features of the internal control system and compliance management systems failed. All of these questions are generally not fully answered by the public prosecutor's office and the police due to the principle of procedural economy.

However, company bodies like the supervisory board, management board, or audit committee are obligated to prevent all damage to the company. In the immediate aftermath of a case where damage was caused to the company by white-collar crime, the issue must be completely investigated so that any findings can be used to implement a damage reduction strategy. This includes, for example, making attempts to recover misappropriated assets or holding people in positions of responsibility liable for the resulting damage under civil law. Sometimes this can even go as far as the supervisory board taking measures against the management board because they acted too passively or were actually aware of certain facts—facts that played no role in the investigation conducted by the public prosecutor's office but were nevertheless important when evaluating the case from the standpoint of the company.

In addition to simply investigating the case, company bodies are now also legally obligated to take appropriate measures for the prevention of similar cases in the future. Therefore, an investigation into these types of crimes must go above and beyond looking into the actual offenses and questions of guilt, and also examine the causes of the crime. Was this an isolated case that could not have been prevented even with the best control systems? Did the control systems fail? Does a structural problem exist that facilitates white-collar crime? Or has the situation developed to such an extent that a subculture has developed within the company, which practices fraud and manipulation in an organized manner? The relevant parameters that investigators can tweak will be presented in more detail in the next chapter where the early prevention of white-collar crime using compliance management systems will be discussed.

Once an offense becomes known, a company cannot simply choose whether it is a matter for the police or for auditors and lawyers. In order to give themselves proper protection against liability risks, supervisory bodies need both—especially if the authorities are already actively involved in the case.

The American model already takes account of this development to a large extent by ensuring that the company, the criminal proceedings, and the actual investigation of the case are already much more strongly linked once the investigative process begins. In this sense, there is no competition between the police and the forensic audit investigating white-collar crime. Companies even benefit from this mutual cooperation, which incidentally is now much more socially acceptable than it was before the turn of the millennium.

3.1.3 The Crime Enforcement Authorities and Companies: An Increasing Level of Cooperation

The level of willingness in companies to directly include independent auditing firms or even crime enforcement authorities in the process of solving white-collar crime from the very beginning has increased, not least due to the strict manner in which managers are made liable in the economy and the corresponding judicature. It has become much more rare for a solution to be exclusively found internally (in line with the motto: We can deal with this ourselves). Strictly speaking, it is not compulsory for companies to notify the police when they become aware of "deviant behavior." There are only a handful of crimes that require the police to be notified in Germany and white-collar crimes are not generally included in this list. As long as none of the sales representatives is preparing for a war of aggression[3] against a neighboring state, the accounting department is not entangled in a case of extortion,[4] and no one in your office is taking hostages, there is no need in the eyes of the law to report their misconduct to the authorities.[5]

Whether and when a company decides to include the investigative authorities is certainly dependent on the relevant conditions in each individual case. How strict is the regulatory pressure? What is the legal form of the business and the ownership

[3] See Article 80 StGB "Preparing for a war of aggression."

[4] See Article 255 StGB "Extortion."

[5] See Article 138 StGB "Failure to report offenses."

structure? Those companies listed on the capital markets are required to behave differently than owner-managed companies or medium-sized enterprises. Does the company have previous history of this type of crime or was it perhaps recently involved in a legal process? It makes sense in many cases to cooperate as a matter of course with the authorities and to engage the services of audit firms to provide the company with protection from all sides. Experience has shown that when commissioning an investigation—whether it is carried out by the crime enforcement authorities, auditing firms, or both—the dangers of indecision are often underestimated. If a tangible initial suspicion materializes and there are convincing indications of misconduct, it is important to act without delay. An attitude of "I'll deal with it later" is simply not acceptable, if only to serve the purpose of fulfilling your duties, ensuring your employer suffers no further damage, and to avoid being drawn into the line of fire yourself as far as liability is concerned. A significant proportion of white-collar crime and corruption-related offenses are impossible to properly resolve because they were not dealt with quickly or purposefully enough.

3.2 The Process of a Forensic Investigation

Especially newcomers to the profession of forensic auditing often imagine that fraud investigations are much more spectacular than they really are. Naturally, you can find yourself in thrilling situations as an auditor that are played out in dramatic circumstances. Almost every forensic auditor will have their own "war stories" with plenty of related anecdotes to tell.

Nevertheless, auditors working in the private sector should not make the mistake of believing they are a "detective" playing the star role in their own small corporate thriller. Ultimately, every forensic audit should be viewed as a consultancy service that is to be carried out in close consultation with the clients. This process must be carried out—in contrast to the assumptions made by many newcomers to the profession—in accordance with budget constraints and cannot afford to focus on anything other than the implementation of target-oriented measures.

Forensics is nothing more than a structured analysis with the sole aim of gaining knowledge. It is a professional trade that is offered on the market. Any evaluation of how this new knowledge may impact on the company only follows at the second stage. This second stage of the process is the task of a company commissioned for precisely this purpose, and which will often also seek legal advice along the way. Experience has demonstrated that those people who are truly guilty of these types of offenses are not always held to account for their actions—this is something that a forensic auditor investigating white-collar crime also needs to be able to handle.

Forensic auditors must be clear from the very beginning about their mandate and about how their actions could be restricted (Fig. 3.1).

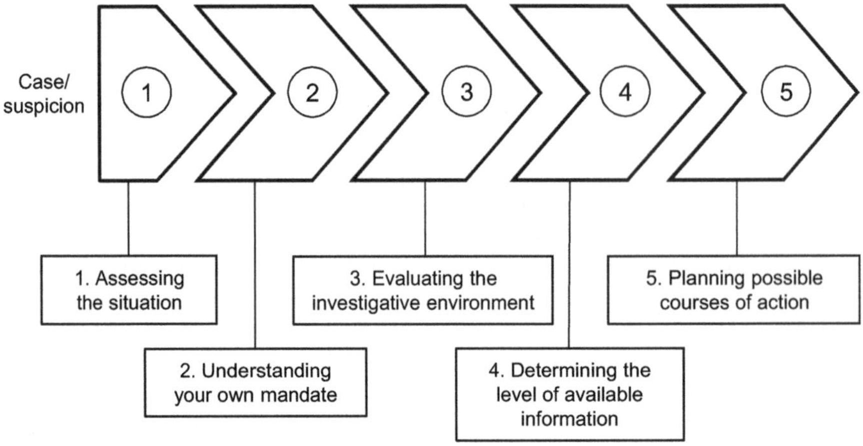

Fig. 3.1 Steps to be followed at the beginning of a forensic investigation

3.2.1 Assessing the Current Situation and Tactical Considerations for the Investigation

The first and most important question that needs to be asked by every auditor when investigating white-collar crime is: What is the current situation? In precisely the same way as in other criminal investigations or during military operations, there needs to be an assessment of the current situation before further investigative steps can be carried out. As already described, the situation at the company in which the investigation is to be conducted can vary greatly. Therefore, there is no unique standardized process for assessing the situation in the case of white-collar crime. Individual elements and key questions can be taken from the principles used to assess the situation in a military setting (for example, according to Army Regulations 100/100 "Military Leadership") and from the criminalistic processes followed for investigating capital crimes (Police Service Regulations 100 "Management and Deployment of Police Forces").[6] The elements of both can serve as a blueprint. An assessment of the current situation—in the context of white-collar crime—basically involves considering the following key aspects: Critically evaluating the mandate itself, visually inspecting and evaluating the environment under investigation, determining the level of information available, and lastly planning possible courses of action.

3.2.1.1 Understanding Your Own Mandate

- Who initiated the investigation? Will it deal only with an investigation commissioned by the company bodies, or are crime enforcement authorities

[6] It is already clear at this stage that experience in the police and military service is crucial for developing the skills to carry out forensic investigations in commercial enterprises – naturally in cooperation with auditors in the traditional sense.

already involved? If so have they already formulated a clear request for information and only want to know how the investigative process will be organized?

- When planning and designing the investigative methods, a different approach should be taken—and may prove more productive—depending on the reason for the initiation of the investigation. This is because the aim of the investigation could be very broadly defined or it could be very detailed and focused on individual events.
- What conditions have been set for the investigative measures? Have the offenses come to an end or are they ongoing?
- The investigative measures will be subject to a set of conditions that must be formulated for every commissioned investigation. Fundamental conditions include time constraints and the methodological framework for the investigation. The conditions governing your own actions can also be slightly more unusual; for example, if only a few people in the company are actually aware of the investigation, certain investigative methods will not be permitted or are not generally permitted due to data protection regulations or corporate principles. Or if it is known that offenses are still being carried out at the time of the investigation and you must deal discreetly with ongoing crimes.
- What type of offenses needs to be investigated? What expertise is required to complete this task? How extensive and time consuming is the investigation likely to be?
- Even urgent and unavoidable investigations still need to be organized, and a calculation made to evaluate the time and effort required. In order to evaluate a mandate, it is thus also necessary to consider the fee for the investigation, external costs, and the deployment of personnel, and to come to an agreement with the client in advance—making sure this is completed before the first file has even been opened.

3.2.1.2 Evaluating the Investigative Environment

- What is the overall economic situation of the company? Is the company in a healthy state or is it in a state of crisis? What effect has this had on the "mood" within the company?
- The current state of the company or organization can already provide clues about the roots of white-collar crime. Those who carry out investigations or commission these types of investigations would be well advised to also keep an eye on soft factors such as the corporate culture and the internal company mindset as a "battleground," and to develop an awareness for them. It is also important not to lose sight of informal networks and to try and get a feeling for the political currents within the company in order to be able to anticipate the threat of conflict.
- Who else is involved in the investigation—who can influence the investigation?
- It is necessary to involve all of the parties actively and passively linked to the investigation in the process of designing the forensic investigation. This includes of course those people who actively commissioned the investigation as

representatives of the company and could also include in-house councils, law firms, the works council, or supervisory board committees such as the audit committee. Naturally, it is also necessary to take into account external players such as the law enforcement authorities.

- Does the company have a previous history of white-collar crime? How were cases of white-collar crime dealt with in the past?
- Every assessment of a situation—whether military or criminalistic—requires a study of similar or previous cases that may play a role. In a similar way to every newly admitted patient in a hospital, every company will bring with it a "medical history" for the areas of noncompliance, corruption, and white-collar crime. Forensic auditors need to familiarize themselves with the details of this history should it be available.

3.2.1.3 Determining the Level of Available Information

- What cases of white-collar crime are already known? What are the sources of evidence?
- In order to assess the situation at the start, it is necessary to study and evaluate the actual reasons for commissioning an investigation: the initial suspicion described earlier or the already existing evidence. It is thus necessary to ascertain what facts there are that point to a case of damage in the company and the information about where this evidence originates.
- How aware of these cases are people both inside and outside of the company? Who knows that an investigation is being carried out?
- In order to determine the level of available information, it is also necessary to evaluate the current level of awareness about the case. The success of an investigation can be significantly influenced by avoiding the shock caused externally by an investigation and a case of white-collar crime becoming known or, conversely, by using public awareness to advance the investigative work.

3.2.1.4 Courses of Action

- How can information be obtained and from what sources? What subsequent steps will be most appropriate? As part of the preparation phase before the investigation, the planning of possible courses of action follows on almost as a logical consequence to assessing the situation at the start and examining the overall aim. In general, there is no ideal way to investigate a case where the company has incurred damage. It is much more probable that there will be a range of different strategies for obtaining necessary information. Depending on how well and diligently the assessment of the situation is carried out, it may be possible to design, schedule, and then implement an appropriate mix of investigative methods.

After the assessment of the situation, inexperienced auditors or investigators are often overcome by a feeling of euphoria. However, it does not make sense for any of the parties involved to blindly plough ahead or set to work too enthusiastically. There are fundamental aspects that everyone needs to take into account when dealing with white-collar crime, especially at the beginning of an investigation.

3.2.2 Three Basic Rules at the Start of an Investigation

As I mentioned before, no two investigations are alike and hence there is no ideal way to investigate these crimes. It is thus necessary to be very careful when discussing concepts like "basic rules." Nevertheless, working for over 20 years in the fields of criminal investigation and forensic auditing provides you with a wealth of experience that enables you to avoid making critical errors at the start of an investigation. The best methodology and the most competent team are worthless if beginner's errors are made right at the very start.

Basic Rule No. 1: Protect the Information

"At this point in the investigation, we are not able to reveal any details about the ongoing proceedings." This sentence is heard often at press conferences held by the police, especially for example, when special commissions are investigating capital crimes. This apparently meaningless phrase with which police spokesmen attempt to fob off journalists already embodies the fundamental task of all investigators—protecting the information.

In the example where an individual within a company has had the aforementioned anonymous letter containing alleged details of corruption slipped under their door, one thing is crucial. They must be extremely careful with whom they discuss this matter and also about how they discuss it. Should they immediately attempt to talk to the accused? Should they turn to a confidant within the company? Or do they even send the information on in e-mails, which can then be forwarded, printed out, and left forgotten on the photocopier?

It is not without reason that the investigative authorities shroud themselves in secrecy after a murder has been committed. It would be negligent or even plain stupid to reveal precisely what had happened to the public because this would only make all other investigative measures more difficult. Let us assume that there are multiple suspects who need to be questioned individually. If the precise course of events has already been printed in the newspapers, investigators lose the opportunity to compare statements or identify irregularities in the statements. For example, when suspects are forced to reveal information about the crime due to skilful interviewing techniques that he or she shouldn't actually know—so-called "perpetrator knowledge."

What is true for capital crimes can equally be applied to cases of corruption or white-collar crime. The skilful screening, protection, and utilization of information simplifies the investigative process and prevents, in particular, perpetrators becoming aware that they have been found out and covering up evidence of their crime.

Basic Rule No. 2: Protect the Employees

Irrespective of how large or small the investigation is, it is not only important to protect information at the start of an investigation but also to protect those employees who provide this information. This is because there is hardly any other environment where carelessly formulated suspicions such as "it could only be so and so" can lead to serious threats to individual employees and the entire corporate culture. This alleged involvement in corruption and fraud will stay with an employee as if they had been branded a criminal—and they will generally never be able to free themselves of this suspicion, irrespective of whether they were actually embroiled in the case or not. This is the reason why most whistleblowers leave their companies after the case has been investigated. The effects on a person's job and life as a result of bullying or being ostracized as a "traitor" or "informer" are enormous. Whistleblowers are generally not celebrated as heroes.

Yet these people certainly do act heroically. This is especially true in cases involving highly charged issues such as arms trafficking, organized crime, or, in certain countries, corruption at a government level in which whistleblowers have been known to suddenly disappear, die with no apparent explanation, or even commit suicide. In some countries, whistleblowers are thus afforded special legal protection. In the USA, the Sarbanes-Oxley Act contains, for example, a number of paragraphs on whistleblower protection, which protect the confidentiality of informants and stipulate that they must not be disadvantaged as a result. However, experience has shown that the employee is already disadvantaged as soon as their name becomes connected with the case.

White-collar crime is a highly emotional subject and almost always an exceptional situation. You could either find yourself in the firing line or find that your closest and most trusted friends and colleagues in the company are suddenly accused of fraud. Only very few management boards and supervisory boards have been forced to witness how the safe day-to-day environment in the company is suddenly turned on its head as a result of white-collar crime, triggering a culture of general suspicion and in turn making all colleagues and employees into suspects themselves.

As a consultant commissioned to investigate these types of crimes, it will often also be necessary to slow down your counterpart at the company and very carefully sensitize them to the situation in order to prevent their own employees, others who may be involved, or the company from being damaged even more than they are already due to the crime.

The managing director who declares that they will fight crime in their company tooth and nail has probably underestimated the impact this approach can have on employees if he or she acts too hastily. The same also applies to heavy-handed consultants.

Basic Rule No. 3: Immediately Secure Data

When it comes to the third basic rule for fraud investigations, we find ourselves almost directly involved in the investigation itself. As soon as the situation has been assessed and the goals have been agreed with the client, all available information, data, and files that could play a role in the case need to be secured as quickly as possible. At this stage, this has much less to do with the actual forensic data analysis itself and more to do with obtaining access to and mirroring the data before it can be falsified, deleted, or smuggled out of the company. This is particularly important in those parts of the company that work in close proximity to the money, and therefore where a great deal of assets can be moved very quickly.

It sounds trivial but more than a few of the prominently conducted corruption, antitrust, and fraud investigations simply peter out after months or even years or completely fail because all the necessary company data was not secured within literally the first few minutes of the investigation, presenting the perpetrators with the opportunity to conceal their crimes.

3.2.3 Concealment and Cover-Ups: Examples from Purchasing and Sales Departments

Concealment and cover-ups make it more difficult for auditors to completely decipher the puzzle of manipulation, corruption, and fraud. In many cases it proves impossible because the crimes are too convoluted or complex and have been concealed for too long. This is not to say that white-collar crime cannot be solved if the perpetrators have not been identified. They are in fact almost always identified, but completely solving the case in a textbook manner akin to the finale of a detective novel simply does not happen often in real life. This is because the possibilities for concealment within an economic system are endlessly diverse and fraudsters now sometimes employ complex processes with the sole purpose of ensuring that an investigation cannot be concluded within the prescribed time frame and with the limited available resources. Depending on the company department, there are also weak spots in relation to corruption and white-collar crime that a good auditor can utilize in almost all cases to identify if, when, and where manipulation has taken place.

The following examples taken from two critical areas of a company—purchasing and sales—will provide a good illustration of these concepts.

3.2.3.1 Corruption in Purchasing: Extremely Difficult to Prove Unequivocally

If a purchaser has been bribed and thus gives a certain bidder or supplier preferential treatment, the level of information in the company is naturally very sparse. However, the damage to the company could be serious because it must then pay inflated prices for poorer products than could be procured on the market. The possibilities for concealment are extremely diverse, if concealment is necessary at all. In many companies and corporate groups, the purchasing department exists on its own as a highly specialized parallel organization—outside of all controls and transparency obligations. The challenges facing corruption investigators, especially in purchasing departments, will be briefly presented below.

- Payments to purchasers are barely traceable

  The bribes paid to purchasers are never actually seen by the commissioning company. They are transferred directly to the private bank accounts of the purchaser, a spouse, or an accomplice—if any money is transferred at all and not just simply handed over in cash. Without being able to investigate the private assets of the purchaser, it is in effect impossible to actually prove these payments unless it is possible to trace them through the books of the sales organization bribing the purchaser.
- Invitations to tender, quotations, and contracts are extremely complex

  Purchasing is a highly specialized area of the company that, depending on the sector and the product, represents a science unto itself. The crucial factor in the selection of a service provider or supplier is often a product detail hidden within a specific context that is extremely complex and difficult for a layperson to understand. Therefore, it is possible in the way that the specifications for an invitation to tender are written to discreetly limit the possible contenders to a group of favorites or to benefit certain individuals. For example, the specifications could be directly adapted to fit the profile of the desired candidate or exclusion criteria introduced that only select suppliers can fulfil. The high level of complexity found in invitations to tender, quotations, and contracts makes it almost impossible for investigators and auditors to extract strong evidence of corruption. If you consider major infrastructure projects such as airports or train stations for a moment, it is hardly possible to comprehend the sheer scope and scale of the individual components involved.
- It is almost impossible to evaluate quality in a neutral manner

  It is only in the unlikely event that products from different suppliers are absolutely identical and their quality cannot be disputed that a corrupt purchaser will be forced to legitimize their selection of a more expensive supplier. In all other cases, preferential treatment given to a certain supplier is often justified using the quality argument. It is hardly possible to provide a neutral evaluation of the quality of a product—irrespective of whether it is yoghurt, strategic consulting, or hose pumps—and this makes it incredibly difficult to find key evidence that some suppliers have enjoyed preferential treatment and the company has incurred damage due to the payment of inflated prices.
- Informal communication and personal relationships

  Only the most incompetent of corrupt purchasers would allow any agreement on an invitation to tender or details about the receipt of kickbacks to be formally documented or recorded. In many cases, a personal relationship—or often even a friendship—has existed between the purchaser and the sales representative for many years. If decisive and detailed information about a future invitation to tender is thus quietly revealed at the weekend at a sports event or on the golf course, there is almost no possibility of finding evidence that any arrangement ever existed. This is also true for antitrust offenses that often only become public because whistleblowers have had the courage to reveal the situation or key witnesses have been promised lighter punishments.

3.2.3.2 Fraud and Bribery in Sales: Identifying Critical Areas

The opportunities available for concealing white-collar crime and corruption in sales are probably just as great as in purchasing. However, fraud in the sales department is a great deal easier to investigate than corruption in purchasing. This is because company documents need to be falsified or changed in order for fraud to be committed through sales activities. If bribes are paid, for example, the money has to leave the company somehow—this money trail is already an example of a decisive piece of evidence that does not exist in the case of corruption in purchasing. When money leaves a company, there are always key areas that can be identified and thoroughly examined.

Following the Money Trail

Money leaves a trail. It does so in the form of fake invoices, fictitious projects, or dummy employees. Every euro that unlawfully enriches the fraudsters is linked to some form of background story that costs the company money. Anybody who takes sufficient time to precisely check whether an incoming invoice is really being paid for a service that the company actually received, will sooner or later inevitably uncover the source of the leak in the company, finally identifying the fraudulent measure being used to siphon away money—even though the creativity of perpetrators knows no bounds.

The employment of agents and consultants was a classic ruse used for many years to help money disappear from the company. This involved invoicing the company for services that in reality had never been provided. Naturally, this relatively unsophisticated form of manipulation does not really present a well-trained criminalistic or forensic auditor with any great difficulty. The example is merely designed to illustrate that corruption in sales, and its associated concealment, offers only one further starting point for the investigation than corruption in purchasing does. Namely, the trail left by the necessity to channel money out of the company through fraudulent means.

Generally speaking, there are a wide variety of possibilities that could have been used to carry out and conceal these types of offenses. This makes the criminalistics process of formulating hypotheses a key skill for forensic auditors.

3.3 The Criminalistic Process and the Formulation of Hypotheses

With the exception of ongoing offenses in which the instruments of prevention and detection must be deployed to a much greater extent, the challenge facing those investigating corruption and white-collar crime is to try to understand events that have already happened in the past. Despite comprehensively protecting the available data, this means investigators of these crimes will often only be in possession of small fragments of the overall picture of what has happened. These fragments must be investigated, evaluated, and put back together in their correct context. It is necessary at this point to make something clear: Even the best investigators will generally be unable to reconstruct the whole picture and with it the offense down to the tiniest detail—no matter whether they are a detective superintendent or a forensic auditor. Naturally, private investigators can still ultimately always fall back on criminal prosecutions because criminal investigators have greater access to information—such as the private assets of suspected fraudsters.

In principle, companies possess a huge amount of information that can be inspected, checked, and evaluated. In terms of the broad range of skills required, it is not so important whether a forensic auditor is capable of doing everything themselves and putting everything they have available to use, but rather whether they are capable of selecting the correct investigative methods in advance and implementing them in a targeted way. This can be achieved by the formulation of a logical hypothesis.

A criminalistic hypothesis is a tentative explanation based on the existing facts for an as yet unproven event that acts as an intermediate stage in the collection of evidence. It represents an attempt to explain offenses that will, in principle, almost inevitably provide starting points for implementing investigative measures. As a result, questions always need to be formulated as follows: "If employee XY is supposed to have carried out this or that offense, what would they have had to falsify in order to avoid being exposed? Who must have known about it and what documents (contracts, authorizations, etc.) would it have been necessary to create?

A criminalist will work through the set of suspicious circumstances using these types of hypothetical questions and constantly compare results with the findings of the investigation. This continues until only one explanation for the crime exists: The right one.

It is only logical that there could be many different starting points for corresponding investigative methods. These so-called "sources of information," as well as their methodology and application, will be presented in the following section. It should be noted that this evaluation of the relevant sources of information and the related forensic methodology covers only key features to avoid this overview becoming too specialist and thus incomprehensible—and to also ensure that the general context is not lost (Fig. 3.2).

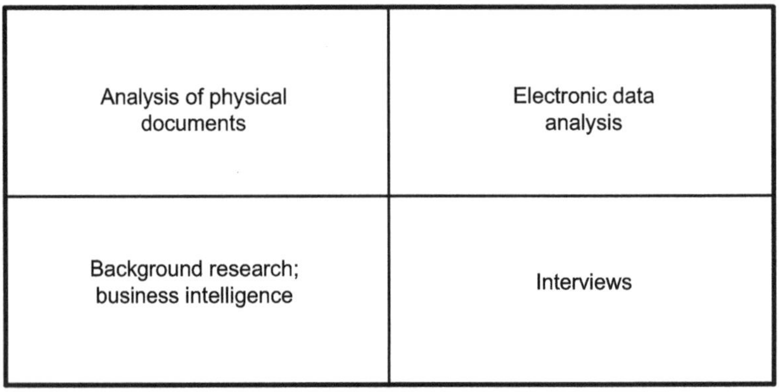

Fig. 3.2 Sources of information in forensic auditing

3.3.1 Physical Documentation as a Source of Information

Even in these times of extensive digitalization of almost all business processes in companies, securing and analyzing physical documents remains indispensable. This is because of the fact that, in contrast to electronic data, it is hard to manipulate documents that have been printed or written by employees themselves. The only possibilities for concealment are the subsequent falsification, substitution, or even destruction of the documents. As mentioned earlier, the quicker the company can react and auditors secure the relevant files, the less opportunity there is to manipulate them. In the modern world, hectic attempts to black out, rip up, or shred documents at the last minute have relatively little prospect of success. There are now certain scanning and reconstruction technologies that in many cases enable these documents to be recreated. In a similar way to making a break for it in a criminal case, an obvious attempt to manipulate documents is increasingly being seen as a clear admission of guilt.

3.3.1.1 Collecting Documents and Sealing Access to Them

In order to protect yourself as an auditor or consultant against possible dispute on the part of the client, it is not only necessary to ensure the authenticity but also the completeness of relevant company documents. There is nothing worse or more embarrassing than when a file suddenly appears shortly before the end of the investigation, turning the whole chain of evidence upside down.

Especially when dealing with large companies and complex manipulations, which can generate an almost endless jumble of documentation, it is important to carefully record when the investigation team received which documents. This is important for the simple reason of protecting the investigation itself. It will help to prevent mysterious files belatedly appearing that have been more or less put together overnight and just happen by chance to contain the commercial documentation for the business transaction being investigated. Attempts to do this sort of thing have certainly been made in the past.

For this reason, no concessions should be made when an excuse is given such as "We'll give you the file tomorrow." All documents need to be immediately safeguarded. If somebody does not want to, or is allegedly unable to, provide the documentation, this situation should be particularly carefully examined and appropriate action taken at an early stage. The fact is that even the willingness to provide documentation itself provides investigators with clues to both the offense and who was perhaps involved.

Once all documentation that could possibly be relevant has been secured, it is a good idea to turn a large conference room within the company itself into the investigative headquarters, or to transport the documentation to a location that is inaccessible to all those not involved in the investigation. It also doesn't cause any harm to change the locks in the relevant locations and create a list of people authorized to have access to this room.[7] If necessary, caretakers and cleaning

[7] Auditing firms such as EY also possess rooms that are secured with alarms and approved by the police for the storage of evidence.

staff with master keys must also be considered. It is essential that nobody outside of the investigative team has any access whatsoever to this room. If there is any doubt, an independent security company should be commissioned to safeguard the access documentation.

Criminal prosecution and antitrust authorities often act in a much more radical way than an auditing firm when they carry out an investigation and secure documents in a company. Here, the rooms may even be sealed. This happened at the end of 2012 when the electricity company e.on had to pay a fine totaling millions because a door seal had been damaged—in all probability by one of the cleaning staff. In these cases, even a scratch on the sticker is sufficient for a fine to be issued.

Once the investigative headquarters have been established and made safe, all of the secured documentation must firstly be copied and then paginated. This means that the documentation is issued with consecutive numbers—making it obvious very quickly if documents are removed or added, and making it possible to uniquely identify each piece of evidence. The purpose of having a copy of the documentation is to ensure that no changes must be made to the structure and content of the original documents and it provides investigators with something with which they can work—meaning they can mark text passages and add references. The original documentation must remain under lock and key at all times during the investigation and is of course not used itself during the audit.

It already becomes clear at this point that during the process of evaluating the physical documentation as a source of information, ensuring the accurate preparation and legal compliance of the documentation is absolutely indispensable. In many cases this proves to be more difficult, time consuming, and significant than the actual auditing procedure itself.

What form do these audits take? Will they deal with checking physical documentation exclusively? Do good auditors always focus on key areas and then commence their search for suspicious activity in a targeted manner? The question should be: What is it that could only be found in physical documentation that would not be recorded in electronic documentation? Naturally, it could be possible to check all money flows, master data from creditors, or time stamps by hand and only using physical documentation. However, this process generally runs much faster and more precisely using electronic tables, forensic software, or full-text analyses. And this sort of repetitive work does not benefit anybody. Nevertheless, there are areas of criminalistics in which humans can outperform machines and the physical documentation becomes an indispensable source of information. For example, in order to reconstruct the case of white-collar crime or corruption, the authenticity of written documents must be checked or certain actions must be traced and their meaningfulness understood. It is generally milestones such as quotations or the actual outgoing invoices that are mainly documented in physical form—rarely intermediate steps or correspondence. A criminalistic feeling for the case and a solid starting hypothesis are fundamental factors in carrying out a truly productive analysis of physical documentation.

3.3.1.2 The Forensic Analysis of Documents Suspected of Being Falsified

Authorizations, checks, internal directives and approvals, contracts, invoices, and personnel documents—everything can be falsified or altered. However, forensic auditors with experienced criminalists in their team possess a relatively large set of technical tools for checking the authenticity of documents. One good place to start is with personal handwriting styles and signatures. Handwritten notes can be matched up relatively quickly with their authors because the human body cannot simply unlearn repetitive forms of letters and movement patterns. For example, even if someone were to make an effort to change their handwriting style, they will still always tend to place the pen in the same position when they begin to write the letter "g". In the same way, it is very difficult to imitate fluidity of movement, application of pressure, or the proportions of the different letters—and these are just a few of the unique characteristics of a person's handwriting.

No forger in the world can avoid the problem of needing to imitate personal signatures—for example, if contracts or budget approvals need to be falsified. A good forger can have great success in this area. What member of the management board can at the end of the day remember everything that they have had to sign? The natural deviations between the signatures of one person—even if the two signatures are only signed a few seconds apart—can never really be reliably falsified. In general, forgers betray themselves due to the fact that they have done their work so well and the falsified signatures are exactly the same as previous signatures. It would be absolutely impossible to achieve this in real life as can be proven using criminalistic analyses.

With payment documents and receipts or cashier's checks, the manipulation involves, for example, changing the original amounts on the crossed checks. This is achieved by either adding, erasing, or even scraping off numbers. By using infra-red light and chemical techniques, this type of falsification can be almost unequivocally exposed should the naked eye or a magnifying glass ultimately prove inadequate.

Besides the handwriting, the paper itself may provide information as to whether you are dealing with a falsified or manipulated document. This could involve the type, weight, pattern, and composition of the paper, as well as the printed image and the origin of the ink on the paper. It is thus possible to determine whether the allegedly falsified purchase invoice originated from a printer within the company or from a private printer—the printed image and the ink composition hold clues about the manufacturer, age, and condition of the printers or pens.

3.3.1.3 The Reconstruction of Business Processes Based on Company Documentation

If technical analyses do not indicate any obvious falsification of documents or there are no suspicious circumstances, physical documents can still be used as milestones and starting points for understanding various courses of action. As described above, a large proportion of the company's documents are stored electronically, so that it makes little sense to view both forms of documentation separately. The details of the individual case will influence precisely what to look for and which hypothesis should be used to investigate the documents.

The approach used to complete a document analysis always seeks to reconstruct business processes and search for conspicuous features and irregularities. These conspicuous features could be that receipts or outgoing invoices are missing, have a different name, or are made out to a different address for a certain period of time, or suddenly contain unusual items—these can all be traced through the company's commercial documentation. In construction and infrastructure projects, it is common for kickbacks or bribes to be hidden within technical details that can be difficult to fully understand. If a type of wall paint is listed as being an expensive fire-retardant paint but a standard paint from a DIY store was used instead, a monetary value is realized that hardly anybody would notice. This can still be detected, however, if an appropriate investigation is carried out where the technical and commercial documentation are compared with each other. This method can be used to reveal which vehicle was used for paying bribes in corruption offenses.

A comparison of the record of activities in the front office and documentation stored in the accounting department will often reveal, especially in corruption cases, a lack of plausibility in the orders compared to the bookings—which is precisely what every corruption investigator is searching for. If the internal company documentation shows, for example, that a business transaction was initiated in a foreign country and then, shortly before the deal is concluded, receipts or invoices suddenly appeared from a consultant who was previously uninvolved in the process, the alarm bells should start to ring. If the investigator traces what services were really provided by the consultant, where money was transferred, and whether the consultant was previously registered as a creditor or debtor, a large number of inconsistencies will come to light over time with more and more in-depth examination. It is then possible to examine these inconsistencies further through background research or by interviewing those involved in order to comprehensively investigate the offense.

3.3.2 Electronic Data Analysis as a Source of Information

In the wake of the digitalization of all corporate processes, the volumes of data held on servers maintained by German companies have increased exponentially: e-mail archives, text files, invoices, balance sheets—terabyte on terabyte and exabyte on exabyte.[8] In addition, there are also many companies who maintain outdated or duplicated data records. This doesn't only cost a great deal of money but also makes the process of finding data in an investigation a real challenge.

The fact that companies are sometimes no longer the master of their own data was demonstrated by an EY survey (see Ernst & Young 2012) that asked for the reasons why companies were poorly prepared for fraud investigations or so-called

[8] An exabyte corresponds to a billion gigabytes.

"e-discovery orders" as part of an investigation. Alongside the lack of software (25 %), a too diverse IT system environment (25 %), and a lack of expertise (26 %), the companies remarked that the data volumes were too large (40 %) and the data structures too complex (40 %).

3.3.2.1 Safeguarding Electronic Data and Data Media During a Fraud Investigation

What is true for physical documentation must naturally also be true for digital documentation. In the event of a fraud investigation, it is crucial to safeguard this data as quickly as possible. Depending on how the IT infrastructure in a company has been designed and the extent to which investigators are permitted to access this system, there are a wide variety of possibilities for safeguarding this data. Investigations that are only carried out internally within a company are subject in many cases to data protection restrictions, meaning it is not possible to utilize the full scope of the technical possibilities as it would invade, for example, the privacy of individual employees. Therefore, it is important to receive legally watertight clarification on certain points before beginning the investigation and starting to collect, evaluate, and process data. What data and data media really need to be safeguarded? What type of data are you dealing with and what technical expertise is required to evaluate this data? And if it is possible to access the data from a purely technical standpoint, is it permitted to backup or view this data? It is necessary at this point to make a brief comment on the subject of data protection: no internal company auditor or external investigator will be content to gain unlawful access to data and make themselves party to an act of noncompliance. For this reason, a process should be mutually agreed for handling the data analysis in cooperation with the company and, if required, lawyers. Otherwise, the entire investigation could be put at risk as the counterparty would be able to use this as ammunition, or it could mean that the evidence will be deemed inadmissible before the court.

Once both legal and political hurdles have been overcome, investigators have a broad range of possibilities for securing and evaluating company data. In general, hard drives, data servers, and mobile end devices are initially secured in one location. The data stored on these devices is then mirrored. This means that physical copies of the data media are produced.

Following this type of court-approved, digital preservation of evidence, any deleted or damaged data may be restored and encrypted or masked data decoded. In reality, data on hard drives or mobile devices is never really deleted when you press the "delete" button. It is merely removed from the hard drive's index and then sooner or later overwritten. It is possible, however, to recover this data using a range of different technologies. This makes the concealment of crimes within company data difficult for those perpetrators who are not proven IT experts.

3.3.2.2 Making Different Types of Data Useful

While murder investigators rely on ballistics experts or pathologists, fraud investigators are similarly reliant on forensic data analysts. They help to reconstruct the concealed actions of the perpetrator and trace the manipulation of data. And in these times of electronic business documentation, these methods offer much greater potential than those based on "printed" physical documentation as a source of information. This is because electronic data traffic in a company encompasses much more than just those documents that need to be archived according to law. This includes e-mails, telephone directories, and document histories—correspondence and intermediate stages of documents that cover far more than just the commercial and technical milestones that are archived in a physical file. The ability to make this data useful—for the purposes of securing evidence and carrying out a criminalistic appraisal of white-collar crime—is a core skill required by investigators in the modern world. This data reveals a great deal if you know how to use it correctly—and the important point is that data does not forget, or at least not very much.

Even if the company reacts quickly to suspicious activities being uncovered, there is still always the chance that a file may disappear or a few pages will be ripped out and destroyed. There have even been cases in which incriminating documents have simply been eaten. Therefore, anybody who thinks that electronic company data is easier to manipulate than physical documents is mistaken. This is because electronic data is significantly less "digestible" and can only really be completely destroyed or masked by extremely accomplished perpetrators. Naturally, it is always possible that the perpetrator arranges for a computer, notebook, or USB stick with incriminating material to simply disappear. Nevertheless, the pool of electronic data in a company remains large. This is because almost every company regularly makes backups of their data—every year, every month, and sometimes every week. This data is saved and kept on specially stored tapes for at least 10 years.

There are even companies where, for example, the archiving of e-mails is controlled by the server—meaning that the users do not decide themselves what or how things are archived when they empty their inbox. The process for backing up e-mail correspondence thus takes place in real time and is permanently documented. In general, e-mails and practically all company data are normally saved to a server whose inventory is regularly backed up. The use of media such as cloud services and social networks that are outside of the company's data structures is a new trend causing increasing problems for these types of investigation.

If suspicious activities relating to white-collar crime come to light, the process of collecting information increasingly ends in the digital cloud. Even criminal prosecution authorities are not permitted to simply view this data—which could include messages dealing with, for example, price fixing or irregular deals that are stored on social network sites like LinkedIn or Facebook. In the case of the large majority of encrypted cloud services and file sharing platforms, they are based on server environments in countries in which the authorities have practically no jurisdiction, let alone the possibility for viewing the data. A judge in Reutlingen issued both Facebook Germany and the European headquarters of this social network in Dublin with a seizure order to receive access to the Facebook account of a potential criminal (see German Press Agency 2012), including access to private messages. He then subsequently issued a request for mutual legal assistance from the responsible authorities in Ireland. If the judge had been successful, it would possibly have proved to be a landmark case, which would have significantly simplified investigations into compliance infringements and white-collar crime within social networks.

3.3.2.3 Forensic Data Analyses

IT specialists carrying out analyses of company data for criminal prosecution authorities and internal company auditors differentiate between two different types of data—structured data and unstructured data. The methods used to investigate these different forms of data differ fundamentally. The basic features will be briefly presented below.

The Analysis of Structured Data

Structured data deals with information that is uniformly arranged and structured in such a way that it can be sorted into a table with rows and columns allowing it to be evaluated. Therefore, the nature of the individual records does not vary, which allows this kind of data to be normally saved in databases. Large parts of a company's internal documentation are stored as structured data, such as time sheets, stock levels in materials management systems, and financial accounting. An analysis of structured data is thus always designed to find patterns, irregularities, contradictions, or logical breaks in a large amount of identical-looking records. These are tasks that even those gifted enough to perform difficult calculations in their own heads could not achieve on their own.

IT forensic auditors are assisted here by specially designed computer programs that search documents being investigated for fraud patterns, arrange and filter data, delete duplicate data, check cross-referenced data, and perform clustering and regression calculations—thus making interrelationships easy to see. Ultimately, this all describes a statistical evaluation process that incorporates formulas used in accountancy and mathematics, such as "Benford's Law" described at the beginning of this chapter, with the goal of creating an algorithm that detects and displays evidence of manipulation and fraud.

The Analysis of Unstructured Data

A completely different type of information can be gained from so-called unstructured data. This type of data cannot be evaluated in table form because its very nature means it can contain very diverse pieces of information. Examples of this type of data are communication and text files such as e-mails, Word documents, PowerPoint presentations, or digital post-it notes, although it can also include images, videos, and sound recordings. A new dimension in this area is the evaluation of web services such as instant messaging protocols, short messages, or message histories in social networks such as Facebook. The most valuable information from an analysis of unstructured data can be found when searching for proof of arrangements made between perpetrators and involved parties, such as in the area of corruption.

In cooperation with the FBI (Federal Bureau of Investigation), EY has developed a software program that focuses on precisely this area and takes the analysis of unstructured data to a completely new level. A linguistic software is used to evaluate e-mails, SMS, or instant messages that searches through all correspondence found in the entire data inventory for suspicious phrases. These could include phrases like: “Nobody will find out,” “Do it off the books,” “Cover it up,” “Charge a special fee,” and so on.[9]

The program also raises the alarm when employees ask their colleagues by e-mail to “discuss it in person” or suggest “it would be better to talk on the phone.” Naturally, these types of linguistic programs need to be handled very carefully and used exclusively for phrases relevant to fraud. However, it perhaps comes as no surprise that Americans have less qualms about using this kind of technology.

There are now forensic analysis systems that can create a kind of global text from the available data material by interlinking all of the relevant documents. Information can be traced throughout this global text by marking key words or file signatures that are subsequently searched across all of the segments of the global text.

If the key word is, for example, “Guatemala”—maybe because bribes have allegedly been paid in this country for an infrastructure project—the system will output all texts, images, and files in which the word Guatemala is either present or implicitly stored in the so-called “meta description” of a file. Depending on the quality of this type of forensic data analysis software, the system can also take into account whether the search word has been spelt incorrectly, abbreviated, or written in another language. This technology is known as fuzzy logic or as a “string-matching algorithm.”

There are now even programs that have a certain level of intelligence built into their full text searches. By applying statistical tools and search algorithms that “learn,” it is possible to filter out duplicated or irrelevant search results that do not fit the search criteria. This makes it easier to sort many files into categories and according to their relevance.

However, modern forensic data analysis programs are much more capable of making use of unstructured data and extracting data from it than by simply searching for key words. For example, if the objective is to reconstruct the actions of, or agreements made by, perpetrators, the programs can read e-mails including their attachments and produce a virtual map that graphically represents the conversations and their subjects at the push of a button. The lines on the screen link pieces of information enabling investigators to trace who wrote to whom, when and how often, what the subject of the e-mail was, or even whether the subject fitted the e-mail content or attachment. Similarly to booking data or material movement data, this data makes it possible to understand how processes were controlled or

[9] There have also already been reports about this software in Germany: See Kaiser (2013).

crimes committed—insofar as this information can be extracted or decoded from the e-mails.

Assessment: Use in a Criminalistic Context

The use of forensic data analyses can deliver an almost endless stream of information about possible acts committed by perpetrators. However, this does not mean that this information alone immediately provides all the answers. Even the most technically sophisticated investigator still needs to examine the analyzed data in a criminalistic context. Investigators can only really work effectively if they are able to correctly read and interpret the digital clues that they have uncovered—and do not simply rely on the feeling of power bestowed on them by technical analyses and evaluations.

This makes the already discussed process of formulating hypotheses all the more important for uncovering the actions of the perpetrators from among the dense jungle of company data. Experience gained through working on many cases investigating "deviant behavior" using electronic data analysis has demonstrated that anyone who switches on the analysis tool but disengages their brain at the same time will only achieve limited success, especially because perpetrators are extremely skilled and hide their crimes well within the masses of data. Nevertheless, the perpetrator is in general not able to think of everything. Those people who carry out manipulations always leave behind traces of their actions. Data analyses alone, even when implemented in combination with criminalistic hypotheses, still only make up one piece of the puzzle—especially when dealing with complex cases. Questions such as "What motives are hidden behind these cases?" and "What happened to enable this type of fraud to be committed?" should never be forgotten when combating fraud, despite the availability of first-class technical measures.

In this sense, the fight against white-collar crime is really quite similar to a murder case: the perpetrators had to act, make the weapon disappear, and eliminate possible witnesses. Depending on the crime, these are precisely the same actions taken by white-collar criminals—actions that even an expertly conducted data analysis will sometimes not reveal.

3.3.3 Background Research/Business Intelligence as a Source of Information

The term intelligence is used in business for a wide variety of information-gathering processes, ranging from researching the market and the competition through to the full analysis and utilization of internal company information for the purpose of managing the company.

The meaning of the word intelligence in the area of forensic auditing is often incorrectly understood or misinterpreted. The focus in this area is the procurement and evaluation of information that deals with people's integrity. This means IT-based background research into publically accessible sources for the purpose of gathering information about the white-collar crime that lies outside of the damaged company.

Background research in the sense of business intelligence is a highly effective and almost always necessary tool that is used during a fraud investigation to follow up suspicions and fully explain cases of white-collar crime. In a large number of cases, relevant information is often found far outside the sphere of influence of the damaged company and firstly needs to be researched or procured. Business intelligence in a forensic audit has two different roles in this area: one is reactive and provides information for helping to explain white-collar crime; while the other is preventative and deals to a much greater extent with checking the integrity of business partners and target markets in advance.

Despite the fact that the term "intelligence" is primarily associated with the American foreign intelligence service, the CIA (Central Intelligence Agency), business intelligence has nothing to do with spying, observation, or undercover operations. The purpose of business intelligence is thus not to uncover the enemy hidden in the economy. The background research required for the purpose of shedding more light on white-collar crime has a much more legal or journalistic character and is utilized for gaining knowledge when the client has a justifiable interest in explaining a crime.

What can business intelligence be used for in an investigation? The starting points are generally any findings from the analysis of relevant documentation and the forensic data analysis. These analyses very often reveal links between the company and the private lives of the perpetrator, or links to other economic activities of the perpetrators, which in turn lead even further into the twilight world of dubious business addresses. This is where business intelligence comes into play in order to follow the clues and uncover the relevant background story. The following applications for business intelligence provide examples of how this instrument can be used in a fraud investigation.

3.3.3.1 Tracing Money Flows

Invoices apparently falsified lead abroad or secured data from a subledger account quote the names of companies as the recipients of money who were not entered as a creditor in the accounting department—embezzled money has to leave the company somehow. Background research can trace money flows and guarantee the integrity of business partners. This could involve, for example, checking whether you are dealing with a bogus company or whether the recipient company has a personal relationship with the suspect or suspects.

3.3.3.2 Tracing Fraudulent Networks

To be able to maintain a complex case of fraud, it is often necessary to set up a large number of bogus companies that will keep it concealed, either to document the transfer of bribes in the correct manner or to be able to offset the payments against tax. After all, the stereotypical briefcase stuffed full of cash is no longer suitable for the purposes of moving assets or laundering money.

At the start there is much that is not clear. How do the people involved fit into these types of fraudulent networks? What is really hidden behind the invoice address? Who exactly are the founders, partners, or website architects of these suspect companies? Therefore, another goal of background research is also to trace fraudulent networks. It turns out to be quite common for fraudsters to lure their families, friends, and acquaintances into their schemes, too.

3.3.3.3 Identifying Individual People

Who is the consultant that is talked about in the e-mails shortly before the business transaction was concluded? Who could have known about the events who is no longer employed by the company, or who perhaps never was? When investigating crimes, it is also important to identify anyone who had anything to do with the events or could be useful as a witness or whistleblower.

3.3.3.4 Checking the Facts

Particularly in so-called "high-risk countries" (see here Transparency International 2012), it is difficult to get very far without business intelligence because these investigations often lead deep into local social structures. Business intelligence fulfils the role of getting to the very source of dubious actions and ascertaining whether the named people, companies, construction projects, or stated ownership structures actually exist. The sources dealt with by a business intelligence unit can be arranged in a cascade, from Internet research and examining registers through to on-site visits. In the case of a fraud investigation, an on-site visit means nothing more than on-site research.

3.3.3.5 Research on the Internet and in Online Databases

Well-trained Internet researchers possess techniques that go far beyond simply using "Google." Those who carry out research on the Internet are limiting themselves to a significant extent if they only use Google and other well-known search engines. This is because the search algorithms used by Google sort the search results according to the user and the frequency with which these search queries have been entered in the past. It is much more sensible to use so-called "metasearch engines." Metasearch engines send their search queries to multiple search engines at the same time and are already smart enough to collect, sort, and evaluate the results depending on how they are configured.

The current generation of metasearch engines also allow syntax translation, so that much more complex search queries can be sent to the relevant search engines than has ever been the case with Google or Yahoo. Metasearch engines are particularly useful when it is comes to carrying out international research, for example, if you are searching for people or company addresses abroad.

However, professional online research comprises much more than simply the use of search engines. In an infinitely large cyberspace, careless perpetrators of white-collar crime in particular will leave clues that can be followed. This begins with researching the press and databases and ends with chat rooms or social networks, in which perpetrators openly brag about their crimes under a pseudonym. This has certainly been known to happen in the past.

Another possibility for following leads on the Internet is provided by those offices that register Internet addresses such as DENIC. They can provide assistance in identifying the creators of websites. It is also possible to look for leads in the HTML source codes for websites in order to find more detailed information. These source codes can be viewed in every browser and viewing them has nothing to do with hacking or breaking into third-party computers. Business intelligence exclusively uses legal research methods and is never illegal, unethical, or simply carried out just for the sake of curiosity. It is based at all times on a legal or justifiable interest from the perspective of the client.

3.3.3.6 Research in Registers and Archives

The Internet contains plenty but not all of the available information required to properly investigate white-collar crime and corruption. Business intelligence also utilizes publicly accessible registers and archives for the purpose of background research. In some cases, these sources are in the public domain but can only be viewed on the condition there is a justifiable or legal interest. The commercial register or the land register in Germany can, for example, be viewed or accessed by anyone. In contrast, information held by resident registration offices or in insolvency registers is only accessible if a justifiable or legal interest can be proven—for example, if there are exigent circumstances and the information can prevent further damage or even prevent criminal acts. However, an independent auditing firm will generally be able to obtain permission to access the required information as part of a fraud investigation. This could be, for example, if the request deals with finding out the last registered address or personal data of suspects or missing witnesses. If a registration office provides information about a person, the person themselves will be automatically informed about the enquiry. If this person must not be informed, then it must be explicitly demonstrated that this is necessary in order to protect legal interests or to prevent criminal acts when the request is made.

These requests for information are naturally not just limited to Germany but take place around the world. Companies with global networks, for example EY with offices in 150 countries, are capable of extracting information within 48 h from official registers in every country in the world, be it India, Morocco, Honduras, or even Switzerland.

3.3.3.7 On-Site Visits

In certain cases, database research and information from official sources may not prove helpful for the investigation or background research. For example, when the quality of the information stored in official registers proves inadequate. A good example here is Greece, where commercial registers or land registers for real estate are practically nonexistent. It often makes sense, particularly when trying to trace the flow of money, to make an on-site visit to try to visualize where the money is really going. This step could reveal, for example, that a company does not even exist or that in reality only a mailbox can be found concealed behind the company's snazzy Internet presence. It could even prove that the street in Islamabad named in the order book was never actually built in real life and formed part of the ruse for moving money for the payment of bribes.

Naturally, it is not possible to check the authenticity of every single component of an infrastructure project by making an on-site visit. However, if tangible evidence has already been found, an on-site visit along with corresponding photographic confirmation will generally deliver sound proof of the existence or nonexistence of already suspicious companies, projects, and people.

Another form of on-site research, although only used in exceptional cases, is cooperation with journalists who are familiar with the local social structures. Appearances can often be deceptive and someone who at first seems to be a person of integrity and a celebrated businessperson who promotes their region could actually lead a double life as the head of the local Mafia. Local journalists with the right connections often possess this type of knowledge and can provide useful hints for investigating corruption and criminality, even if they themselves would never write about it. Why is this type of cooperation only possible in exceptional cases? Because the safety and protection of the informants must be 100 % guaranteed and the journalist or the knowledgeable local source must never be placed in danger as a result of this cooperation.

3.3.4 Interviews and Audits as a Source of Information

The questioning of those involved, known as interrogation in the area of criminal law, is generally known as conducting interviews in the private sector. Alongside the examination of physical files, data analyses, and background research, interviewing witnesses, accessories, or those accused of the crime offers a further source of information for forensic auditors. In particular, interviews should be used if the available documentation or level of information in the company is not sufficient to properly reconstruct the criminal actions. In a criminalistic sense, interviews also provide investigators with an opportunity to compare different statements, uncover the personal backgrounds behind the offenses, or extract knowledge from the perpetrator through skilful interviewing techniques. Despite the fact that interviews are part of almost every investigation, the quality of the evidence provided by witnesses is rarely as good as that provided by the material evidence. This is because statements can be retracted, the transcripts of the interview contested, and confessions withdrawn. Hard facts do not lie to serve their own purpose, which cannot be said of witnesses or those accused of the crimes—and nowhere more so than in commercial enterprises. Conducting interviews as a source of information is, therefore, the weakest tool to be found in the repertoire of forensic auditing.

During the hectic events that are usually triggered by an investigation in a company, and under pressure to quickly solve these types of cases, there is often no time to properly prepare for the interviews or to plan the discussions down to the last detail. Nevertheless, some fundamental and organizational aspects need to be taken into account, which will be briefly covered in the following section, before investigators become more actively engaged in carrying out interviews.

3.3.4.1 Deciding the Order in Which Interviews Are Conducted

Experience has shown that it is advisable to carry out interviews from the bottom up. Why is this the case? These crimes often spread through a number of hierarchical levels. At the lowest levels, there is still often the possibility of making it clear to confidants or accomplices that it is not worth protecting higher hierarchical levels and that it would thus be better to instead cooperate and help resolve the case. In addition, the people employed at these levels often possess detailed knowledge that is simply not present in the same form at higher management levels, and which can be ideally compared with associated documentation from files or electronic data.

3.3.4.2 Creating a Suitable Atmosphere

The fundamental rule when selecting a room to conduct the interviews is the exclusion of all possible interruptions. It should be guaranteed that during the discussions nobody can listen in to the interview, telephone the room, or barge in unannounced. After all, it isn't always the perpetrator themselves that should be coaxed into giving a confession. Interviews are often conducted with other employees who have been put under pressure and who require safe and pleasant surroundings before it is possible to establish trust between the investigator and the interviewee. Many guides to criminalistic interviewing techniques often state that interviews conducted with suspected perpetrators should never be held in familiar surroundings. Instead, they should be conducted in a clinically clean environment (see Odenthal 2009, p. 194)—meaning, among other things, that it is important to ensure that a suspect cannot hide behind the desk during the interview. Such recommendations must naturally be treated with caution. A forensic auditor is not conducting an interrogation, but is reliant on the cooperation of the interviewee—irrespective of how well the room layout has been conceived.

3.3.4.3 Limit the Topics of Discussion

The following rule is valid for interviews: less is more. Obtaining high-quality information must always be more important than recording lots of needless waffle on tape—which assistants then have to type up night after night. A structured interview guide will help to limit the proceedings to important discussion topics and avoid becoming entangled in unnecessary altercations. Nevertheless, a good interviewer should be able to deviate from their guidelines, steer the conversation using active listening techniques (for this term see Rogers 2010), and sensibly limit and define the scope of the discussion.

3.3.4.4 Interviewing Skills and Critical Appraisals

Skilful criminalistic interviewing techniques are something that can only be learned or taught to a limited extent. Interviews are dynamic and can quickly change course, especially if the interviewer is dealing with a practiced speaker. The fundamental rule of "the person who asks, leads" is only partially true in this situation because only one party generally has a real interest in the discussion and thus will be asking all of the questions.

Nevertheless, it is equally important not to forget that the skill of being able to formulate questions in different ways is invaluable as an interview technique and can be decisive when it comes to extracting information. Most people subconsciously formulate questions in different ways yet underestimate the power of a cleverly worded question.

For example, if it is necessary to slow down a particularly talkative interviewee and stop them from rambling too much then closed-ended questions should be used: "Yes or No?" "Did you know anything about it or not?"

It is also possible to use so-called "alternative questions" in this situation: "Did you learn about these offenses from Mr. X or Mrs. Y?"

On the other hand, if you want to encourage the interviewee to talk and use free association, the questions are often formulated more openly: "What could have led him to do that?" Sometimes it is also helpful to emphasize the significance of the question by providing supplementary information. "In order to exclude all other possibilities, we need to know who had access to the computer. When did you last use the computer?"

Hypothetical questions can also be used to break down the barriers between the interviewer and interviewee or to increase the quality of the information provided in the answer (see Bohm in Hlavica et al. 2011, p. 227). "If you had been in his position, what would you have done?" However, leading questions that attempt to influence the answers provided by the interviewee or have the purpose of increasing pressure should be avoided: "Why not just admit it, you would also have taken the money!"

In contrast to a criminal investigation, it is not possible to apply more pressure or even utilize legal force when carrying out an investigation into crimes committed within a company.

A forensic investigator acting as a consultant or an internal auditor is reliant on the cooperation of the people involved. He or she could even endanger the entire mandate if their demeanor was considered unacceptable by the clients, or if the works council is forced to intervene because employees are being interrogated in the true definition of the word. The mandate issued for the investigation is a civil contract and can be terminated at any time. This is especially true when fraud cases result in complicated political circumstances within the company. Being caught in the crossfire is the last thing that a client who is just interested in resolving the case wants. Investigators are thus faced with a completely different environment in the business world than, for example, in the investigation of a capital crime. Some actions simply do not work in a free market, such as applying more pressure, alleging incidents that bear no relation to the facts, misleading business partners, or creating bewildering interview situations. This is not the time or place for a "good cop, bad cop" routine.

Naturally, one constantly reads about special techniques to expose liars, or becomes aware of them through television. One example is that fraudsters look up and to the right when they are lying because the eyes supposedly turn towards the creative part of the brain. These types of myths are naturally nonsense. In most cases, it is not necessary to be able to read somebody's thoughts in order to find out whom is lying or not. It is usually sufficient to simply listen carefully, employ perceptive criminalistic skills, and possess a little experience in dealing with white-collar crime.

Nevertheless, there are of course a few psychological tricks that can be used without hesitation in order to be able to use interviews as a source of information. This primarily involves creating a feeling of trust, while clearly signaling that there is a way out of the situation and making it clear that holding back information will only make everything worse. The message to bring across is "We want to help you" instead of "It all looks very bad for you. Why don't you just come clean?" The nature of the situation also means that investigators of white-collar crime can find themselves stuck in interview situations where they are faced by slick interviewees who skillfully deny everything. "I've done nothing wrong and can't explain why it happened. I just want a coffee and then to head off home."

In truth, an internal auditor has no power to force the situation in such a case. An auditing firm, which is obligated to remain independent according to the law, can at least take the following action: it can recommend in its role as a third party that the private assets of an employee suspected of wrongdoing should be subjected to an external check. The details will be handled confidentially and the client will merely be informed whether the evaluation was "clean" or "unclean." It is always amazing how many people who later turn out to be guilty nevertheless agree to this type of check because they cannot see a way to escape from the situation.

3.4 Investigations in the Future

Investigating white-collar crime is a game of cat and mouse. It has always been the case, and will continue to remain so. The perpetrators continue to learn, auditors become more professional, and the chase is never ending.

Nevertheless, we should permit ourselves to look briefly into the future at this point and outline from the viewpoint of a former police detective and active forensic auditor what developments are likely to occur in the future. Because just like investigators—irrespective of whether they are engaged in the private sector or public service—perpetrators also learn constantly and adapt to the latest technological and methodological developments.

3.4.1 Offenses and Investigations Are Increasingly Driven by Technology

The most recent major corruption and fraud cases have already demonstrated that the investigation of white-collar crime is being increasingly driven by forensic technology. What were previously expensive and very complex applications for the evaluation of large volumes of company data—so-called "big data"—will become standard in the medium term. The corresponding computer programs will then be capable, for example, of grouping and simplifying large volumes of data and master data, and be able to flag up indications of fraud using intelligent algorithms. Nevertheless, in contrast to making the skills possessed by "old school" criminalists superfluous, their work will just become more digitalized over the long term.

Yet what is true for the investigation is naturally also true in reverse for the offenses themselves: white-collar crime is itself becoming more digitalized. It is already possible to clearly identify a trend towards ever-more threatening computer and cybercrime (see Federal Criminal Police Office 2011)—which continue to deal with the manipulation of company data. White-collar crime of the future will increasingly focus on misappropriating sensitive data and information from companies—digitalization has heralded a new chapter in the history of industrial espionage. It is now no longer necessary to get your hands on files or prototypes in order to steal company secrets. It is almost possible today to fit the entire data inventory of a company onto a mobile data storage medium, where it can be deleted, hidden, and copied in seconds. And yet companies are not even remotely prepared to defend themselves against these threats.

3.4.2 Investigative Work Is Becoming Increasingly More Specialized

By using sophisticated and technical detection methods, investigators are attempting to reduce the advantage that perpetrators hold when it comes to committing and concealing their crimes. But the innovations introduced for the investigation and prosecution of these crimes have naturally not gone unnoticed by the fraudsters. This means that fewer and fewer fraudsters will make the mistake of transferring suspect amounts of money to offshore accounts or discuss their activities via e-mail because they know that the systems available today can not only quickly find evidence of this, but also make it legible. Instead, misappropriated funds will be more cleverly integrated into a company's ongoing business—for example, using obscure items on quotations or service contracts.

Investigative work will therefore become increasingly more specialized and focus to a much greater degree on individual business divisions and sectors. If fraud is thus committed within an infrastructure project in the form of a minor detail hidden within the construction work, the investigators involved must be able to expertly evaluate the prices, products, and processes used in order to detect irregularities in the calculations and quotations.

3.4.3 Investigation and Prevention Are Becoming More Closely Linked

It is rare today for forensic auditors or district attorneys to still encounter companies that are or were totally unprepared for a case of damage in the company. The methods for investigating white-collar crime and the systems for preventing it will become even more closely linked in the future. The diverse range of compliance and anti-fraud systems will lead to more frequent investigations, but that does not necessarily mean that companies are becoming more corrupt. As white-collar crime is a classic control-related offense, the more controls that are introduced, the more anomalies will be discovered that require investigation mainly for the purpose of ruling out the risk of liability for managers. Investigations will no longer be considered special events in the future but will instead be embedded in the control loop of a management system that comprises all the different steps for combating white-collar crime, from the occurrence of an acute case through to the transfer of the gained knowledge into corresponding preventative measures.

We will be looking at precisely this control loop in the following chapter. How can the results of the investigation be transferred to this type of system? What elements make up a compliance management or anti-fraud system? And what operative measures for their implementation and effectiveness are ultimately hidden behind the key phrase "compliance management"?

Literature

Editorial of Süddeutsche Zeitung. (2012). *Studie zur Wirtschaftskriminalität: Der Feind im Inneren* (Study of white-collar crime: The enemy within). Süddeutsche.de. Accessed February 1, 2013, from http://www.sueddeutsche.de/wirtschaft/studie-zu-wirtschaftskriminalitaet-derfeind-im-inneren-1.1534302

Editorial of the Thüringer Allgemeine. (2011). *TU Ilmenau weist Schummelei Griechenlands nach* [Ilmenau University of Technology Proves Greece Cheated]. Thüringer-allgemeine.de. Accessed January 29, 2012, from http://www.thueringer-allgemeine.de/startseite/detail/-specific/TU-Ilmenau-weist-Schummelei-Griechenlands-nach-1811171608

Ernst & Young. (2012). *Enabling Compliance Welche Rolle spielt Technologie?* [What role is played by technology?] Ernst & Young GmbH. Accessed June 26, 2013, from http://www.ey.com/Publication/vwLUAssets/Enabling_Compliance/$FILE/Enabling_Compliance_Welche_Rolle_Spielt_Technologie.pdf

Federal Criminal Police Office (Bundeskriminalamt). (2011). *Cybercrime, Bundeslagebild 2011* [Situation Report on Cybercrime 2011]. Bundeskriminalamt (Federal Criminal Police Office). Accessed June 26, 2013, from www.bka.de/DE/Publikationen/JahresberichteUndLagebilder/Cybercrime/cybercrime__node.html?__nnn=true

German Press Agency (Deutsche Presse Agentur). (2012). *Internet-Machtkampf zwischen Richter und Facebook könnte ausfallen* [Internet power struggle between judge and facebook could end]. Zeit online. Accessed February 1, 2013, from http://www.zeit.de/news/2012-02/23/internet-machtkampf-zwischen-richterund-facebook-koennte-ausfallen-23151027

Hlavica, C., Klapproth, U., & Hülsberg, F. M. (2011). *Tax Fraud & Forensic Accounting, Umgang mit Wirtschaftskriminalität* [Dealing with white-collar crime]. Wiesbaden: Gabler.

Hofmann, P. (2008). *Handbuch Anti-Fraud-Management, Bilanzbetrug erkennen–vorbeugen–bekämpfen* [Manual for anti-fraud management, detect–prevent–fight balance sheet fraud]. Berlin: Erich Schmidt Verlag GmbH.

Kaiser, T. (2013). IT-Sicherheit, Software prüft E-Mails von Angestellten auf Betrug [IT security, software checks employee e-mails for fraud]. Die Welt. Accessed February 1, 2013, from http://www.welt.de/wirtschaft/webwelt/article112478404/Software-prueft-E-Mails-von-Angestellten-auf-Betrug.html

Odenthal, R. (2009). *Korruption und Mitarbeiterkriminalität, Wirtschaftskriminalität vorbeugen, erkennen und aufdecken* [Corruption and employee criminality, prevent, detect and uncover white-collar crime]. Wiesbaden: Gabler.

Rogers, C. R. (2010). *Die nicht-direktive Beratung: Counselling and Psychotherapy* [Non-directive consultancy: Counselling and psychotherapy]. Frankfurt a. M.: Fischer.

Transparency International. (2012). *Corruption perceptions index 2012*. Transparency International. Accessed June 26, 2013, from http://www.transparency.org/cpi2012/results

Systems for Combating Criminality 4

Designing and Implementing Compliance Management Systems

In 1969 in Palo Alto, California, Philip Zimbardo smashes the windshield of his dark blue car with a sledgehammer—and secures his place in the history of crime-fighting forever.

However, the man with the sledgehammer is not a notorious vandal. Zimbardo is a psychologist and a very renowned one at that. He is also a young man. On the day that he smashed the windshield of his car, Zimbardo was 36 years old and one of the youngest professors in the USA.[1] The destruction of his car was not simply an outburst of rage but part of a social experiment that has significantly changed the way in which criminality is currently understood and combated.

A few weeks before the event in Palo Alto, Zimbardo parked a different car in the Bronx area of New York. He unscrewed the number plate and opened the hood of the car. Then he simply sat back to watch what happened. After only a few minutes, a family started to take the car apart and demolish it. He later found the car completely gutted after 3 days. A seemingly clear lesson: This is what happens if you park your car in one of the worst neighborhoods in the country.

Until Zimbardo took matters into his own hands and reached for the sledgehammer, the same experiment had been running for 1 week in sunny California without any vandalism—in fact, entirely in vain. A passer-by had even closed the hood of the car when it started to rain. But something remarkable happened later. Once Zimbardo had smashed the windshield of the car himself, other passers-by also started to vandalize the car. And the vandalism continued here until the car was also completely gutted. And all this in a sleepy American town where the crime rate was insignificantly low in comparison to the Bronx area of New York.

[1] Zimbardo quickly became a much discussed psychologist due in particular to his sensational social experiments. Probably the most well known was the "Stanford Prison Experiment" in which the test subjects took on the role of inmates and guards in a prison. The experiment had to be aborted after 6 days because the test subjects were faced with serious physical and psychological danger.

S. Heissner, *Managing Business Integrity*, Management for Professionals,
DOI 10.1007/978-3-319-12721-7_4

The observations made by Zimbardo were used by the sociologists James Q. Wilson and George L. Kelling in 1982 for their "Broken Windows Theory" (see Wilson and Kelling 1982; as well as Hess 2004). The theory proposes that large criminal acts can be triggered by smaller crimes. A good metaphor for this idea is a broken window in a house that leads to the decline and criminalization of the whole city district if it is not immediately repaired. According to the theory, the first signs of social disorder will already lead to a causal chain reaction that increases the general level of insecurity and breaks down social control—thus promoting criminality (see Laue 2002).

Yet how do broken windows fit into the context of this book? The purpose of this small excursion into experimental criminology is to clearly indicate those areas where it is really necessary to act in the fight against white-collar crime and corruption—namely, prevention and early detection. In a figurative sense, it is also possible to find broken windows in commercial companies that will gradually lead to major losses—and which subsequently develop into huge scandals. The process for identifying and repairing these windows, or even better, preventing them being broken in the first place, has become a key focus of corporate management in recent years—this concept is often substituted by the keyword "compliance."

It should be clear to everyone that simply responding in a selective manner cannot be the solution to protecting company assets against criminality. Anybody who wants to effectively exclude the general risk of damage and personal liability will not be compelled to take systematic precautions as a result of entrepreneurial thinking alone. A contribution will also be made by the national and international legislative environment. After introducing the basic concepts behind "deviant behavior" from a criminological viewpoint and describing the methods used in forensic investigation, this chapter will then focus, as a result, on systematic protection against white-collar crime and corruption.

Ultimately, the purpose is to ensure that all employees abide by existing rules—meaning they observe legal, ethical, and sector-specific rules, as well as operational and behavioral rules within an organization. Managers describe this observance of the rules today as "compliance[2]." Therefore, the targeted control and influence over this observance of the rules is called "compliance management." The central organizational measures that a manager utilizes in order to establish, test, and strengthen this observance of the rules are combined together to form a "compliance management system."

However, the intention is not and should not be to safeguard against every single conceivable misdemeanor. No compliance management system in the world is

[2] Compliance means in the first instance "observing the rules." This could be any form of compliance—the term does not originate from the field of economics. It became popular due to its use in the field of medicine. Compliance was used in this context to describe how willing patients were to follow the instructions issued by their doctors or those issued on the leaflet found inside their prescribed medication.

capable of achieving that goal. What compliance management should actually achieve is the prevention and early detection of systematic misdemeanors.

How this type of preventative system is created, and which processes, methods, and responsibilities are incorporated into it, will be extremely dependent on those areas of the company that are specifically at risk. This means that effective compliance management systems are—across the board—designer solutions. The reason for this is that they are directly based on the individual risks faced by a company, as well as its cultural and organizational characteristics.

The phrases "anti-fraud management," "internal control system," and "risk management" are often uttered together in the same breath as compliance management. However, it is not possible to clearly differentiate between these concepts without there being any overlap. These concepts are briefly explained below to help avoid any confusion.

The different terms have primarily developed over time and describe systems designed to identify and manage company risk from different perspectives. The "Internal Control System" (ICS) has its roots in accountancy and primarily focuses on the proper handling of accounting-related processes; for example, processes such as the separation of functions or the "four-eye" principle.

Over the years, these basic principles have also been adopted in other areas that do not have anything directly to do with accountancy. "Risk management" was initially based on a generic view of the detailed risks faced by a company, which are then systematically identified, analyzed, evaluated, monitored, and controlled. It is already possible to notice some overlap here with an internal control system. "Anti-fraud management" originated during the establishment of a more stringent internal control system following investigations into the financial scandals facing Enron, WorldCom, etc., and the term can be found, in particular, in the wording of the Sarbanes-Oxley Act (SOX).

"Compliance management" was motivated by similar events and developed, in particular, as a result of high profile competition violations in the areas of cartels and corruption.

Anti-fraud management and compliance management are currently moving closer and closer together. This is because measures incorporated into an anti-fraud management system to combat "fraud against a company" are often based on the same principles as measures found in compliance management that focus on "fraud by employees of a company." A common feature here is that both disciplines aim to prevent intentional or negligent behavior that breaks the regulations or laws. The difference is that noncompliance can benefit the company in a superficial sense, while fraud always damages the company directly.

Alongside the issue of fraud, an internal control system is also designed to avoid errors—meaning damage caused due to negligent behavior. For this reason, it is self-evident from a criminological/criminalistic standpoint that the concepts of anti-fraud management and compliance management are set to converge.

It becomes clear at this point that the precise components incorporated into a fully functional compliance management system remain flexible to a certain degree, and can never be exactly the same due to the range of different business activities and the nature of each company's corporate culture. This chapter will focus on the various steps that can be taken on the path to developing a tailor-made preventative system. A model will be presented that has proven itself effective both in the field of consultancy and in practical application—namely, the closed loop compliance system. This model aims to determine individual risk and create a system that protects, sensitizes, detects, solves, and learns—meaning it attempts to sustainably minimize damage caused by "deviant behavior" over the long term.

The fact that many more aspects apart from just controls and regulations play a role in the design and implementation of compliance management systems is part of a holistic approach to compliance consultancy that is gradually becoming established in the world of business. Especially if the objective is to use compliance management as an instrument for actively creating value, an approach that is based too strictly on the concept of control is more likely to achieve the opposite effect. Ultimately, it will prevent more business transactions than it enables. Practical experience has shown that anchoring the concept of compliance into corporate culture and management is a decisive factor in the success or failure of a system and it is increasingly important to "strike the right tone." Interpreting compliance as a restrictive monitoring system is a completely understandable reaction, which unfortunately in practice very rarely achieves the desired goal. This is because it excludes the positive aspects that compliance can deliver to the company as part of the management system—especially in terms of value creation.

It is particularly these aspects, which are in essence of a commercial nature, that should be included in the discussions about a compliance management system. The fact is that targeted management measures do not only enable compliance to be tested but also increase the efficiency of internal processes.

The conflict between culture and control is an aspect that is only dealt with to a limited extent in the fight against crime outside of the business environment. For example, the American police authorities—particularly in New York—reacted to the "Broken Windows Theory" from Wilson and Kelling in the 1980s by almost universally introducing the concept of "zero tolerance" (see Dreher and Feltes 1997). In other words, by cracking down hard on crime. However, the fact that this strict approach is only one side of the coin when it comes to compliance management will also be part of this and the next chapter.

4.1 Critical Preliminary Remark on the Design of Compliance Management Systems

Whether there is really an explicitly stated legal obligation in Germany for managers to establish a compliance management system is not clear from a purely legal standpoint (see Moosmayer 2012, p. 5). Nevertheless, the facts gleaned from a range of recent court judgments send a clear message. In accordance with the Stock Corporation Law (especially Article 91 of AktG) and the German Regulatory Offenses Act (especially Article 130 of OWiG), the management of the company has a responsibility to ensure that the company does not suffer damage due to white-collar crime and corruption.[3] This includes, at least indirectly, the development and supervision of protective measures. In an international context, the requirement to set up and maintain this type of preventative system is much more clearly formulated in SOX and the UK Bribery Act. These laws even predefine some of the content and individual elements required in a compliance management system.

Despite this obligation to protect the company, experience has shown that the way "deviant behavior" is handled is still characterized to a major extent by reactive thinking. A substantial proportion of companies still only respond once it is too late and misconduct has already caused damage to the company. There are only very few companies who really give any thought in advance to providing adequate protection against existing risk, even though the generation of companies and managers who treat occurrences of white-collar crime as isolated cases and either do not respond or only do the bare minimum required are indeed threatened with extinction. The consequences in terms of criminal liability are now simply too serious and sure to catch up with all those who do not emphatically embrace this subject sooner or later.

It is still likely that the extent to which a fully comprehensive preventative system can be established in a company is primarily dependent on the level of pressure perceived within the company. In purely objective terms: the more a company has suffered in this area, the more willing they are to protect themselves with preventative measures in the form of a compliance management system. Once misconduct and the resulting investigation become public, it does not take long before there will be a clamor for compliance. It appears that getting your fingers burnt still seems to be the best lesson when it comes to white-collar crime and corruption.

Following internal investigations or investigations carried out by the criminal prosecution authorities, the pressure to respond could, however, result in an excessive desire to take action. In many cases, this stems from a panic reaction to the increase in supervisory duties and personal liability. Otherwise it could result from a completely inappropriate overreaction to the act of deceit itself. Taking action for the sake of it and panicking when it comes to issues of compliance will almost inevitably lead to disproportionate controls being placed on employees. This is because anyone who is not aware of the types of risk faced in their various business areas, or how to tackle them in a targeted manner, will simply introduce control systems based on a "one size fits all" approach along the lines of the motto: "the more controls, the better." Yet it has been observed time and again in practice that management systems that are hastily stitched together will fail sooner or later, or will progressively reveal their fragmentary nature.

The fact that this type of approach to compliance creates more problems than it solves will be discussed and demonstrated in Chap. 5. In this critical preliminary remark on the design of really effective compliance management systems, it is nevertheless vital to underline the fact that compliance systems introduced as

[3] For more details, see Chap. 1.

control-oriented reactions to cases of damage often prove insufficient. Truly effective compliance management systems need to delve deep into the heart of the company and its business activities and, most importantly, deal with the relevant compliance risks in an interdisciplinary manner. In order to design and implement these types of programs, a certain degree of calm and careful planning is required, which is probably something that is only possible to a very limited extent after a case of damage in the company. However, there is something else that is even more important in the design process: Proper expertise and, where necessary, good consulting services.

It is not difficult to imagine how the boom in compliance, triggered directly by the events at Enron and WorldCom and the effect they had on the relevant legislature, also saw new providers of corresponding management systems spring up everywhere like mushrooms after a rain storm. What actually qualified these consultants to design, implement, or evaluate compliance management systems was not, for a long time, defined by any documented criteria. The IDW PS 980[4] standard from the Institute of Public Auditors in Germany now provides some standardization in this area, although the differences in quality within the field of compliance consulting remain huge. This can prove both costly and dangerous for anyone with an acute desire to take action but who does not have much experience with the subject matter.

There are in fact many possible approaches to compliance management and the methodological models used to implement it. Consultants constantly attempt to outdo one another with flowcharts, organograms, and particularly clever schematics to illustrate how the implementation of the "perfect" compliance management system can be realized. At the real heart of the matter, however, lies the interplay between the various areas of expertise that are required to make a compliance management system function properly. Therefore, it is helpful to briefly describe these specialist areas and which types of consultant are necessary to develop a properly functioning system.

An **auditor (1)** who is able to understand commercial business relationships and apply the right methodology to reliably check the correctness of balance sheets and reports will almost always be required. A **lawyer (2)**, whose specialist knowledge guarantees that processes in the company will be implemented in a legally watertight manner and that the content of the compliance management system fulfils all of the national and international regulatory requirements, will also be very helpful. To be able to determine how white-collar crime and corruption develop in a company and how individual crimes run their course—or in other words what the modus operandi is (for this term see Berthel et al. 2006, p. 36 ff.)—there is no alternative but to engage the services of a **criminalist (3)**, who can use their knowledge gained from the investigation of previous fraud cases to design precisely those mechanisms that are effective in real life. Finally, there needs to be a **process**

[4] The subject of auditing standards will be addressed in more detail at the end of this chapter in Sect. 4.5.1.

consultant (4) who can integrate the developed system and its elements into the everyday business of the company and into all the company processes.

None of the different consultants mentioned here could develop and implement a comprehensive protective mechanism, able to withstand the threats faced in reality, on their own—irrespective of how large, small, specialized, or even one-dimensional the company may be. A lawyer lacks the criminalistic knowledge, while a process consultant has not mastered the auditing methodology, and so on. All of them thus benefit from each other. It is hard to say which expertise is most important in this team and it is certainly dependent on the individual company and the risks it faces. However, the consultant that is likely to be the most difficult to find on the market is the criminalist, as this specialist expertise can usually only be gained by working in the police service or public prosecutor's office. It is naturally possible to participate in a training course and study relevant literature on forensic auditing, etc. However, there is no weekend seminar in the world that can really replace the experience gained from fighting corruption and criminality on a daily basis.

In the final analysis, precautionary compliance management involves the application of investigative methodology for the prevention of white-collar crime. Consultants and system architects that do not possess or cannot purchase this type of core expertise in forensic criminalistics are always faced with the danger that, while the early warning systems and controls they develop are methodologically sound, they themselves will nevertheless only really understand and hence be able to prevent the sociological phenomenon of "deviant behavior" to a limited extent. Crimes and the methods used to commit them will simply slip by their controls.

Experience has shown that many lawyers or process consultants who develop and provide compliance management systems tend to set them up in a very formal and systematic manner, with the result that they only scratch the surface of the real problem. Therefore, the focus should always be placed on identifying critically afflicted areas of the company and from there develop precisely those controls that can really help to prevent manipulations or other "deviant behavior" in the long term. It is certainly also clear that a compliance management system can only be effective if it "understands" the company. The system will then in turn be understood, accepted, and sustainably implemented within the company.

Before we follow this preliminary remark by looking at the "compliance loop" as an effective model for compliance management systems, it is first necessary to reflect on the basic concepts and fundamental principles of compliance management. This is because no matter how well a compliance measure is designed, it remains nothing more than a patchwork solution if the right prerequisites have not been met in order to effectively integrate it into the company. In simple terms, this means that something along the lines of a "compliance organization" must be installed and networked throughout the company—based on fundamental concepts that will ultimately guide the entire system.

4.2 Methodological Principles for Compliance Management

Anyone who wishes to tackle the subject of compliance in a structured manner by setting up a management system and anchoring the concept firmly in the company should not make the error of pressing ahead without proper consideration—even if the regulatory pressure is high. In a similar way to every other strategic company issue, good and solid planning will always prove more successful than hectically rushing around and giving in to the desire to simply take action for the sake of it. This is particularly important because compliance is a subject that can have a profound effect on the whole company—both for the good and for the bad. Therefore, before we outline an example model of a compliance management system with all its elements and interrelationships, it is necessary to answer some fundamental questions: What form could a compliance organization in the company take? How is it possible to prevent this organization existing in isolation within the company? How can it be guaranteed that the subject will be taken seriously throughout the company and also by business partners? Where can and should compliance be anchored in the company and backed up with personnel and processes?

Before we even give any further thought to the concrete risks faced by the company or the organizational approaches for implementing compliance measures, it is necessary to clarify some basic methodological principles. These form the foundations upon which everything else will be built. If these foundations are unstable, there is a danger that the whole system will collapse in on itself like a pack of cards at a later point in time. What do we mean precisely when we talk about these basic foundations?

The first thing to realize when talking about the subject of compliance management is that we should really be discussing integrity management. This is because persuading employees not to infringe on the legal regulations or other defined rules is what lies at the core of the issue. In other words, they must act with integrity.

This type of infringement can be carried out intentionally—with the person's full knowledge—or also due to negligence. Or in some cases it could also originate due to a mistake or because the wrong priorities were set. In this context, regulations or controls act as nothing more than aids because they only limit a person's freedom of action to a certain degree and can be overcome or disregarded. A brief look at the daily events reported in the economic press and the lessons learned from the latest fraud and corruption cases will certainly support this presumption.

Therefore, compliance management is basically the responsibility of personnel management. Yet it is also much more: compliance is also a social responsibility. After all, employees do not change their personality when they enter the company premises, but are shaped by the influences in their private and social environments. Nobody should deceive themselves by assuming that white-collar criminals are socially isolated beasts. This fact alone implies that corporate culture plays a crucial role in what lies behind all of the measures for guaranteeing integrity in everyday business practices. If this culture tolerates corruption then all of the measures constituting the compliance management system are ultimately pointless. Both the innate creativity of humans and their drive to break the rules are simply too great.

The key phrase here is "integrity management." The objective behind compliance management systems is to prevent negligent or intentional misconduct by employees. The boundaries independently imposed within these systems regularly go above and beyond the legally defined limits. Why is this the case? On the one hand, because the company is aware of their social responsibilities and does not want to be perceived to be a company that pushes the legal boundaries. On the other, it is to try and avoid further measures being taken by the criminal prosecution authorities or other supervisory bodies that would result in legal regulations being introduced to prevent even the smallest hint of noncompliance.

It is thus only logical to take advantage of crime prevention models when faced with the question of how to systematically prevent misconduct. When one looks at leading compliance management systems around the world, which are based on the so-called "3-pillar model" (prevention—detection—reaction), this only confirms the rationale behind using crime prevention instruments.

For the purpose of clarification, measures for "prevention" focus on the awareness of the employee and are also designed to help support correct behavior. "Detection" involves management measures that serve to monitor the system. And the area of "reaction" covers all actions dedicated to handling cases of noncompliance, as well as making any necessary adaptations to the system when the risk landscape changes.

The question that now naturally arises is how can this type of system be integrated into a company. The so-called "Three Lines of Defense" model[5] provides practical assistance in this area (Fig. 4.1).

The first line of defense against noncompliance is the operative business of the company itself. The employees working in this area must be able to recognize and manage those risks that arise in their everyday business. This requires, as already mentioned, a corresponding level of awareness about the risks and additional measures for providing assistance—such as guidelines or software and applications that control the relevant processes. Employees must be fully aware of their responsibility for their own actions during everyday business. They must not get the impression that their colleagues in the compliance organization are solely responsible for reducing risk.

The compliance organization itself represents the next line of defense. For example, it is there to clarify the situation where there is doubt or handle inquiries relating to specialist analyses for pending business transactions. The legal department or the corporate security department can also provide assistance in this area. A good example here would be a planned business transaction abroad in a high-risk country that involves the intended engagement of an agent.

[5] The model can be originally traced back to the European Institute of Internal Auditors; see here Burger and Schmelter (2012, p. 105).

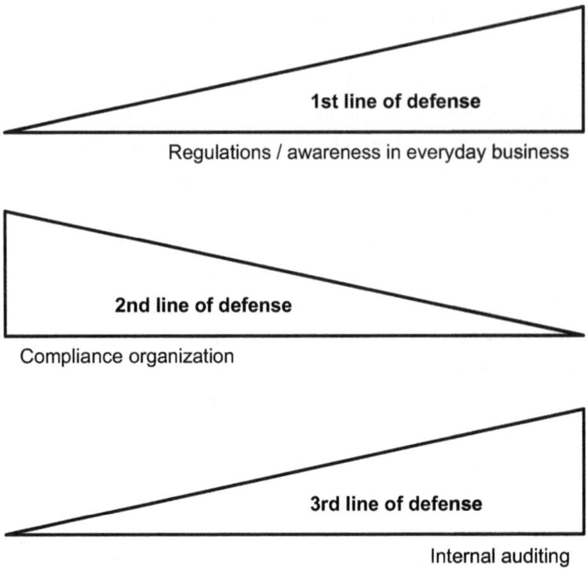

Fig. 4.1 The three lines of defense model

The third line of defense is auditing. Downstream and targeted auditing of compliance guarantees that the compliance management system is working as designed. Alongside process-related auditing, this level of defense also requires transaction-related auditing—so-called "ex-post" auditing.

Here is a brief summary: it is particularly important that management personnel take a serious approach to compliance. This approach, together with the corporate culture, will form the backbone of the entire system. The 3-pillar model and the "Three Lines of Defense" will ensure that the system will be designed to prevent crime and guarantee that the concepts behind it become securely anchored in the company.

So far so good, but now the question of what precisely the compliance management system should be targeting naturally arises. A brief anecdote provides a good insight into the problem. The managing director of a company explained once that his compliance officer had identified over 200 laws that were relevant to the business and with which it was necessary for the employees of the company to comply in future. Among others, they included the Dog Owner's Ordinance (Hundehalterverordnung) issued by the city council in Berlin, because the company had a guard dog at one of the company locations.

This clearly illustrates that while one cannot simply state that things such as the Dog Owner's Ordinance are unimportant when (further) developing compliance management systems, it is also not necessary to set out to rediscover the world. Rather the goal should be to establish the strategic priorities for the company. The real reason for dealing with the subject of compliance is primarily the fact that the massive corruption, fraud, and cartel cases, as well as data protection infringements, have demonstrated that previous management systems in these companies did not have this subject sufficiently under control.

Nevertheless, compliance management systems have actually been used in most companies for a while now. And management systems have been around for even longer, for example, to ensure that tax laws are correctly observed in the tax department. Accounting departments also have systems for properly managing financial reporting requirements and the accounting process. In the example above, the situation would, in all probability, already have been handled by the corporate security department responsible for the guard dog.

This perspective on compliance management was given to demonstrate the next requirement, now that the perspective of the management personnel/corporate culture has also already been discussed above. And that is that once the organizational elements have been clarified, it is important to decide which risk areas or legal spheres should be targeted by the newly implemented or refined compliance management system.

A short tour of the methodological principles here should highlight the fundamental elements that need to be included in a compliance management system: compliance culture, compliance objectives, risk management, compliance organization, compliance program, compliance communication, and the permanent monitoring and improvement of the system. Incidentally, these seven basic elements are found in IDW PS 980, which is the auditing standard for testing compliance management systems. This standard is formulated quite generically on purpose and will be discussed in more detail at the end of the chapter.

4.3 Compliance Culture, Compliance Objectives, and Compliance Communication: Elements of Strategic Corporate Management and the Management of Personnel

The corporate culture, compliance objectives, and compliance communication are inextricably linked in the compliance system and thus also in the strategic corporate management and the management of personnel. Before we consider these elements and their interrelationships in a little more detail, it is necessary to first take a look at the abstract concepts behind this subject. It is worth examining the prevailing general management culture, which has been influenced by the economization of incentive structures over recent decades in the Western world.

Comments on the Prevailing General Management Culture The prevailing management culture continues to be strongly influenced by the "Chicago School" (for more on this term see Reder et al. 2008), whose guidelines and economic concepts have developed from their origins in North America in the 1960s into the paradigm of the modern global economy. The Chicago School and probably its best-known and leading thinker Milton Friedman (1912–2006) understood the economy as follows: the state must not constantly control and reprimand its citizens in their search for prosperity. Entrepreneurial activity can only develop for the good of society if there are free markets that regulate themselves (see Friedman 2004).

These ideas are based on a concept of humankind that has increasingly started to crumble. Economic behavior—according to the representatives of the Chicago School—can be almost totally explained by the neoclassical price theory. At the center of this explanation is the concept of "homo economicus," whose purpose in life is to maximize his or her own benefits (see Franz 2004).

In order to demonstrate the relevance of these ideas for the modern world, one interpretation of the financial and economic crisis in 2009 stated that the dogma of self-regulation had turned out to be a disastrous fallacy. This was a dogma that had symbolically collapsed along with the investment bank Lehman Brothers and large parts of the global banking sector.

It is not possible at this point to conclusively evaluate whether those events surrounding the recent banking crisis will really lead to a fundamental and enduring rethink of management culture. A rethink of the general management and leadership culture would nevertheless be desirable. There is certainly room for improvement, above all when it comes to handling risk. The financial crisis clearly demonstrated that the neoclassical school did not help to spread corporate risk but at best helped to obscure it (see Faller and Otte 2011).

Paul Volcker, former Chairman of the Federal Reserve in the USA and a somewhat controversial national hero, was correct when he stated that the "financial markets are not mathematical but rather human creations" (see ibid.). Therefore, it is not possible in any way to predict human behavior using statistical models and economic theories.

This rethink also needs to play a role in the design of compliance management systems. The design process should not focus on standard procedures and formal legal considerations. Instead, it should place the spotlight on people—not as purely economic creatures but first and foremost as social beings. This makes an examination of employees and the corporate culture indispensable to the development of a compliance management system.

4.3.1 Examining Employees and the Corporate Culture

"Deviant behavior" is more than just a mathematical phenomenon and its genesis is strongly shaped by the social environment of those people involved. Therefore, a risk assessment used to provide the foundations for a compliance management system must get right inside the company and put out feelers to identify attitudes and, in a broad sense, the customs found within the corporate culture. In contrast to the process-oriented examination of risk, the focus here must be placed to a much greater extent on management personnel and the whole area of human resources (HR).

What kinds of characters and personalities are there working in the company? How is the market and market behavior determined overall? How high is the turnover of employees? Do employees challenge work directives or do they follow every order without question? How fairly or unfairly does the company remunerate its employees? Is the company active in different cultural circles? If so, have the different cultural values held by employees been adequately integrated into the evaluation of culture as a factor for compliance?

There is currently still a lack of measurement instruments for gaining a clear understanding of the bigger picture at the level of "corporate ethics." A feasible alternative could be to hold discussions or design questionnaires on, for example, perceptions about leadership styles, working atmosphere, awareness of controls, or the emphasis placed on success—carried out at all company levels and within all of the different cultural circles.

4.3.2 Harmonizing Compliance Objectives and Compliance Communication

In order to avoid unnecessarily isolating the idea of compliance in the company before it has even been born, it is advisable at the very least to compare the compliance objectives with the general business objectives. Designers of compliance management systems will have created a true masterpiece if the compliance objectives are as congruent as possible with the strategic company objectives. After all, conforming to the regulations and achieving business success seem to stand in opposition to each other often enough in real life—consider the whole area of corruption and the dilemma in the examples that have been described here between breaking the rules and achieving success.

The process of defining and formulating the objectives will impact on the cultural components of compliance. The term compliance culture encourages us to imagine that a concept such as culture can be managed. It isn't possible—at least not directly. However, it is certainly possible to create the conditions in which the compliance culture can exist. This could mean holding discussions internally about the integrity-related principles of the company and deriving elementary behavioral guidelines from them—providing a frame of reference in which a culture of compliance can develop over time.

One aspect is particularly important in such a process. The so-called "tone from the top"—meaning a clear commitment from the management of the company to integrity, observance of the regulations, and the management of compliance with all of its implications. In contrast to other management programs, the acknowledgement and active involvement of the CEO/managing director is not just something that is nice to have. It is an absolute necessity. If this tone from the top is missing then nothing can be achieved in the area of compliance—at least nothing that will prove effective in the long term. Why is this so? Because a lack of credibility and assertiveness will be used as an excuse by every manager to the management board as to why they should not have to stick to the rules. Compliance will remain just a phrase and the measures merely a tempest in a teapot—and in the final reckoning it will all be a waste of money.

If the chairman of the management board can only muster up enough enthusiasm to read out a speech announcing the compliance management system and then endure the rest of the ceremony until he can at last delegate this bothersome subject to the deepest echelons of the company, it will be very plain to every employee just how seriously he is taking it. Yet it could be so easy to have the opposite effect!

The chairman of the management board could credibly convince his board members—the executive level of the company—and all other employees that he is serious about the subject of compliance. By behaving as a role model, his actions will have a knock-on effect in many places, ensuring that the subject can be sustainably positioned within the company and be effectively maintained.

So the decisive factor in this context is the philosophy of "walk the talk," meaning that all of those at a management level must fulfil the obligations they have themselves made and which they also expect their employees to fulfil. In the worst case of an incident of noncompliance, this means that when applying sanctions, there can be no difference between how white-collar employees and blue-collar employees are handled. In the event of misconduct, even the best horse in the barn must also be liable for punishment. In other words, even top-performing sales employees must be made to leave the company in the event of misconduct.

4.4 From the Risk Assessment, Through the Compliance Program and Compliance Organization to Constant Improvement: The Control Loop for an Effective and Sustainable System

4.4.1 Compliance Risk Assessment

At the heart of every compliance management system is the risk assessment. As already described above, the first step is to identify the significant compliance risks faced by the company. The examination of these risks must be carried out from a number of different perspectives.

1. "In what regulatory and legislative environment are my business activities conducted?" It is important to take into account here any special features that relate to the specific sector or country.
2. "Do I want to obligate myself to additional voluntary commitments that go above and beyond these regulations and laws?" For example, the UN Global Compact or voluntary national recommendations relating to corporate compliance.
3. "Does my company already have management systems in place for the identified regulations, laws, and voluntary commitments that could be described as compliance management systems?"

It is now necessary to carry out a detailed risk assessment for the relevant legal areas and voluntary commitments. A common error at this point is to dispense with a further detailed assessment of the relevant legal areas and to turn to a "one size fits all" solution offered on the market.

This is why many compliance officers often make statements about the subject of corruption such as "we require a whistleblower or ombudsman solution," "we require guidelines for the issuing and receipt of gifts," "we require a process for checking business partners," "we require training," and so on.

Yet questions about which business areas, employees, and business events are actually exposed to corruption risks often remain unanswered, leaving many follow-up questions also unresolved: How exactly does the problem look on-site? What could be a possible solution? In what form could these manipulations actually occur so that, for example, bribes are not immediately noticed? Relatively little thought is given to all of these issues.

Instead, organizations are loaded with standard solutions whose effectiveness or efficiency has not been satisfactorily evaluated. The consequences are that in difficult and unclear situations, organizations will face a greater burden rather than a lesser one, and employees will start to complain about the rats' nest that is the compliance system.

It is for this reason that it is absolutely necessary to carry out a risk assessment at the level of the daily activities carried out by vulnerable employees in business areas that are fraught with risk. In the practical example of the fight against corruption, this could mean reproducing step by step the processes carried out by the sales employees.

However, this does not mean that the assessment has to be carried out for all sales employees individually. Groups should be progressively formed based on risk profile, existing decision-making authority, the standardized processes followed, the characteristics of business partners, or the employment of agents.

The completion of an adequate risk assessment is very important. All of the information gained in this process delivers starting points for developing the risk-reducing measures that will become part of the compliance management system. They could be measures in the areas of prevention, detection, and reaction—or the focus could be on the question of which line of defense should be used to define relevant responsibilities.

It is not possible to provide sweeping answers to these questions as the standard solutions offered by many consultancy and compliance system companies attempt to do. These answers need to be individually compiled and tailored to the type of business activity or culture upon which the company is based. Incidentally, there is not just one culture within a company. In international business transactions involving national companies within large corporations, a wide range of different cultures can be encountered with differing practices and behavioral patterns when it comes to the acquisition and processing of orders.

Of course, no company starts with a blank sheet of paper when it comes to a risk assessment. In many cases, it is likely that the critical areas of the company have already been identified. Construction companies will probably place their focus on the area of corruption, while commercial companies will need to provide more protection in the area of cartelization. And those companies that have to manage a lot of company data will focus on the area of data protection and concentrate their activities accordingly. The area of data protection is always also linked to the question of how the works council should be involved. Meanwhile, banks and insurance funds are increasingly confronted with issues of money laundering and transaction integrity. Chemical and energy companies are required to deal with the issues of work safety, environmental protection, and production risks to an ever-greater extent. And a subject that is becoming increasingly relevant, especially for technology companies involved in foreign trade, is global sanctions. Let us briefly look at the example of a company that manufactures metal alloys and operates as a supplier for the aviation or arms industries. The management of the company needs to ensure that their products are not delivered to countries on international sanctions lists or those subject to other restrictions according to the Military Weapons Control Act (Kriegswaffenkontrollgesetz—KrWaffKontrG). As it is an extremely sensitive area, no tolerance is usually shown for negligence. In companies whose business activities involve the manufacture of military weapons, compliance management must thus pay particular attention to the supplier chain and customer network in order to guarantee that their company is not unknowingly arming the dictators of this world with fighter jets or rocket technology.

This example alone demonstrates that a risk assessment must generally encompass much more than just the area of corruption in purchasing and sales. Although these areas have been forced into the center of public attention—to a major extent due to recent large cases of corruption—they only actually account for a small proportion of the risks that a company must identify, evaluate, and cover. The fact that there is constant need for adjustment within a compliance management system is also due in some respects to the current trends in criminal investigations and the increasing level of regulation. For example, the sanctioning of antitrust crimes has become so professional in the last few years that it makes a lot of sense to once again carry out a root and branch review in this area—and to introduce any necessary improvements.

Those who carry out risk assessments naturally find themselves in a state of conflict between acting appropriately or overzealously. How much is enough? When have all of the relevant risks really been covered and sufficiently integrated into the design process for the compliance system? Can some legal regulations be treated as poor relations just because they do not represent a threat to the existence of the company? In this context, it is once again all about the interplay between, and utilization of, those different areas of expertise described above. If a company only commissions a lawyer to collect information on areas of risk in the company then it is possible that he or she will search out hundreds of laws and regulations with which the company should comply—dealing with issues from military weapons through to guard dogs. In cooperation with experienced criminalists and auditors, however, it is then possible to determine which of the many regulations are really relevant and already covered by existing management systems, or which ones still need to be covered by a separate compliance management system.

The key to a really beneficial risk assessment is, therefore, to find the right focus. What is the result of integrating all of the conceivable risks to the same extent into the compliance management system? In the first instance, it will result in lots of duplicated work and unnecessary bureaucracy. This is because the company that is now developing a compliance program did not only start up in business yesterday. Lots of areas that are identified as playing a significant role in terms of compliance in the review of the current situation will already have been dealt with by other organizations within the company. As already mentioned, the tax department at the company will already have looked closely at those regulations relevant to them. The same will also be true for individual areas such as work safety or environmental protection. Thus to inspect all these areas again in order to evaluate them from a compliance perspective at the top decision-making level only makes sense to a limited extent. It is much more important that all of these components are brought together, coordinated, and kept up to date by a—perhaps newly created—specialist compliance department.

The purpose of focusing on risk in this design process is to give the resulting compliance management system a clear direction. This will help avoid searching in vain for a miraculous, oversimplified solution, or attempting to integrate everything possible to an equal degree. The more clearly and precisely top management can identify those really acute areas of risk and secure against them by employing sensible measures, the more understandable and acceptable these measures will be for the employees themselves. A standard solution that can "do everything" will simply be perceived as less urgent and less significant—and will be implemented as such—than a focused solution that starts working precisely where the need for action is the greatest.

The need for action is basically driven by two factors that will give the risk assessment some direction. These two factors are the previous cases of misconduct within the company and the prevailing risk potential. It is worth taking a brief look at other high profile cases either within the sector or which developed across related sectors, in order to develop a feeling for your own risk. When these two factors are examined in relation to one another, the real areas where action in the area of compliance is needed very quickly become apparent. The result will also naturally depend on the level of willingness to honestly evaluate the situation. And this in turn depends on the question of how much emphasis is given to each area. Is it worthwhile investing a lot of work in the development of compliance measures in the area of data protection or money laundering if this type of misconduct has never occurred in the company? At first glance the answer would be "not really"—except if the risk potential is so high that one single case of misconduct would immediately lead to criminal charges, arrests, cover stories, disgorgement settlements, or exclusion from certain markets.

This small example is designed to show that risk, from the perspective of the previous exposure of the company, needs to be balanced against the probability that noncompliance will occur[6] together with the possible consequences for the

[6] It is interesting that empirical studies have shown that managers attribute almost no significance to the calculated probabilities that risks will occur. Most managers base their risk assessments more on subjective convictions (see Hofmann 2008, p. 374).

company. There is nothing else that clearly distinguishes a sensible risk assessment from a useless one.

This also explains why the majority of compliance measures implemented in German companies are likely to concentrate on corruption and cartelization. There is a need for action in these areas because the payment of bribes and corruptibility were for a long time routine and were practically part of the business culture. However, these offenses are now forcefully pursued and punished by legislators, crime prosecution authorities, and, not least, the public. The same is also true for the area of cartelization in which fines totaling millions and even billions now appear to be normal. The subject of data protection is a similar burning issue for companies, fuelled by a diverse range of public scandals, for example eavesdropping on employees at Deutsche Bahn or the theft of customer data at Deutsche Telekom.

Viewed in a pragmatic sense, compliance takes two types of risk into account. On the one hand, those risks that are a priority for the company and which result from the direct business activities of the company. There is a real probability that these risks will occur and they are correspondingly sanctioned by legislators. Prevention in the form of compliance management clearly focuses on these risks and is designed to systematically reveal and prevent misconduct in these areas. The compliance organization and top management clearly and precisely identify these risks and handle them as a priority when it comes to the company's public image.

On the other hand, there are also so-called "secondary risks" that result to a lesser extent from the direct business activities of the company and which could occur in practically every company. A good example of this type of risk is taxation law. Every company is obligated to pay tax and ensure that they do not evade tax or defraud the government. However, focusing the entire compliance program on this subject would only really make sense for a handful of companies—such as banks. This does not mean that companies should simply disregard the secondary risks. The role of the compliance organization and the corresponding compliance management system is less to act as a direct driver of compliant behavior in this area and more to act as an intermediary between existing departments in the company who are already actively involved in these issues.

After looking at the fundamental approaches to the risk assessment and the "plea" for the prioritization of risks, it is now necessary to examine each of the questions that must be asked in the risk assessment. The starting point is the relevant laws. The subject of corruption will be used as an example here because it provides a very tangible and vivid representation of the methodology behind a professional risk assessment. The majority of those compliance management systems that are actually being applied will focus on the area of corruption—which is once again due to the consequences of major corruption cases.

Step 1: Gain an Overview of the Relevant Legislation

As already mentioned, the relevant legislation and the corresponding enforcement of this legislation form both the basis and main driving force behind systematic compliance management systems. Although it is true that compliance management systems often go above and beyond the current legal framework, their fundamental function is nevertheless to establish compliance with the law in the operationally active areas of the company. Therefore, there is generally no way to avoid having to take full stock of all of the legislation relevant to the company. It can usually be expected, however, that any normal legal requirements will already be covered by existing systems.

Step 2: Compare International Standards

The business activities of most companies in Germany are not only limited to Germany. It is therefore necessary in Step 2 to compare the already introduced compliance "guidelines" with international legislation at a state or EU level. Of course in the first instance, this means observing the operative regulations that are in place at a local level. Anybody building a dam in Brazil must naturally ensure that all of the relevant construction regulations and guidelines according to Brazilian law are observed. The greatest areas of risk in this example would probably be work safety and environmental protection.

As every form of business abroad—whether it is the construction of a dam or anything else—now represents a possible gateway for corruption, the examination of the legal regulations valid in the respective country becomes a self-contained step in the risk assessment. The reason for this is that the various legal regulations and provisions, which were already introduced in part in Chap. 1, differ across the world. The question should always be formulated as follows: "What international laws are valid for my business activities and what standards do they impose on the compliance management system that I am establishing?"

Here are a few examples. The most complex law with the greatest level of detail in its requirements is the UK Bribery Act. It is currently the only known law that prescribes concrete due-diligence checks—in other words integrity checks—for business partners. And this is a legal obligation not just a sensible recommendation. In their guidance papers, the authors of the UK Bribery Act, the UK Ministry of Justice, and the UK Serious Fraud Office (SFO), also specify additional elements that must be incorporated into a compliance management system (see Ministry of Justice 2011). These include:

- Proportionate procedures—clear and unambiguous guidelines, regulations, and processes dealing with fraud and corruption
- Top-level commitment—obligation for the top management level to clearly commit and actively contribute to compliance
- Risk assessment—a company-specific risk assessment
- The already mentioned due-diligence checks on business partners
- Communication and training—sustainable implementation and adequate training of all employees
- Monitoring and review—monitoring, auditing, and further development of the compliance program

If the UK Bribery Act is considered not just in terms of the elements dealing with criminal prosecutions, but also in terms of its implications for compliance management, it becomes clear what a hugely significant piece of legislation this is. It leaves those responsible in the company with almost no scope for deciding how to design their own preventative systems, but instead clearly dictates very concrete procedures. Even if existing compliance programs already meet the required standards set by the regulations from the FCPA or IDW PS 980, they could nevertheless still prove insufficient in the eyes of the UK Bribery Act and thus require some adaptation. Therefore, it is necessary to check very carefully whether your own company could fall under the jurisdiction of the UK Bribery Act.

The prerequisite for the application of the UK Bribery Act is proof of "carrying on a business or part of a business 'in any part of the United Kingdom'". The country or the affiliated company in which the questionable action took place is irrelevant in this context. As long as the action is considered punishable in Great Britain, it can now also be pursued worldwide under the UK Bribery Act as a punishable offense. This means in practice that it could be possible for British crime enforcement authorities to carry out investigations at German companies in Germany. In accordance with the guidance papers issued by the UK Ministry of Justice, a company is regarded as carrying on a business or part of a business, for example, if:

- a German company conducts or has conducted business activities in Great Britain
- the employee that carried out the questionable action is a British citizen or is considered to be subject to British law for other reasons
- the affected company used British service providers to develop its business activities. This means, for example, maintaining a British bank account, operating a British Internet domain, etc.

In the area of compliance standards, the British with the UK Bribery Act are without doubt setting the pace in the area of global corruption legislation. The Federal Republic of Germany is handling this subject a little differently. German legislation more or less only stipulates that business is to be conducted cleanly. Meanwhile, the interpretation of these laws is being established slowly but surely through court judgments. These developments have also gradually led to standards of a sort. However, these standards do not stipulate actual concrete steps, such as a due-diligence check for business partners or the institutionalization of compliance training.

In American legislation, the situation has developed in almost the reverse order. The precise elements of a compliance system are not formulated very clearly in American law. For example, SOX also only mentions the provision of an "adequate preventative system." The yardstick for designing compliance management systems according to American standards is instead the US Federal Sentencing Guidelines.[7] These guidelines control the sentencing policies used for infringements against American federal laws.

[7] See: http://www.ussc.gov/

If a company appears in court to answer to a case of corruption, it will generally receive a lighter punishment if it operates a compliance management system. The US Federal Sentencing Guidelines define the components that need to be included in the compliance management system before the mechanism to enable leaner sentencing can take effect: for example, compliance with the regulations is incentivized in the company, whistle-blowing systems have been installed to motivate informants, or regular compliance reviews are carried out. The compliance standards are thus not part of the wording of the law like in Great Britain, but can nevertheless be found by looking a little deeper into the judicature.

In order to fall under the jurisdiction of the American legislature according to the FCPA or SOX, it is simply sufficient—as described in Chap. 1—to have a subsidiary listed on the American stock market or to have paid or received bribes in US dollars. The Americans, in the form of the SEC or the Department of Justice (DOJ), have—to put it mildly—been extremely aggressive when it comes to interpreting their right of jurisdiction. It is possible, for example, that the US authorities will intervene if they become aware of, or feel they have jurisdiction over, a German company with "significant business relationships"[8] in the USA that has become embroiled in a case of corruption somewhere else in the world. This could be for the simple reason that they are perturbed by the fact that one of their market participants has apparently not been maintaining clean business practices.

Representatives of the American authorities may then formulate their concerns perhaps so: "We are currently examining whether this case falls under our jurisdiction. In order to avoid any difficulties, it would be helpful if you could answer a few questions about the case for us." The company in question on the other side of the Atlantic may then respond: "Dear DOJ, you are welcome to check the legal situation but it does not fall under your jurisdiction." This exchange initially sounds harmless but there is a certain level of threat nevertheless involved: does the company answer the questions or not? After all, the company does not want to sour their relationship with the Americans or possibly be excluded from the American market. If it cannot be demonstrated in such a situation that the American compliance standards in terms of the US Federal Sentencing Guidelines were properly fulfilled, there could remain the threat of fines or subsequent criminal prosecutions.[9]

Whether and to what extent international standards and jurisdiction apply beyond German borders, and as such should be integrated into the development of a compliance management system, must be checked in each individual case and must subsequently be kept up to date. As part of the evaluation of the current risk, this process should be carried out for all countries in which the company operates and for all countries where there are companies with which business is conducted.

Ideally, a map should be created that illustrates the relevant legal and regulatory situation in all countries. When implementing this first pillar of an effective

[8] For definition see DOJ Online http://www.justice.gov/criminal/fraud/fcpa/

[9] Economic policy motivations cannot be excluded in such a process, the role of the SEC and their conduct in transnational investigations needs to be critically examined from case to case.

compliance management system, there are two possible approaches: take either the highest legal standard from across all countries and apply it to all company affairs, or deal with the situation individually for each country. If each country is dealt with individually, there will of course be the risk that at some time or other a regulation or provision may be overlooked. This choice also presents the architects of the compliance management system with a dilemma: the country-specific solution requires more effort as it will involve many different independent cells, which must each be kept up to date. The more comprehensive solution of taking the highest standard can, however, cause a lack of understanding in the national companies. "Why are we now being audited in this area? It is not even relevant to us." This is the type of statement often heard from employees at middle management levels.

If both approaches are weighed against one another, the solution using an overarching, higher compliance standard implemented across the company appears to be much more feasible and will provide greater security from an organizational and commercial standpoint. In this solution, it will be necessary to make only minor improvements later on, while the key aspects were already defined when the compliance measures were rolled out. In addition, it will reduce the need to diversify the communication of these measures within a large organization, which in turn will help limit the freedom of scope for interpretation and flexibility.

In summary, the first steps of a risk assessment should involve an examination of the relevant legislature together with any international equivalents, and the question of which laws and regulations apply for the company worldwide. In what areas is it absolutely necessary to guarantee compliance everywhere? In the next step, the company and its different areas will be examined in more depth in order to compare legal regulations with day-to-day reality. The goal here will be to develop preventative measures that bring the required and the actual behavior closer together.

Step 3: Identify Concrete Areas of Risk in the Company

Once the legal environment has been clearly defined, the next question covers what areas of the company will be affected by the legislation. To answer this question it is necessary to delve deep into the company processes and find starting points that will help to decide which control or measure will best cover the risks in which areas. As the range of possible risks is simply enormous, there will be a greater focus at this stage on the methodology behind the risk assessment rather than on providing a full list of all imaginable risks faced by the company. We will once again look in more detail here at the example of a risk assessment for corruption. Ultimately, this concluding step in the risk assessment requires fundamental knowledge from the area of criminology relating to the development of white-collar crime. Against the background of the relevant laws and regulations, it is important at this stage to ask the right questions about how misconduct arises. These questions will then be subsequently answered in the next phase of the process, "detection."

In order to identify critical areas of risk in the company, a number of practical approaches are recommended.

4.4.1.1 Evaluating Previous Cases of Misconduct

No company is keen to delve into its own cases of misconduct from the past. If the people who were involved are still employed at the company or cases of "deviant behavior" were locked away and treated as a taboo subject then a serious reappraisal of the events is particularly difficult. However, an external risk consultant should not make any allowances for these issues. Gathering precise information about the cases of corruption or fraud experienced in the past will help the consultant enormously: What exactly happened back then? Which control measure failed? What was the response to the case? How great was the damage to the company? What motivated the perpetrator? Were the controls subsequently improved? What contribution did leadership and incentivization play in the misconduct?

An experienced criminalist can use any available fraud and corruption reports to identify patterns in, and starting points for, systematic misconduct. The consultant will derive little joy from examining each individual case in detail. However, the consultant will certainly notice if the same patterns of fraud and corruption have reoccurred in different areas of the same company. For example, if engineers have bribed the same construction company in different countries in the same way, or if repeated cases of similar inconsistencies are identified in goods purchasing or stocktaking. It is thus already possible here to recognize any systematic risks and thus go on to examine them in more depth.

4.4.1.2 Analyzing the Organization and Processes

As described in Chap. 2, complexity is a major driver of white-collar crime and corruption. The more complex a company structure is and the more convoluted and incomprehensible its process are, the larger the shadowy realm in which crimes can be committed and concealed will be. It is—as explained—only a question of time until somebody exploits this complexity to create an advantage for themselves. In the course of a risk assessment, there is thus also a very comprehensive examination of the organization and processes. What are the approval processes? Is the four-eye principle followed? Is there documentation of what was signed by whom and when? Are the stock levels continuously monitored and documented? What are the process steps involved in carrying out purchases and orders? An important factor in this evaluation is the clarity and understandability of internal directives and existing regulations. A common symptom for the development of blind spots in risk management is fast growth. When a company is growing quickly, the monitoring system is not generally able to grow at the same pace.

4.4.1.3 Scrutinizing the Company Finances and the Accounts Department

One further stage in the development of a structural risk assessment is to examine the current state of the company finances. This stands to reason because hardly any case of fraud or corruption develops without some form of manipulation or deception of the financial accounting in the company. The handling of transactions is thus a core area of the risk assessment that must be used to identify weak spots. On the one hand, this involves authorizations and processes for initiating a transaction and, on the other, looks at the documentation of the flow of money and payments. In the prevention of corruption and money laundering, it is especially relevant to be able to chronicle and trace all of the money flows extremely cleanly.

Are all service providers registered as creditors at the company and entered along with a corresponding contract? Are payments really only made through registered bank accounts? Who can set up bank accounts for the company or a national subsidiary? Who has access to cash on-site? Construction companies, in particular, always have a cash box containing sufficient money to cover all of the ongoing costs on-site. The use of these types of physical and mobile cash boxes naturally also represents a risk.

4.4.1.4 Example Application: Corruption Risks

Most compliance management systems are likely to have been specifically developed for the systematic prevention of corruption. This provides us with reason enough to once again look at the types of corruption risk that need to be part of every risk assessment. In contrast to the very different types of risk found in the areas of fraud and balance sheet manipulation, it is much easier to provide a general overview of the risk patterns found in the area of corruption.

In Chap. 2, we already looked at the different ways that corruption in sales or purchasing could be effectively concealed.[10] Here is a short recap: both corruptibility in purchasing or bribes and antitrust manipulations in sales are sources of risk. A corrupt purchaser damages the company by purchasing poorer-quality products at inflated prices. And a corrupt sales employee risks profit disgorgement settlements and weakens the innovation of the company over the long term. This is because they purchase the illusion of business success through supplementary payments. Corruption—whether it is bribery or corruptibility—often occurs in those areas of the company where everything revolves around successfully winning a contract at the pitching or invitation to tender stage. Therefore, those who want to assess the risk of corruption in their company should critically assess their own business structure. The well-known five W's and one H questions from the area of journalism can provide some orientation.

Who Do I Conduct Business With?

Do you deal with private companies or the public sector? In the case of a public invitation to tender, the risk is per se higher because the fact that granting an advantage is treated as a criminal offense means that an additional safety margin has been introduced against bribery. In contrast to private customers, it is now not only bribery or corruptibility that is punishable in Germany,[11] but even the receipt of "benefits for the performance of your duties." The risks faced when dealing with the public sector also increase exponentially in so-called high-risk countries, where

[10] See Chap. 2.

[11] See Articles 331, 333 of StGB.

public employees are not sufficiently monitored or the issuing of a contract can be politically influenced.

In combination with the client, there is also the question of the invitation to tender itself. Is the briefing complete and understandable? Are the competitive conditions transparent and product-oriented? Or is the contract issued by guess and by gosh without any controlled process?

Where Do I Conduct My Business?

The organization Transparency International creates a global corruption map every year with the assistance of EY—the Corruption Perceptions Index.[12] This index allows you to keep very good track of how pronounced and taken for granted corruption is in countries around the world. If your company generates a large proportion of its turnover through business transactions abroad, you should thoroughly examine this map and its methodology and critically ask why your company in particular has managed to clinch a succession of public contracts in this or that high-risk country while others have been left empty handed. Having business success here is a reason to take a closer look and examine in detail how the process of issuing contracts works and how your colleagues in the relevant business unit portray the local situation themselves.

What Business Do I Conduct?

It would be presumptuous to claim that construction companies and the armaments industry—which are almost always highlighted when examining the risk of corruption—are the only sectors that have to fight corruption. Transparency International also issues a special index in the form of the BPI[13] that names those sectors in which the most bribes allegedly flow (see here the Editorial of Wirtschaftswoche 2012). The index shows that the risk of corruption is higher in some sectors than in others. This is not at all due to the individual sectors having any intrinsic depravity or virtue, but is entirely due to the complexity of the product and lack of product transparency. Therefore, it is also necessary for a risk assessment to focus on this area: "How complex are my products? Do I conduct business in such a multifaceted and non-transparent way that it enables bribes to be concealed? Can the invitation to tender be manipulated via the technical details? How many employees in my company have any idea at all about the product that we sell there?" It is an obvious fact that the complexity of industrial plants, fighter jets, or medicines with tens of thousands of either ingredients or components is so high that no layperson, let alone a controller in the accounting department back at headquarters, can truly comprehend what is good, bad, too expensive, too cheap, or even just right.

---

[12] Transparency International: http://www.transparency.org/research/cpi/overview

[13] Bribe Payers Index: http://www.transparency.org/research/bpi/overview

How Do I Conduct My Business?

This question is ultimately the one that delivers the most tangible impetus for implementing a preventative system against corruption. Those who take a close look at how business transactions are arranged and carried out in a company encounter numerous possible areas where corruption can develop. An important role is played in this area by "consultants" or "agents." Moosmayer also takes the view that systematic corruption is increasingly characterized by the involvement of "sales-driven business agents" (see Moosmayer 2012, p. 27). These people are acting on behalf of the company as authorized representatives or commercial agents and possess the corresponding power of procuration and funds (cash) to influence the issuing of contracts. Experience has demonstrated that it is impossible to generate sales in some countries without the help of expert local agents to arrange the business deals, even if this assistance eschews every form of corruption that could lead to prosecution. The utilization of these types of agents is thus not inevitably linked to corruption—but is close to it.

Those analyzing their corruption risk must pay particularly attention to the mechanisms by which business is conducted in the company: Are agents being used? What are these people actually paid for? How did the business relationship originate? In what environment do these agents operate? Which of their services are documented and comprehensible? If external third parties are used as a vehicle for the payment of bribes, they require money or other assets that can be used for this purpose. The aspects on financial controlling and accounting described above also naturally play a role here.

4.4.1.5 Summary of the Subject of Risk Assessments

As already mentioned, corruption is certainly only one of the areas of application for this type of risk assessment—which forms the foundations and starting points for all subsequent compliance measures. It is completely irrelevant in this process which type of "deviant behavior" is under consideration. The methodology behind the risk assessment is always the same: Identify the relevant laws and regulations, transfer these to the areas of risk in the company, and specifically apply them.

The risk map created for the company serves as the foundation upon which all other preventative measures will be developed.

4.4.2 The Compliance Loop

The following key question will be posed sooner or later by those involved in compliance management: What elements should an effective compliance management system include? Which individual process steps and functional areas are involved? How can a systematic protective mechanism be set up in a company that ultimately makes it possible to evaluate risk, make employees aware of risk, train them in regulatory matters, recognize misconduct, and, at the same time, learn from cases of white-collar crime? By starting with the principles behind the compliance objectives, utilizing the cultural influence of the "tone from the top," and taking into account the possible organizational forms behind the measures, an effective mechanism for protecting against "deviant behavior" can be built on the following three pillars: **Prevention, (early) detection, and investigation and remediation**.

The compliance loop presented here is not, by a long stretch, the only model that can be used to implement compliance in a company. In precisely the same way as every other type of management system, compliance measures are never piecemeal or a one-off solution but follow previously defined process routines. Even if it necessary to define the processes and responsibilities at the very beginning, the system will remain in a state of continuous change, updating and improving itself constantly—although its basic orientation or base content will not ever actually structurally change. This makes it extremely important to create a meticulously designed model as a template—otherwise the measures are damned to be simply one-off therapies for systematic misconduct.

If we assume that a compliance management system is developed without previous experience or a history of misconduct in the company—although this is practically never the case in reality—then the first step in the process is prevention. **Prevention is always based on the preceding risk assessment**. This step defines and establishes all of the structural, organizational, and content-related principles upon which future measures will be based. Prevention is thus essentially the heart of a compliance management system.

The controls and mechanisms established as part of the **detection** step are equally as dependent on the risk assessment in order to be able to identify, uncover, and test those typical patterns of "deviant behavior" relevant to the company at an early stage. Detection thus operationalizes the hypotheses derived from the risk assessment.

If the controls take effect and provide indications of fraud or corruption, an **investigation** is added to the compliance loop of the management system. An investigation into irregularities is carried out in line with the options presented in Chap. 3, although every investigation must be adapted to the individual circumstances in the company, as well as the concrete evidence or existing regulations. If an effective early warning system has been established, the investigations themselves will tend to be smaller and more specialized. This is why the detailed considerations found below will focus, in particular, on how these types of investigation should be conducted as part of the system to avoid causing unnecessary disruption in the company every time.

Any cases of white-collar crime that have been investigated and solved are then analyzed in context during the subsequent phase of **remediation**. Noncompliance is sanctioned, other legal requirements are handled, and the lessons learned integrated into the preventative mechanisms, driving the entire system through a continuous process of learning and improvement. An example of remediation would be the provision of new risk reduction measures to cover previous blind spots (Fig. 4.2).

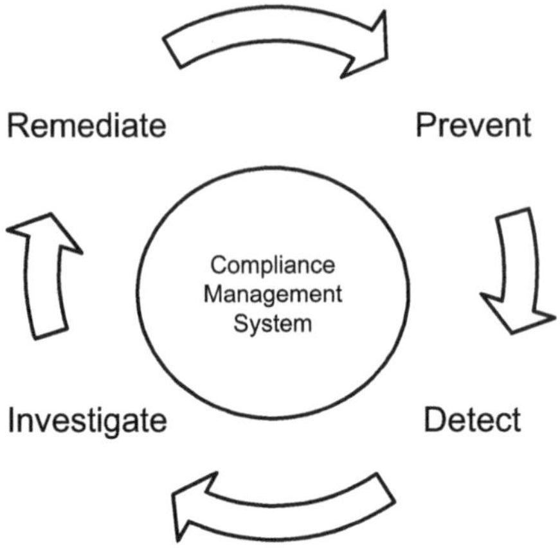

Fig. 4.2 The compliance loop

4.4.2.1 Prevention

Prevention combines all of the concepts for preventative measures into a compliance management system—working out the regulations and voluntary obligations, standard processes, compliance training, and opportunities for developing incentives for compliant behavior. The precise measures that form part of the prevention step and what these look like in detail are significantly dependent—as previously described—on the risk assessment. This will show exactly what the compliance mechanisms need to address.

Policies and Procedures: Creating a Core Content

Putting down compliance regulations, guidelines, and working aids in writing and then communicating them is a central part of every compliance management system. What should be precisely written in this documentation and how it should be communicated both externally and internally is directly dependent on the results of the risk assessment that was carried out. Irrespective of their form, format, and content, the development of binding definitions for regulations and processes is the central measure for preventing damage caused by "deviant behavior"—and thus forms the core content and the ideological nucleus of the corporate management system.

The objective should be to create a comprehensive set of rules that is valid for all employees in the company. The lowest level at which this codification of the compliance measures takes place is in the specialist departments. The findings from the risk assessment are translated into directives for action, in the form of work regulations or supplementary conditions in the work contracts issued to employees. Even if extremely tangible statements are made here about which behavior is desirable and which is not desirable, it is not necessary to formulate individual instructions for every conceivable dilemma or regulation dealing with the acceptance of gifts. The decisive criteria are that employees are provided with proper orientation, and the legal requirements are translated into the language of the company's daily activities—within the freedom of maneuver of those employees working in high-risk positions.

Anybody attempting to put compliance regulations into words and define policies and procedures cannot just stop at producing operative regulations. Whether these regulations are accepted and implemented by employees is dependent to a significant extent on the way they have been formulated and the relevance attributed to them. Therefore, basic compliance regulations need to be supplemented with a declaration of the company's fundamental values. Here, the responsibility lies with top management. In the best-case scenario, the chairman of the management board will address their employees with an unambiguous statement that actively promotes compliance. This involves briefing employees in the simplest possible terms about the principles embodied within the company's corporate values and explaining to them what compliance actually means. Whether the result of this turns out to be a vision, a code of conduct, a value statement, an ethical code, or a governance policy is quite frankly incidental. The main point is that the content has been adapted to the individual company and its specific areas of risk, while at the same time symbolizing the clear commitment of company management to integrity and compliance. This "tone from the top" is much more than just the icing on top of the compliance cake. It is demanded to some extent by law and is an important part of the overall compliance structure. This is because it gives the newly created regulations in the company meaning, context, and authority—and hugely simplifies the implementation process for a compliance management system as a result. This basic commitment to compliance is of course not just communicated internally but also externally—for example, via the company's website or their own publications. Many companies publish these types of compliance statements or ethical codes, or even devote parts of their annual reports to the superordinate theme of governance.

The next step deals with those processes that need to be immediately adapted to the newly created or updated set of rules. Ultimately, all of the available controls and concepts must have been adapted to the principles contained within this set of rules at the latest by the launch of the compliance management system. Preventative mechanisms will, as a rule, already be present in the company and these now need to be supplemented or adapted in accordance with the results of the completed risk assessment. These compliance procedures include, for example, setting up process-related controls in the different company departments. This could involve institutionalizing the four-eye principle, segregating duties and functions, introducing guidelines for conflicts of interest and dilemmas, and documenting rules and clear procedures for authorization and approval processes.

An example will be discussed below, once again from the fight against corruption that will also be picked up later on in the section on detection. If the risk assessment indicates, for example, that there is a risk of corruption due to cooperation with consultancy firms who have business addresses in offshore financial centers, the corresponding work directives for the accounting department or the process controls behind these directives must logically be designed to make it impossible to enter suspicious master data in the first place. The company would thus adapt the application used by the accounting department, or the calculation tool used by the sales department at a programming level to make it impossible for business addresses from the Cayman Islands or the Isle of Man to be entered. A less restrictive measure could be to make it necessary when entering corresponding master data to at least add certain additional information, or could be to set up a map of high-risk countries within the system.

This would mean that whenever a creditor from, for example, one of the countries on the risk list issued by the OECD or the Financial Stability Forums[14] is entered, a warning in the Compliance Office will be triggered and the process frozen until the Compliance Officer has checked the integrity of the creditor added to the system.

Compliance Awareness: Combining Theory and Practice

Strictly speaking, the definition of policies and procedures for a compliance management system is a preliminary exercise. The set of rules as such initially represents the theoretical foundations for the management of compliance and employee integrity. An important component of institutionalized compliance is thus the combination of theory and practice, in other words raising awareness about the rules (compliance awareness). It is important to bear in mind that as soon as the compliance management system is implemented, employees in different business units will suddenly be confronted with numerous laws and regulations that someone with very little legal training can only grasp to a limited extent. This can happen irrespective of how briefly, concisely, understandably, or user-friendly the compliance rules have been formulated. Internalizing these rules using practical exercises and training as an element of prevention is an important part of the overall program.

At this point, a decisive factor is sensibly extending the validity of the existing rules to include the business units themselves. All compliance management systems run the risk of fizzling out somewhere between the group headquarters and the front lines of the business. A compliance program does not even have to be poorly designed for this to happen. It often occurs when, for example, the program produces rules that are too bureaucratic and incomprehensible, and which hinder normal operations in the company.

It will suffice if the objectives and the meaning behind compliance and the developed measures are not effectively explained, or there are too few training programs for them to be put into practice. What is actually written down on paper is only a formality. The short period of time in which German companies have been dealing with compliance has shown that it cannot be effectively implemented if employees are simply instructed from on high to cram in order to learn the regulations. It is only through a critical examination of compliance, an exchange of ideas and information, and an explanation of the wider context that the desired awareness will develop within the corporate culture, forming the basis upon which

[14] Can be followed for example at http://www.financialstabilityboard.org/index.htm

many other measures can then be built. Corresponding advisory services for employees could also be included, for example, in the form of a hotline or personal advice center in the company. And this too is an awareness issue: "Where can I find out more information on this subject?" "Who can I talk to if I have any questions?" The point is that it is not sufficient simply to mail the latest version of the code of conduct or compliance standards to sales employees abroad. These employees must be offered the opportunity to critically scrutinize the information or, in the best-case scenario, be integrated into the process at an earlier stage. And the training offered to these employees must be carried out where they are located: on-site in the relevant country where their business is being conducted. Training provided on the subject of compliance should, in a similar way to the set of rules themselves, be adapted to the individual business units.

The goal is thus to provide orientation beyond the regulations. After all, it is not possible to define a standard process for every conceivable situation. In particular, employees in sales and purchasing repeatedly find themselves in situations where they have to deal with a dilemma or a conflict of interest. Regular training courses could be arranged to examine the common dilemmas experienced in each business unit, and to provide recommendations for compliant action in these situations.

These types of dilemma workshops will more likely deal with corruption and conflicts of interest in their broadest sense, protecting against criminal behavior carried out by third parties in high-risk countries, avoiding gifts, and managing markets in which nothing seems to be possible without a bribe. Similar training sessions on fraud and manipulation topics could then be tailored specially to the relevant target groups. It is important in this process not to engineer cases or to dream up examples that colleagues in the business units themselves cannot even comprehend. It is much better to learn from real cases, which means using existing knowledge in the company and examples illustrating day-to-day problems to specifically identify gray areas in the field of compliance and to adapt the training provisions correspondingly. A method that is very popular in many companies is for former employees with decades of professional experience on the front line to share their experience and knowledge about daily conflict situations. This method provides an excellent foundation on which to base practical "insider secrets workshops."

Incentivization: Creating Positive Incentives

Another component in the architecture of a compliance management system is the incentivization of compliance, meaning the creation of positive incentives to encourage correct behavior and observance of the rules. Now some people may ask why they should reward their employees for observing the applicable legislation. This type of behavior should simply go without saying.

Unfortunately it doesn't, but anyway this is not what is actually meant by incentivization here, but rather something completely different. Compliance-related incentive systems mainly focus on middle management and link part of their annual bonus to the achievement of targets dealing with compliance. This ensures that managers are encouraged to give their employees positive incentives for observing the regulations. The basic philosophy behind these types of incentivization systems is that compliance should always represent a better alternative than corruption and manipulation. Management personnel should thus create the corresponding prerequisites for clean business practices. There has not been any general consensus up to now on the validation logic that should be applied in evaluating the performance of management personnel in the area of compliance, and it thus differs from company to company. The first step is often to remove any incentives in the already formulated objectives that may appear dysfunctional from a compliance perspective. For example, this could be the formulation of really tough and completely immoveable sales targets that must be reached at any cost.

It is possible to incentivize a great deal of things when it comes to compliance, with regular training of employees, personal commitment in the form of further education and attending lectures, the observance of compliance controls, or the quick investigation of cases of damage—should any offenses actually occur. Siemens, for example, additionally evaluates the performance of its management personnel in the area of compliance on the basis of an employee survey. Those who score well on the survey and otherwise demonstrate that they are taking the subject seriously with training courses, controls, etc., also receive more money.[15]

Nevertheless, it is necessary to make a critical observation at this point. Nobody has really thought through these value-oriented remuneration systems to their logical conclusion up to now—even though Siemens with their previous negative experiences of white-collar crime have made great strides. The fundamental conflict between compliance objectives and sales targets still remains. How does a company react when billion euro contracts suddenly fail to materialize because bribes are no longer being paid? How is it possible to harmonize concepts such as values and integrity with the actual corporate objectives of the company? The path that the company must take is sure to lead far beyond pure compliance management, and will thus be discussed at another time, namely when dealing with good business management as a whole—or more precisely—the future model of good corporate governance.

4.4.2.2 Detection

This part of the compliance loop deals with the early detection of compliance risks and infringements. In the first instance, people tend to think of technical controls. However, the means and methods used to detect misconduct and pursue indications of white-collar crime are a little more varied. In particular, it is important to look in more detail at the importance of whistleblowing and the simultaneous creation of exit strategies to allow perpetrators to escape the spiral of crime. In contrast to mass data analyses and compliance screening, the significance of these measures in the ongoing compliance process is often overlooked. In a purely pragmatic sense, an important part of detection is also the development of controls that do not interfere

[15] Also see here Siemens (2008): http://www.siemens.com/responsibility/report/08/de/management/compliance/incentivierung.htm

with or limit the company's actual business activities. A criticism that is often heard from many quarters is that compliance degenerates into a sort of regulation frenzy and the resulting controls require so much time and effort that the organization as a whole loses much of its ability to properly conduct business. How should these types of controls be developed? And on what kind of expertise should they be based?

Risk Assessments and the Formulation of Criminalistic Hypotheses as the Foundation for Non-event-Based Controls

The task of detection is thus the early recognition of misconduct. If we once again consider the expertise required for the development of a compliance management system, it will be precisely here that a criminalist can make a major contribution. This is because early detection combines at its core two aspects: the findings from the risk assessment and the formation of criminalistic hypotheses. The risk assessment demonstrates which parts of the company need to be controlled and weights them according to risk areas. Then the areas at risk are assigned a manipulation hypothesis according to the freedom of maneuver held by the respective employees. Ultimately, criminalists formulate these types of hypotheses in exactly the same way as they do during an investigation. Depending on the conceivable modus operandi, testable indicators of misconduct are identified. It's at this point that it often becomes clear that the documentation necessary to identify these indicators is not available for this stage of the process. This documentation needs to be already defined in the prevention phase so that it can be used for creating the tests later on in the early detection phase.

A couple of practical examples now follow, starting with the broad field of corruption. What methods can actually be used for the payment of bribes? Who can judge within the company whether the invoiced amounts are too high, services were genuinely provided, or bank accounts truly exist? Could cash from cash boxes be used to grease someone's palm? If the answer to the previous question was yes, who has access to the cash box and how is the cash balance documented? Are there ways that money from project teams could be siphoned off? All of these questions need to be worked through and evaluated in the development of suitable anti-corruption measures—the objective being to track and therefore prevent opportunities for misconduct.

Here is an example from the area of securities trading. What do investment bankers have to do in order to be still able to report their massive losses as profits? What records need to be falsified? What ways are there for them to falsify these records on their own? Or where will they need, for example, an accomplice from the back office? Which reporting systems apply to both of these employees and how could this system be outsmarted?

Let us now look briefly at the different subject of industrial espionage. Who actually possesses the knowledge and authorization to access sensitive documentation? How are electronic documents protected? What legal and illegal methods could still be used to view confidential documents from the research and development department (R&D)? And in what ways could these documents be leaked out of the company?

As already mentioned, the range of possible hypotheses is at least as diverse and complex as the offenses themselves. In contrast to the investigation of a concrete case of white-collar crime, the criminalist must formulate a lot more hypotheses in the detection phase—the offense has, after all, not yet been committed and in principle everything could still be possible. In the development of a functioning apparatus for detecting white-collar crime, it is thus necessary for the architects of a compliance management system to delve a level deeper into both the offenses themselves and the actual processes carried out in the company. In this way, they can gradually develop scenarios for the most dangerous cases of damage. Critical paths within each of these scenarios will then become apparent and these then need to be issued with corresponding controls.

In the case of fraudulent investment bankers, it may be ascertained, for example, that they would need some sort of secret account to "park" the phantom profits so they can conceal future losses and carry out fictitious deals. If the bankers do not have the authority themselves to set up this type of account, they would require an accomplice in the controlling department. The two employees would then need to communicate with one another—special computer programs can evaluate this type of communication and search for suspicious phrases or code words without having to spy on every single e-mail sent by every employee. In the previously described case surrounding Kweku Adoboli, the code word was incidentally "umbrella".[16] Among other things, the trading limits were exceeded by using this "umbrella account" and it was also used to park profits from fictitious securities transactions in order to conceal risks and offset losses from other transactions. A similar approach is conceivable for any comparable offense in the area of market speculation. The modus operandi follows clear patterns that need to be understood, evaluated, and correspondingly taken into account.

When it comes to protecting knowledge in the company against industrial espionage, an almost inevitable intrinsic control measure that will be arrived at sooner or later is the need-to-know principle. Here, technical access controls, data encryption, and the controlled distribution of knowledge are used to try to guarantee that no one can view, copy, or record data, send it by e-mail, or smuggle it out of the company on a data medium without explicit authorization. This is all essentially centered on the maintenance of IT standards. One principle that is well known in law firms and auditing firms is for all computers to be equipped with a script that immediately sets up a code and a password for any USB device inserted into the system. This renders them practically unusable on any third-party devices and means they cannot be accessed by an unauthorized user.

[16] Ruwan Weerasekera, Chief Operating Officer of Securities at UBS, revealed during the proceedings that the "umbrella account" would have been more carefully examined if there had been appropriate controls of the communication data and relevant logs; refer to publications such as Bloomberg (2012).

However, with respect to industrial espionage it may be useful to mention that one of the best control mechanisms to guard against losing expertise has always been to deal fairly with top employees. This is because the easiest way to procure knowledge from competitors is still to simply poach the head of development or R&D experts from your competitors. The protection of employees with key expertise could also be included as part of compliance management if there is a risk posed to the company in this area.

In the case of corruption and bribery, the controls would be sure to include such things as checking business partners and agents, preventing creditors with business address on the Cayman Islands or other tax havens from being added by the accounting department, the centralized payment of transactions, and insisting on the most precise receipts possible for cash payments and bank transfers. However, the risks faced in the area of corruption are becoming increasingly complex, which makes it necessary to constantly adapt control mechanisms. The perpetrators will also at some point realize that compliance screenings and data analyses are now checking the integrity of agents and consultants. This means that they will have to find new methods for concealing the payment of bribes. And the creativity shown here knows no limits: for example, founding a joint venture in which loans are granted as part of the agreement that are never actually repaid. Or the trick of embedding items with inflated prices or fictitious services into quotations or into the calculations themselves.

The good news is that the more stringent and systematic the controls become, the more creative and elaborate the fraudulent actions need to be. The bad news is that in order to become wise to these manipulations, it will no longer be sufficient to only check consultants and the flow of money. The compliance controls will be required to delve deeper into quotations, calculations, and product details in order to identify fraudulent actions. And what is valid for investigation is thus also true for detection: this field is becoming more specialized and increasingly complex. This is because the offenses also adapt to the current standards and become less transparent and more convoluted as a result. The fight against white-collar crime is, and will remain, a game of cat and mouse.

Those who look after compliance management systems need to keep an eye on cross-sector trends in order to continue to effectively protect their companies by adapting their controls to the latest possibilities for fraud and corruption. After all, each sector has their own individual key areas of risk, which should be studied and used to make tailored adaptations.

Basic Instruments of Detection: Data and Contract Analyses

Despite the fact that detection makes use of the criminalistic expertise applied in an investigation, the difference between detection and investigation lies in the fact that there is no initial suspicion being followed during detection. The process thus involves scanning practically the whole company based upon potential risk and permanently carrying out structured analyses or controls in order to identify misconduct. Although it would be possible at this point to list corresponding indicators and suitable controls for all offenses, it would not really be conducive to explaining which individual components make up a fully functioning compliance management system.

Every single company ultimately requires a different set of compliance measures that need to be very precisely tailored to the existing conditions. It would be disastrous to simply purchase a compliance solution off the peg. The mechanisms used in the area of detection, in particular, are exclusive designer pieces—despite the fact that the market occasionally tries to claim otherwise.

Nonetheless, there are basic instruments of detection that should be briefly described at this point: namely the analysis of data and the analysis of contracts. Both of these instruments can often provide practical starting points for developing structured compliance controls, which are then further refined later on in the process. Data and contract analyses can also be utilized on an ad hoc basis and do not necessarily need to be part of a complete compliance management system.

Let us look at a typical example: shortly after purchasing a company, the chairman of the management board is concerned about whether the acquired construction services provider in a high-risk country, such as Algeria, has issues with corruption. Despite the fact that the company passed a due-diligence check before the acquisition, they want to make sure that they have not just introduced a bad apple to the barrel—for which they will be ultimately liable in the event of any misconduct. In this case, the situation calls for the company to be checked out without any concrete indications of misconduct. One of the aforementioned starting points for so-called "compliance detection audits"—and therefore for early detection measures—are forensic data analyses. Following the acquisition, the parent company now has full access to the company data. It is thus possible, for example, to run all creditors and debtors at the company through a search mechanism that has been configured to filter out suspicious records. This could include incomplete information, business addresses in offshore locations, or master data that indicates that business partners are related to employees at the company. Any of this information could prove to be an indication of corruption.

For example, if a suspicious data record leads to a company run by the wife of the top salesman that also happens to be located in the Cayman Islands or the Netherlands Antilles, then it would be justified to take a closer look at the business process and the relevant transactions. The transition from detection to investigation is then fluid. If the indications that something is not right become more tangible, it is advisable sooner or later to speak to those involved or to evaluate their communication data[17] in order to clarify what is really going on. However, this would only need to be carried out for this individual case and not as a blanket measure applied throughout the whole company.

A second instrument for detecting misconduct that follows on from the principles of a data analysis is a contract analysis. This ultimately involves monitoring whether services for which the company has paid have also been provided.

[17] For ethical and data protection reasons, this naturally requires valid suspicions or the clear consent of the employee.

The focus is once again placed here on the prevention of corruption and balance sheet manipulation. If a company does not have a central contract management department or central purchasing department, the approval of payments to service providers is generally the responsibility of the individual subsidiaries or the individual business units. As the company's control over its own financial transactions dwindles, the risk of noncompliance naturally increases.

A contract analysis as a basic instrument of detection comprises fundamental controls derived from these risks to the company: standardizing service descriptions in purchasing, linking payments to order numbers and unique receipts, and setting up and monitoring clear approval processes for payments—to name but a few. The control environment is thus designed to indicate whether every contract that is concluded by the company is also fulfilled and is not being misused for the purposes of fraud or corruption. This is because perpetrators are reliant on the conclusion of contracts with dummy companies and consultants in order to keep up the appearance of normal business transactions.

In general, data and contract analyses are applied together. The data analysis provides some initial orientation among the masses of transaction data in a company, while the set of indicators are then checked in a structured manner. In the case of transactions where the indicators reveal suspicious information—so-called "red flags"—a contract analysis is utilized to check the plausibility of the relevant transaction based on the agreed contracts.

Other Examples of Detection Instruments

Without going into too much detail unnecessarily, examples of other instruments for the early detection of noncompliance will be presented at this point—in order to demonstrate the sheer scale of the environment in which companies can and must operate in the field of compliance management. Depending on the legislation valid at an international level, other standards for complying with the relevant regulations need to be created that are reflected in the compliance management system. For example, the UK Bribery Act prescribes due diligence as part of the compliance system.

When describing some of the possible individual measures, it becomes clear that instruments of detection do not always necessarily deal with controls based on internal company information but in their widest sense encompass everything that could contribute to reducing risk. Nevertheless, they always focus on the central ideas of how offenses are committed and how the company can become aware as early as possible about suspicious actions.

Pre-employment Screenings

It may sound harsh but compliance begins with the selection of personnel—from the warehouse clerk right up to the CEO. It is also possible to establish control and detection mechanisms in this area to guarantee compliance in the future. It is particularly true when it comes to filling positions on the management board or other top management positions that hardly anybody will be employed today if they fail to pass an integrity check in advance. These so-called "executive integrity assessments" are a field of prevention that has boomed in the last few years. These assessments involve—in line with the instruments used for business intelligence—background research into publicly accessible sources. This type of background research thus has nothing to do with screening or invading a person's private life. This is despite the fact that dubious detective agencies and spurious private investigators consistently give this field of consultancy a bad name.

Business Intelligence and Third-Party Due Diligence

What has gradually become standard practice in the recruitment of management personnel can also be utilized in regular business operations, such as the use of background research—such as that already presented in Chap. 3 in the section on business intelligence as a source of information. Because of the UK Bribery Act, the focus has been placed, in particular, on integrity checks for business partners. This legislation explicitly prescribes third-party due diligence. Above and beyond the liability implications found in the UK Bribery Act, business intelligence is also relevant as a preventative mechanism in those areas where suppliers, investors, business, and joint venture partners need to be selected. The most common field of application is thus likely to be mergers and acquisitions on both the selling and buying sides. Business intelligence becomes interesting for the purposes of detection within a compliance management system when the possibilities offered by background research are innately integrated as a standard process for dealing with business partners. This will then come into play irrespective of whether large transactions are being dealt with or the company is simply selecting an advertising agency or an agent.

Approval Limits and Access Controls

Many compliance violations begin where internal documentation guidelines and access controls end. Another standard instrument of detection is thus the development of an IT-based authorization concept. On the one hand, this deals with access rights to documents, rooms, funds, or sensitive company data. While on the other hand, authorization concepts also focus on internal approvals for payments and their documentation. The objective must always be to enable companies to precisely determine in real time, or at least in retrospect, what was approved by whom and when, and whose desks did these contentious documents pass over in the process.

Management and Monitoring of Master Data

Especially in the fight against corruption, the risk-oriented management of master data is an indispensable tool. Major cases of corruption and fraud in the past have clearly demonstrated in almost all cases that data from sales-related agents or banking relationships with alleged business partners were manipulated to enable money to disappear from the company. One possible solution for preventing this could certainly be to strictly segregate the use and administration of this master data. If the issue is corruption in the sales department, the company's IT system must already be capable of preventing a sales employee entering or amending master data for a creditor. This type of preventative model can then also be backed up with other controls. For example, by highlighting any changes to the company's master data and ensuring that these changes are traceable.

Accompanying Data Analyses

In view of the completely digitalized commercial enterprises found in the modern world, it is likely that electronic mass data analyses will become the detection and control instruments of the future. Mass data analyses essentially concentrate on isolating suspicious patterns of records that appear out of the ordinary, and automatically checking their plausibility based on threshold limits for standard discrepancies and deviation tolerances. Conspicuous data records can then be checked by hand using forensic methods to shed more light on any suspicious activities.

Physical Stocktaking

In times of completely digital business transactions, the good old process of stocktaking has almost been forgotten. Yet even the slightly outdated process of counting stock levels and assets is also one of the detection mechanisms used in a compliance management system. It is thus advisable to check at regular intervals whether assets recorded on the balance sheet actually exist in reality.

In some cases, these types of control mechanisms need to be set up as a direct requirement of the legislation or supplementary notes made by the responsible authorities. A good example is the circular MaComp II (see Federal Institute for the Supervision of Financial Services 2012) from BaFin, which after the financial crisis defined concrete requirements for compliance functions and the completion of risk evaluations on securities dealers and service providers. These requirements primarily comprised control processes needed to supervise the proper observance of Articles 14 and 20a of the German Securities Trading Act (Wertpapierhandelsgesetz—WpHG). The core concept behind the circular was to make it clear that the requirement for compliance with WpHG at an operational level should be conveyed in the company at an early stage and institutionalized as an independent control function. For example, it should already be introduced at the development stage for financial products and not just downstream.

How company management should translate these requirements into concrete detection mechanisms was naturally not revealed in detail by the legislators—as this would of course be impossible. Once again this is the task for those responsible for compliance in companies in cooperation with specialist consultants.

Whistleblower Systems as an Instrument of Detection

Despite the fact that a substantial part of "deviant behavior" can be detected at an early stage using process-related controls, processes and controls that restrict an employee's freedom of maneuver have their limits. Nobody should exclusively rely on just this area of compliance management. It ultimately only presents the white-collar criminal with hurdles that can be overcome. An important element of the structured detection process is thus the introduction of a whistleblower system into the company.

As already mentioned, there are areas of "deviant behavior" that are almost impossible to detect even with the cleverest controls. Cartelization and price fixing, in particular, operate outside the sphere of influence of most compliance controls. Ultimately, only the most clumsy cartel builders would communicate by e-mail, letter, or telephone. Instead, they meet personally far away from all compliance documentation—perhaps on the golf course over the weekend.

The EU Commission issued the so-called "TV and computer screen cartel" made up of the screen manufacturers Philips, LG Electronics, Samsung SDI, Technicolor, and a number of other illustrious suppliers with a fine totaling 1.47 billion euros. The reason was that high-ranking representatives from these companies had fixed prices of screens for many years and divided up the markets and customers among themselves. And they continuously met up again and again over the years—always over a round of golf. How is it possible to control this? In truth, it is virtually impossible. In the case of antitrust crimes in particular, the orders are often issued at the very top of the company and often appear confusingly similar to normal developments on the market—especially when almost the whole sector regularly meet up for 18 holes of golf.

How is it then at all possible to find these cartels guilty? The answer is using key witnesses. The consequences of the amendment to the key witness regulation by the German Federal Cartel Office (Bundeskartellamt) in 2006 are now being clearly felt. At both a German and EU level, there has been a conveyor belt of cases where cartels have been exposed. And the authorities are regularly outdoing themselves with new record fines totaling billions of euros. The coffee roasters cartel, candy makers cartel, kerosene cartel, and car glass cartel were all exposed by these so-called key witnesses. The deal on offer is reasonably simple. Anybody who is part of a cartel but reports it and cooperates in any subsequent investigation will escape without punishment or will receive reduced fines. The responsible antitrust authorities are making this possible. The story was no different for the TV and computer screen cartel in which the manufacturer Chunghwa from Taiwan snitched to the EU about the clubhouse clique and was allowed to escape from the situation without a fine.

What does this now mean for compliance management systems and the area of detection? The establishment of anonymous whistleblower systems and corresponding key witness regulations in companies makes a very significant contribution to raising awareness about noncompliance. Whistleblowing should be seen here as a supplementary measure to the already existing reporting channels via management personnel or the works council. Anonymous whistleblower systems are particularly advantageous when employees find themselves in a state of conflict and are unable, or do not want to, trust those in their direct environment. For example, if pressure is being placed on these employees, a neutral point of contact or an independent ombudsman can prove very valuable in these situations for the purpose of collecting information first hand.

Criminality in commercial enterprises is a phenomenon that can quickly spread among an apparently very loyal group of perpetrators. These people are linked by their secret crime and the common fate they will experience if it is exposed—which leads to the development of a circle or ring of perpetrators. Depending on the gravity and duration of the crimes, these criminal rings can develop into sworn communities and hold genuine conspiracies of silence. Criminology describes this as the spiral effect within closed systems (for this term see Dewald and Freiling 2011, p. 45). The group moves closer every day to its doom, the height from which they will ultimately fall gets higher, and thus the peer pressure to keep silent grows—which results in a sort of feigned solidarity. As long as nobody breaks the ring, everyone appears to benefit from this association. We also speak of a spiral effect because the ring of insiders becomes ever larger, either because other accomplices need to be recruited in order to conceal the offenses, or confidants want their share of the pie and use their knowledge to apply pressure. The longer this type of group exists, the more money they need to steal—resulting in the already described spiral effect. This spiral effect can also result in other cartels being formed and other corruption or fraud offenses being committed. Therefore, the result is a series of follow-up offenses.

The principle behind the key witness regulations focuses to a large extent on exploiting this spiral effect and offering "weak points" within the group an escape strategy. In general, this will happen as soon as one member of the group feels they have been unfairly treated. Many of the perpetrators who become key witnesses started out in truth as cheated fraudsters. Facilitating and rewarding whistleblowing in a targeted manner is thus an instrument of detection that is much better suited to breaking apart existing criminal circles in a company than process controls.

When viewed from the perspective of corporate culture and how people are dealt with in the company, whistleblowing can, however, cause some unrest. This is because establishing an anonymous whistleblower system can result in a certain degree of controversy. As previously indicated, the cultural perception of whistleblowing differs greatly from company to company—and it can thus also be seen as betrayal or denunciation. An equally important factor is the protection that must be afforded to the whistleblowers themselves. This will also require processes and clear guidelines within the company.

How will the subject of whistleblowing develop in the future? It is once again worth taking a look at this point at the situation in America. The facilitation of whistleblowing in the form of an anonymous whistleblowing system within a compliance management system is not only explicitly prescribed by SOX and the US Federal Sentencing Guidelines. The Dodd-Frank Act even enables whistleblowers to receive attractive rewards if their insider knowledge contributes to white-collar crime and corruption being uncovered. The fact that whistleblowers are not just made up of knights in shining armor but also include extremely dubious personalities is demonstrated by perhaps the most famous recent whistleblower Bradley Birkenfeld. Birkenfeld was an asset manager at the major bank UBS and his job involved assisting wealthy Americans to evade tax. The former financial consultant provided the American financial authority, the IRS (Internal Revenue

Service), with the first conclusive evidence of the wheeling and dealing being carried out at UBS and received a princely sum in return—a reward of $104 million was paid to the whistleblower by the IRS. The unsavory aspect was that Birkenfeld himself served a 2-year prison sentence for tax evasion until August 2012.

Similar endeavors to reward whistleblowers in this way are being currently discussed at an EU level. If the protection and, where possible, the anonymity of the whistleblowers can be guaranteed then the principle also makes sense. The crime prosecution authorities receive information and evidence first hand and can issue correspondingly high fines. The whistleblowers themselves receive the opportunity to escape from these closed criminal systems without ruining their whole professional and private lives at the same time. Corresponding reward systems at a state level, as well as those introduced in companies as part of a compliance system, must nevertheless carefully differentiate between those people who really want to assist with the investigations and those who are only attempting to free their own head from the noose.

Admittedly, it is likely that all whistleblowers are motivated to some extent by the fact that they may escape punishment. Therefore, anonymous whistleblowers should also be handled very carefully. The expertise required to evaluate and classify these leads is much more important than the institution of the whistleblower system itself. This could involve holding personal discussions with whistleblowers, or having the capability needed to check the validity of their statements. What should be avoided at all costs when establishing a whistleblower system is setting up something verging on an in-house inquisition that even follows up totally unfounded accusations and can be exploited for the purpose of denouncing unpopular colleagues.

The way key witnesses are handled is dependent on the circumstances in each individual case. It is especially important when cases of noncompliance subsequently lead to court proceedings and investigations by the public prosecutor's office that key witnesses do not simply walk away totally unpunished—otherwise this would also endanger their own credibility within the company. After all, it is necessary to punish misconduct and any potential whistleblowers must be aware of this fact from the very beginning. Promising a general amnesty to whistleblowers and then subsequently pressing charges or making claims for damages would not only be unethical but would send out completely the wrong signal through the company. Therefore, it is important for the whistleblower system in the company to clearly communicate the exact nature of the deal at the very beginning. "You explain to us what really happened and help us to clear up the case. In return, we will make sure that you are not punished as harshly according to criminal and labor law as your accomplices. The better the information, the better you will escape from your predicament."

It is important to make employees clearly aware of the situation in advance: The earlier the offenses are revealed, the more leniently everyone involved will be handled. In the case of fraud offenses, in particular, the damage caused to the company shoots exponentially upwards after a while. Many cases of fraud and balance sheet manipulation in recent times started off as trifling matters and ended in disaster. The earlier employees are able to escape from the situation, the more damage can be effectively prevented. Yet this is only true if there are corresponding organizations and systems that are ready to properly handle these leads, crimes, perpetrators, and the legal consequences.

Facilitating whistleblowing means much more than just setting up a hotline or installing a mailbox as an assembly point for repentant fraudsters. At the same time, whistleblower systems and those people working in conjunction with them must be able to outline a realistic escape route from the vicious circle created by white-collar crime. The fundamental principles underlying the different types of perpetrators and offenses presented in Chap. 2 can be practically applied in this area. Not everyone who falsifies balance sheets is an unscrupulous criminal. It may be that the person simply ended up in the situation by chance, through a mistake, or due to their relationship with colleagues. The best way out appeared to be by telling a small white lie in the belief that nobody would ever find out about it. Padding out invoices, billing sales revenues early, concealing losses, and sprucing up survey reports—major scandals almost always start out small. It is not uncommon for the snowball effect to take hold, gradually—sometimes over many years—making the consequences of the misconduct increasingly worse. That is until it all ends with a big bang, the involvement of the public prosecutor's office, and a feeling of disbelief that it could all possibly have gotten so bad.

The situation is similar when it comes to corruption. It is also not always the case here that uncontrolled greed and a craving for recognition lie behind these offenses but often also the criminal behavior of third parties. The experts call this "extortion." The principle behind this concept is based on putting people in compromising situations or blackmailing them. The following example illustrates how this works. A business agent advises a sales representative to meet up with customs official XY—ideally in the bar on the corner. At the meeting, an envelope is shoved across the table while an accomplice takes photos of the events. The blameless sales employee now finds themselves in a no-win situation. The sale representative can either let himself be exploited by the criminals and cooperate in the offenses or defend himself and risk the supposed photographic evidence falling into the hands of the German press or being published on the Internet.

However, extortion can also sometimes be conducted in a much more subtle manner: using expensive presents, sponsored vacations, and hotel upgrades, or evenings out in the red light district with overly chummy business partners. All of these events can then subsequently be used against the person who has become entangled in the criminal's web. Although at the end of the day, everybody wants to establish good relationships with their business partners, it can go one step too far and people can become embroiled in compromising situations that can be used later to pressurize them.

In this context, compliance awareness delivered in the form of courses and training sessions becomes increasingly significant. It is precisely these types of scenarios in which attempts are made to lure people into the vicious circle of noncompliance that can be broached in advance. And it is possible to develop courses of action for responding correctly in serious cases.

When we examine the instruments of detection, it immediately becomes clear that knowledge about the different manual and technical methodologies has been obviously borrowed from the area of fraud investigation. One key question that many of those involved with this subject often ask is: Where is the defining line between detection and investigation? When do you reach the point where it is necessary to switch over from a regular control mechanism to a forensic investigation?

In the following section of this chapter, we will look more closely at these questions with the goal of integrating fraud investigations—as previously described—into the compliance loop.

4.4.2.3 Investigation: Integration into the Compliance Loop

The practical aspects of a fraud investigation and the methodology used for forensic auditing were already the subject of Chap. 3 "Forensics." Therefore, the only unanswered question when it comes to compliance management systems is how precisely to integrate the investigation of cases and the preservation of evidence into the described loop of compliance measures. Hence, this section will now describe what should be taken into account before, during, and, most importantly, after these types of investigations in order to avoid any legal pitfalls or additional liability risks. While Chap. 3 principally concentrated on the individual acute cases and the ad hoc commissioning of an investigation, it is especially important when dealing with a continuous compliance management system that the investigated cases of misconduct are collected, carefully documented, and concluded in a legally compliant manner.

But firstly, we need to return to the initial question. At what precise point does the switch flip from detection to investigation? Or, in other words, when do controls turn to practical intervention? From a purely legal standpoint, the compliance office or the management of the company is initially obligated to pursue all indications of misconduct. This also makes sense within the company in order to demonstrate to the workforce that the subject of compliance is taken seriously. However, not every indication of misconduct immediately triggers a major investigation—it is also absolutely essential here to develop a feel for what the correct response to each situation should be and to set up clear routines. Those companies who have just experienced a scandal in the area of noncompliance are particularly likely to lose this knack for selecting the right response.

The presence of external forensic experts, lawyers, or public prosecutors is generally not required to sufficiently clear up cases of misconduct. If the indications of manipulation or other offenses become more tangible, it is then necessary to look in detail at precisely what happened, starting with the physical documentation, through auditing with those parties involved, to forensic data analyses. If sufficient evidence of serious misconduct and corresponding damage is discovered, the response is, so to speak, shifted up a gear: from evaluating the employee's communication data through to reporting a possible criminal offense to the responsible authorities. The process is thus carried out step by step and the case is gradually escalated up through the different levels. It is imperative to observe the following point in this process: it tends to be rare for the investigated cases to be completely solved right down to the very last detail as always seems to happen in a crime novel. Instead, the time available for the investigation should be used to collect together the relevant facts. These facts will allow a sensible decision to be taken in order to reestablish normal operations in the company as quickly as possible.

A compliance management system that includes investigations as one of its modules must, therefore, possess mechanisms for dealing with the findings of the investigations and sensibly bringing cases to a conclusion in line with the valid legislation and corporate standards. The key phrase here is "following up the case." This is not always easy, especially if the crimes cannot be 100 % reconstructed. How does a company handle a situation where accusations have been leveled at an employee but it is not possible to prove them 100 % conclusively? How deeply does the company probe into the confidential communication data of the suspected employee in these cases?

It is important to note at this point that the often-quoted legal principle "in dubio pro reo"[18] is only valid to a limited extent in the investigation of white-collar crime and corruption. This is because even if the corruption cannot be unequivocally proven, there is a legal principle in German criminal law that nevertheless makes representatives of the company who are authorized signatories liable: breach of trust. A breach of trust is a so-called "catch-all" element in law. If money has been lost from the company on a large scale but its whereabouts can no longer be discovered, the responsible management personnel are certainly not free from liability, or out of the woods with respect to criminal prosecution. They are required to prove that the company assets entrusted to them were invested for the good of the company. If they are not able to provide the required proof, this could be regarded as a breach of trust—and thus a criminal offense. Furthermore, this may also be accompanied by a taxation issue. If the investigation demonstrates that the taxed services on the invoice did not correspond to real events or the recipient of the payment does not actually exist then it is not permitted to deduct these taxes from the company's operating costs. There is thus the additional risk of tax evasion if the situation is not immediately reported.

If a criminal act cannot be proven unequivocally but there is a preponderance of suspicious circumstances based on a criminalistic evaluation, there is, however, a solution: The principle of dismissal on the grounds of suspicion[19] can resolve situations in which the company can no longer be expected to honor the working relationship due to the findings of the investigation—meaning the relationship of trust has been irrevocably destroyed.

[18] Translation: "when in doubt, for the accused." This principle has not been made the legal standard under German law but can be derived from various paragraphs of the Code of Criminal Procedure (Strafprozessordnung).

[19] The principle of dismissal on the grounds of suspicion is in line with the consistently taken decisions by the German Federal Labor Court (Bundesarbeitsgerichts—BAG)—it being an important enough reason for the extraordinary termination of an employment contract according to Article 626 of BGB.

Case Management: Setting Up a Case Database

In the hectic events surrounding an investigation, it is possible that the importance of documenting in a legally compliant manner (data protection aspects need to be especially taken into consideration) the investigative steps, the results of the investigation, and the subsequent assessment of the damage caused can be forgotten. Yet this can prove dangerous for the company. On the one hand, the management of the company is obligated to comprehensively investigate all incidents and cases of damage to the company, while on the other hand, the company is depriving itself of the proof that the investigative measures needed for any subsequent legal proceedings were carried out. The lack of this kind of documentation can also massively impair the company's ability to learn from these concrete cases of damage and the crucial examinations of the actual events, as well as any follow-up review of the crimes. It is thus both sensible and advisable to create and continuously maintain a case database.

The case management process involves logging and following up on a case—from the initial suspicion through to its conclusion. Over time, a library of sorts will evolve that details both small and large cases of damage and represents a priceless treasure trove of knowledge for future risk analyses, training sessions, compliance audits, and system updates.

Direct Follow-Up Measures After an Investigation

Before we look in the next section of this chapter at "remediation" and the systematic revision of cases of damage, we will firstly examine the direct measures that should be carried out after an investigation. Keeping these measures in mind and being able to correctly and appropriately implement them in a legally compliant way immediately after any internal investigation will help to eliminate liability risks and prevent any subsequent damage.

Authoritative Assessment of the Damages

An authoritative and independent assessment of the damage caused to the company is a fundamental duty after cases of damage. The evaluation and follow-up of legal judgments basically revolves around the question of which binding losses have resulted from the entire process. An independently drafted damage assessment helps people within the company to understand the scale of the case and can be combined with a commercial report on the events. Practical experience has demonstrated that it is advisable not to carry out the damage assessment internally but to commission an independent auditing firm and—if required—a specialized law firm. Calculations of damage that are not carried out independently will be—particularly in the case of large corporations—too open to criticism.

Claims for Damages Against Responsible Managers

What was up until a few years ago considered to be in bad taste has today become common practice. The Siemens affair also led to a real change in mentality in this area, with the result that managers now face much tougher treatment after cases of damage. In response to pressure from supervisory boards and especially the public, it is now almost impossible to exclude the possibility of claims being made under civil law after a case of damage in the company. There is also pressure for the company to fulfil its duty to stakeholders and do everything in its power to recover the lost or damaged assets and reduce other damages as far as possible.

Disciplinary Measures Against Employees

An effective compliance mechanism should be able to deal with and sanction individual cases. Although the rational and commercial tendency towards standardization is all well and good in the area of compliance, it is not really of benefit to those people responsible when it comes to disciplinary action. It pays off twofold when you take the time in the compliance loop to discuss each case individually and reflect on the precise circumstances surrounding the crime. On the one hand, it is important that the whole compliance organization should not become insensitive to the employees. While on the other hand, the entire workforce will be closely following how each individual case is being handled.

There is in fact no need for blanket judgments to be issued after every case. This is because the options available to the company under labor law cover more than just absolution or termination. Depending on the individual case, the severity of the crime, and the individual circumstances, it is possible to reprimand, serve a written warning, reduce or cancel bonuses, and transfer employees. If offenses are committed, for example, due to ignorance, it may simply be sufficient to obligate employees to regularly attend compliance training sessions.

However, irrespective of the type and severity of the sanction, some form of sanction is absolutely essential. If company management fail to punish compliance violations, they risk the whole system being dismissed as nothing more than a blunt sword. This will be poison to the culture of compliance in the company.

As a consequence of the increasingly stricter scrutiny of how companies deal with these cases of noncompliance, traditional business practices from the times when white-collar crime was still viewed as a mere peccadillo are no longer acceptable. This includes, for example, the golden handshake. This was offered as standard to those employees leaving the company who had served it particularly well in the past but at some time or another stupidly fell foul of the law. Instead of the extraordinary termination of the contract, the employee's contract was prematurely dissolved—combined with a small or large severance payment as compensation for the many unjustified inconveniences caused by the public prosecutor's office or the overzealous auditors in the company.

In order to put this exaggerated view of the situation into perspective, these golden handshakes represented in truth damage to the assets of the company. Anybody who issues a golden handshake to an employee is in fact committing a crime: namely a breach of trust. The result is then a situation where one case of damage that has just been resolved is followed immediately by the next one because the first case was not correctly concluded.

4.4.2.4 Remediation

To remediate means to correct or remedy something. In a compliance loop, remediation describes the important and often neglected final functional stage: following up the cases of damage experienced in the company after an investigation. A well-designed compliance management system is a system that learns and constantly evolves—it should not just incidentally pick up on signals for the further development of the system and integrate what has been learnt when it happens to suit the company, but instead proactively and systematically make inquiries into whether an improvement can be made and institutionalize such processes.

In particular, those companies who do not possess a fully implemented compliance management system and carry out investigations on an ad hoc basis often neglect remediation as a consequence. This is because they lack the standard processes that a company really needs to force itself—if the truth be told—to carry out following a case of damage. Handling "deviant behavior" is never easy and is certainly not a topic that people are pleased to see on their meeting calendar. Most of those affected by white-collar crime are pleased when the investigation has been concluded, the external investigators have left the premises, disciplinary measures have been administered, and legal disputes settled. The company can now finally return to normality.

But the "close your eyes and hope for the best" principle is dangerous and also legally negligent. This is not only because the future liability of those in positions of responsibility at the company is linked to how they individually handle a case, but also because crucial knowledge about possible systematic misconduct at the company will be ignored. The consequence is that the company will repeatedly experience cases of damage in the future that are based on at least a similar design.

How should this remediation process be organized in the sense of a sustainable case management system? The responsible company body should be a newly created working group or an extended compliance committee that discusses the facts leading up to a case through to its conclusion, and develops an extended investigation report focusing on the clear consequences for the current system together with the measures needed to improve it. This committee should not work in a vacuum, but instead use the employees and any others directly involved in the case as sources. After all, these people will deliver the most vivid clues and findings for how the company-wide preventative mechanism can be best improved. The logical questions should thus be:

1. What exactly happened and in what areas of the company?
2. How did it remain undetected (for so long)?
3. How was it uncovered in the end?
4. What motivated the perpetrator?

Those who are able to fully answer these questions will be able to develop the technical and cultural measures that can in turn be input into the system for the purpose of continuous improvement. These measures can then be distributed throughout the company starting with the compliance organization, then to the management board, the works council, the internal auditing department, HR, accounting/controlling departments, and the affected business unit—along with clear instructions to please roll out the catalogue of measures by date X.

This is also the point at which the compliance loop described in this chapter comes full circle. The case-specific improvement measures developed in the remediation phase in turn have an impact on the areas of prevention and detection, turning the compliance management system outlined here into a living organism that constantly learns and adapts. In the course of the remediation process, already existing compliance measures are scrutinized and coordinated, for example existing process controls, previously formulated behavioral rules and work directives, or the established auditing process. It is even theoretically possible for an established compliance control to have proved itself to be completely ineffective. It will then need to be correspondingly corrected or removed from the system. The case management system implemented between the investigation and remediation phases can also be used to update training programs and internal compliance courses. There will almost automatically be a particularly great demand for training in dilemma situations once current cases have been concluded. A company that has recently dealt with a serious case of corruption and is not prepared to talk openly and frankly in a training session about the recent case—and strive to benefit from the lessons that can be learned—will inevitably encounter incomprehension from its employees.

It is quite common and also sensible for a new detection phase to be tagged on after the investigation and the correction of the preventative measures. This acts as a sort of practical test of the updated mechanisms. It may be that during the course of an investigation risks were identified that were not covered properly in the previously completed risk assessment and thus need to be subsequently combined with suitable auditing processes.

One might now assume that the control environment becomes more stringent with every case of noncompliance and every correction cycle carried out on the compliance system—or in other words that an increasing number of controls will gradually be set up until it is simply no longer possible for anything get past the corporate governance system. However, it is necessary to issue a word of warning at this point. Remediation does not mean the senseless addition and tightening of controls but rather represents the search for sensible replacements or improvements to existing measures for the establishment of compliance or the detection of misconduct. There is nowhere else where the true modus operandi of the offenses can be more clearly identified than in the follow-up review of cases—if companies are prepared to complete this step.

The actual control environment has in fact already been limited by the respective data protection regulations and the legitimate right of employee representatives and unions to have their say on the matter. Even if some chairmen of management boards might wish that the situation were different, there will never be a truly transparent sales employee nor control systems that monitor every single action carried out by employees. This would also be far from expedient. Trust between the company and employees would be destroyed and the floodgates would be opened to a culture of suspicion. And it would hardly be possible for the two parties to work successfully together. These ideas will be examined further in Chap. 5.

4.4.3 Organizational Principles: Responsibilities, Reporting Channels, and Setting the System Up as a Company Department

Those who develop a compliance management system also need to create an organization behind it and install it within the company. This raises a further key question about which model to use. What sounds like a formality can sometimes become a political hot potato within the company because a discussion on the organization of compliance always brings with it issues related to responsibilities, hierarchies, and resources.

In terms of the already mentioned expertise required for setting up a compliance management system, this is the process consultant's finest hour. The crucial focus should be placed here on integrating the newly developed compliance department into existing structures and networking it into the various business areas.

However, it is also impossible to provide any perfect and authoritative answers to the questions of where exactly the compliance department should be established, how big it needs to be, to whom it should report, and how precisely it should function. It would be pointless to conduct an overly theoretical discussion on the precise model of the compliance department. Instead, this section will present and comment on different possibilities for the compliance organization based on practical examples.

In general, the management board has overall responsibility for the observance of laws and company regulations. It is, after all, liable in the event that this does not happen. For this reason, it is essential that the compliance organization report directly to the management board. When dealing with compliance measures that directly impact on the management board, the compliance organization will report to the supervisory board. In this case, the contact person on the supervisory board will be the chairman of the auditing committee. The management board cannot escape from its overall responsibility by simply passing this responsibility over to the compliance organization. It can only delegate the individual tasks that need to be completed.

In terms of setting up the organization and the corresponding reporting channels, there are in principle two possible models (see Moosmayer 2012, p. 34 ff.). The first model involves setting up the compliance office as an autonomous department within the company. This department will then develop and control all preventative and reactive measures centrally—across the whole company. The compliance office is thus responsible for the whole process, from developing a set of rules through to disciplinary measures. All other company departments and compliance officers, as well as management personnel both at home and abroad, report to the chief compliance officer (CCO), who is in effect the chairman of this new organization. The CCO then in turn directly reports—preferably in person—to the management board or the supervisory board and is also immediately subordinate to them.

The advantage offered by this autonomous centralized model is that the chief compliance officer is granted a large amount of authority and can exercise this "reach" in critical situations (for term see Moosmayer 2012, p. 34). All matters concerning compliance at the company flow back to one central point and can normally be dealt with more quickly than if the autonomy over compliance were to be split. The organization as a whole is thus probably quicker to react than if other areas of the company were involved.

The major disadvantage of this model is without doubt the possible isolation of the compliance department in the company—which is being increasingly observed in real life. As a completely independent and autonomous company department, it is difficult to fulfil the role as a consultant and partner for the various business units. The compliance office can quickly take on the role of a "foreign body" or even an "occupying power." Although it dictates which rules are to be followed, it does not otherwise get involved with the company and its business affairs. The problem can already surface at a seemingly trivial level, such as where the offices or premises for the newly created company department should be located. If the compliance colleagues are located from the very beginning in their own offices away from the action—or even worse at completely different premises—it naturally makes this type of alienation even more likely. Independence should not necessarily mean isolation.

Another disadvantage of the autonomous model is most definitely the high cost involved in setting up the department—both financially and in terms of the required personnel. The whole compliance organization—from the offices through to the car park—must of course be created from scratch. And an even more difficult problem to solve is the fact that suitable personnel need to be found. After all, compliance is still a very young discipline in companies and there are very few specialists available on the market. The required expertise either needs to be obtained on the free market possibly at great cost to the company, or suitable employees must be transferred from other business units such as the legal department or the auditing department. This situation is again not always welcomed by everybody.

The second model involves setting up a decentralized compliance organization. The compliance office will be much more focused in this model on the task of coordination. Other departments in the company such as the legal department, accounting department, HR, internal auditing, and possibly also the corporate development department will be integrated within a committee in order to control and further develop the compliance process. This compliance committee is then the body in which resolutions relating to the subject of compliance are made within the company.

The advantage is that the sole authority of the compliance organization is removed to some extent and this authority is integrated much deeper within the existing company and its processes. The danger of isolation is thus reduced. At the same time, the financial costs are lower. This option does not require completely new structures and departments to be created but instead taps into existing structures and capacities available in the "compliance committee." This can lead to the impression that the work can be more flexibly distributed. But a word of caution: The decentralized organization of compliance also has some disadvantages, despite the fact that it is the model recommended by many in the relevant literature on the subject.

From a completely practical and strategic group perspective, the argument about greater flexibility is nothing more than a myth. This is because the more departments and people that are involved in the process, the longer, more complex, and laborious it inevitably becomes. It is of course necessary within a committee for all decisions, responsibilities, and schedules to be agreed. The rate at which the compliance organization can react tends to slow down rather than speed up as a result. This can prove dangerous in fast-paced business operations like sales and purchasing, as well as in real-time trading. One only needs to think about the way compliance organizations were originally set up in companies as bulky and cumbersome bureaucratic monstrosities and how important it is to avoid this perception today.

Depending on the relevant situation in the company and the regulatory pressure, another aspect of the decentralized model has an additional influence on the perception of compliance in the company: formal devaluation. Those who decide against a centralized compliance organization are accepting that the subject will lose importance in the company. For a start, an interdisciplinary department will be perceived as having less presence than a newly created organization with a CCO and direct links to the management board. It is thus all the more important that the situation is made clear to all fronts at the company via the corresponding "tone from the top"—irrespective of which model is selected and implemented in the end.

It is often the case in practice that hybrid forms are created where a chief compliance officer is installed in the company and provided with their own organization, but where strong links remain to existing departments. In some cases, the CCO may also hold another role as the head of one of the company departments.

Therefore, there are companies in which the chief compliance officer is, at the same time, the head of the internal auditing department. This is a rather conservative model that will probably steer the specialist compliance department strongly in the direction of investigation and sanctioning of misconduct. The still very strong legal influence exerted on the area of compliance ensures, particularly in major corporations, that the chief compliance officer is often either also the head of the legal department or at least very strongly linked to this person. Depending on the main risks facing the company, it is equally common in practice for the responsibility for compliance to be given to the chief financial officer—resulting in compliance leaning toward the area of controlling. It is much rarer—and this fact is quite telling—for the compliance organization to be attached to the HR department, despite the fact that compliance, including all of its associated concepts, is undoubtedly a personnel management issue and cannot be exclusively broken down into commercial and legal aspects. This point was also elaborated on earlier in this book. It is important not to forget that the subject will receive a different spin depending on which department compliance is attached to and how it is personified. It can thus be assumed that lawyers and accountants will place the focus much more strongly on controls and sets of rules than on open dialogue, training, and "value management".[20] This does not mean, however, that one or the other focus is right or wrong. The conditions and requirements found in individual companies and organizations are simply too varied to make that call. Therefore, it is not possible to give an authoritative recommendation for one particular compliance organization even with the best will in the world.

Nevertheless, this is a good opportunity to present a future-oriented and highly creative model. It also demonstrates the direction in which these discussions are headed: the seemly organic installation of compliance in companies—ensuring they are viewed less and less as a "foreign body" and are more naturally integrated into company structures. This makes great sense not only when it comes to liability issues but also from a commercial standpoint. The more naturally and smoothly the compliance organization can be anchored in the company, the more productive the whole company will become. One model that already takes good account of these concepts is also one that takes its lead to some extent from the system of state government. This model organizes the company in accordance with the principle of a separation of powers.[21]

The compliance organization thus takes the form of the legislative organization. The rules are developed and defined in the form of directives for employees, which are supplemented by consultancy and training courses. The compliance organization thus functions like an in-house legislator with an integrated advisory center. The role of executive in this model is held by the internal auditing department. It attempts to guarantee that all of the rules are observed by introducing controls. If there is misconduct in the company, the auditing department assumes responsibility and coordinates the investigation of the cases as the executive body. In the individual evaluation of these cases, the legal department at the company plays the role of the judiciary to clarify difficult issues and rule on the individual disciplinary measures without having developed the rules behind the system themselves.

No matter how a compliance management system is established, or which elements are set up for the purposes of prevention, detection, investigation, and remediation, one question constantly arises: How effective is the compliance management system in reality? Many managers have been asking for unified standards practically since the birth of compliance in companies. Who can evaluate, and in what way, whether a compliance management system delivers what it has been set up to achieve? Therefore, the final section of this chapter will be dedicated to the aspect of independent auditing and an evaluation of these types of systems.

[20] Although the targeted development and promotion of values in the sense of value management overlaps to a large extent with the subject of compliance, the subject matter has experienced significant developments and will thus not be examined further at this point.

[21] Source in: Montesquieu "The Spirit of the Laws," 1748.

4.5 Testing and Evaluating Compliance Management Systems

A very important question from a practical point of view—which follows on directly from the earlier questions about the necessity and fundamental mechanisms of a compliance system—will conclude this chapter: How can management personnel with a high risk of liability prove in a serious case that the prevention measures they introduced were a sufficient response to the existing risk[22]? Who will provide them with a guarantee that their compliance management system is also actually worth the money that was invested in its development? What it really comes down to is whether their own independently designed and implemented compliance management system actually achieves what it was designed to do: Effectively protect the company against damage caused by misconduct.

In truth, the testing and evaluation of preventative systems has already been the subject of heated debate. These systems can in reality only be compared to one another to a very limited extent. The specific risks and cultural factors, which are found within every single company, are simply too varied for this to be possible—and hence likewise the measures implemented to provide sufficient protection against the risk of "deviant behavior." What is perfectly adequate in one company might be inappropriate and completely ineffective in another. As already mentioned, compliance management systems are exclusive designer pieces. This makes it much more difficult to standardize them.

Nevertheless, the whole industry has been calling for uniform standards since practically the birth of compliance.[23] At that time, the uncertainty and also the ignorance about what precisely an effective system for providing protection against white-collar crime should be able to achieve and deliver was simply too great. It is safe to assume that this desire for standardization also originated from those who held positions of responsibility at companies who wanted to mitigate their personal liability in a case of damage. One way to achieve this would be to prove that the company operated a fully functional compliance management system designed according to international standards and independently tested to verify its effectiveness. In essence, that would mean it would thus not have been possible to prevent the case of noncompliance even with the best will in the world. And hence it would not be possible to be held personally liable for the misconduct.

This desire to provide protection against liability is understandable. In the event of a case of damage, the judge responsible for handling the case and following the investigations conducted by the public prosecutor's office will naturally look into those measures taken by the company to prevent misconduct. An independently tested compliance management system would certainly prove a positive attribute here—even if it does not provide those in responsible positions with a free pass. The

[22] In the sense of the duty of supervision according to Article 130 of OWiG and other relevant laws and ordinances.

[23] For a detailed description of the individual cases: see Chap. 1.

judiciary could still pass judgment that responsible company bodies violated their duty of supervision. A certified system would then prove useless in this situation.

The trend towards standardization and the question of what a compliance management system should include and be able to achieve has already been embraced by individual working groups and sector associations in response to the huge demand on repeated occasions over the years. Yet no solution had really become generally accepted. This situation changed markedly in April 2011 as the Institute of Public Auditors in Germany (Institut der Wirtschaftsprüfer—IDW)[24] published the IDW PS 980 auditing standard. This auditing standard saw the IDW define those requirements expected of a generally accepted compliance management system and laid out the framework that auditors could use as a foundation for testing compliance management systems.

The auditing standard itself brings together and combines internationally valid concepts dealing with compliance, and uses them to derive the basic elements expected of a compliance management system. It does this without ever prescribing in too much detail exactly what should be contained in the individual systems in the process—which is only right and proper. Nevertheless, IDW PS 980 should be treated with some caution. This is reason enough for us to now delve a little deeper into what it entails.

4.5.1 IDW PS 980: A Calibration Tool for Fully Functional Preventative Systems?

The basic idea behind the creation of the auditing standard was simple. The IDW wanted to provide businesses with a framework according to which the effectiveness of compliance management systems could be tested. The aim was to achieve broad acceptance for the auditing standard by integrating internationally recognized auditing methods and regulations.

And this is also precisely what happened in the development of the auditing standard. The working group actually did nothing more than bring together international "conceptual frameworks"[25] for compliance management systems. A compliance management system can, according to IDW PS 980, thus be based on the following generally accepted standards or on the company's own independently created conceptual frameworks (see Ernst and Young 2011):

General Conceptual Frameworks

- Foundations Guidelines "Red Book" (Open Compliance and Ethics Group [OCEG], Phoenix/USA)
- Australian Standard on Compliance Programs (AS 3806-2006)

[24] Sector association for commercial auditors http://www.idw.de/

[25] In this context, this deals with the implications for compliance that can be derived from international "hard law" and "soft law."

- Enterprise Risk Management—Integrated Framework (COSO II)
- OECD Principles of Corporate Governance
- OECD Guidelines for Multinational Enterprises

Specific Conceptual Frameworks
- Specifications document for compliance management in the real estate sector
- Basic principles of proper compliance (Austrian Financial Market Authority)
- United States (US) Federal Sentencing Guidelines
- PACI: Principles for Countering Bribery
- OFT Guide for Compliance with Competition Law
- Fighting Corruption: International Corporate Integrity Handbook—an ICC code of conduct for business (International Chamber of Commerce Berlin)
- Business Principles for Countering Corruption (Transparency International)
- BME Code of Conduct (Bundesverband der Materialwirtschaft, Einkauf und Logistik e. V.—Association of Materials Management, Purchasing, and Logistics)
- ComplianceProgramMonitor from the Centre for Business Ethics (Zentrum für Wirtschaftsethik—ZfW), Constance; monitoring standard for the ZfW value management system

IDW PS 980 remains in principle an open standard. This means that any new and relevant conceptual frameworks can be added where required. For example, this could include the BaFin circular 4/2010 "Minimum Requirements for the Compliance Function (MaComp)" or the Guidance Papers published in 2010 for the UK Bribery Act.

Those conceptual frameworks that do not apply to the individual audit can also be excluded. If a company has no business operations in Great Britain or business dealings with companies based in Great Britain, for example, it is not required according to the auditing standard to integrate the third-party due-diligence tests prescribed by the UK Bribery Act into the company compliance management system. Despite the fact that this might of course be advisable, it is not necessary for it to form either part of the system or part of the audit.

The IDW has thus completed the hard work of bringing together all of these different standards. The job of selecting and applying these standards then rests with the individual auditor. If one reads through all of these conceptual frameworks and organizes their contents in a structured manner, it is possible to define seven fundamental elements of a compliance management system that can be audited in sequence:

1. **Compliance culture** Deals primarily with the fundamental philosophy and attitudes held by the management of the company about compliance ("tone from the top") and the awareness for rules and integrity within the corporate culture.

2. **Compliance objectives** Defines the various individual areas of the company affected by the compliance management system and the rules to be observed.
3. **Compliance organization** Describes the roles and responsibilities within the system, as well as the operational and organizational structures in terms of resource planning.
4. **Compliance risks** Deals with the identification of significant compliance risks and selected methods for recognizing and evaluating these risks.
5. **Compliance program** Includes the evaluation of risk-minimizing measures and also detailed regulations to be followed in the event of concrete compliance violations.
6. **Compliance communication** Deals with the internal communication and conveyance of compliance as a corporate theme and the defined reporting channels within the organization.
7. **Compliance monitoring and improvement** Focuses on reporting and case management, as well as the elimination of weak points and defects in the system after cases of damage and continuous controls.

These seven fundamental elements are then each audited in three steps. It is necessary in this process to ensure that the required step in each case incorporates the preceding one. Anybody who commissions an audit of the effectiveness of their compliance management system also receives an audit of the design and suitability of the system. For the sake of clarity, the auditing steps will be explained below.

Step one: **Audit of the design of the system (1)**. This audit provides information on whether the fundamental compliance principles developed by the company can also be properly applied in the form they have been drafted. The audit thus serves as an evaluation of whether the developed concepts and statements have been correctly described in the outline of the compliance management system and could also function correctly in real life.

Step two: **Audit of the suitability of the system (2)**. This audit determines whether measures for protecting against risk within the designed system are suitable to also adequately curb the prevailing risks found in the company. The key issue here is whether the measures defined in the compliance management system also really deliver what they were designed to achieve? Have the measures been communicated to the affected business units in the organization?

Third and final step: **Audit of the effectiveness of the system (3)**. The audit of the effectiveness of the system discovers whether the defined principles and measures in the compliance management system have also functioned properly in practice. It is thus tested, for example, whether the measures developed within the system were actually part of the general business practices carried out by the company during a defined period of time. The entire system including all of its components is thus audited.

There are currently discussions about whether to unify the audit of the design of the system with the audit of the suitability of the system because, in practice, auditors found that they are already confronted by the question of suitability when testing the design. At the same time, this raises the question of whether a separate audit of the implementation of the system would make any sense because the audit into the effectiveness of the system also tests its implementation.

However, it is not always necessary to carry out the full audit from A to Z. The major benefit of this testing system is its flexibility. These audits must not by definition always cover the entire compliance management system, but can also be adapted to focus on individual sections of the system. This could include specific legal areas, business areas, or regions. For example, if there is a new regulation dealing with the subject of money laundering or a new sales department has been established in a country such as India, an audit of the performance of the compliance system can be adapted to this specific area.

The precise design of the audit is always left to the individual auditors. This is initially another major advantage because it allows more freedom of scope for the audit itself and does not try to impose those standards required of a DAX-listed company onto a medium-sized enterprise in the Munster region of Germany. This creative freedom is, however, also a weakness of the auditing standard because it also allows, at the same time, massive differences in quality between the compliance audits offered on the market. Above and beyond this particular aspect, there are also other common misunderstandings when it comes to IDW PS 980 that will also be briefly examined below.

4.5.1.1 IDW PS 980: A Critical Examination Based on Its Practical Application

Overall, the introduction of IDW PS 980 has admittedly already led to the business community dealing with compliance in a much more structured way. And this is already an important achievement that should not be forgotten. After all, it wasn't clear for a long time what was actually hidden behind the buzzword "compliance." Only a few years after its introduction, IDW PS 980 has thus made an important contribution to breaking down the abstract concept of compliance at a commercial level, making it much more tangible than the mere promise of virtue and decency.

Nevertheless, one should now also be permitted to cast a critical eye over this auditing standard. The criticism here has less to do with the auditing standard itself and more to do with its distorted perception on the market. The standard is understood in many places to be something that it is not, or its significance is simply overestimated.

In order to once again avoid any possible misunderstanding: IDW PS 980 is nothing more and nothing less than a set of guidelines according to which compliance measures in a company can be evaluated. This means it stipulates what should be audited and what basic elements need to be contained in the compliance management system as part of this audit—these are derived from the various conceptual frameworks for compliance that exist in the world.

However, it is certainly not a template for the perfect compliance management system. Neither does it provide any reliable information about how precisely a compliance management system should look. This is because it does not reveal exactly how risks should be identified and evaluated, how effective controls can be designed, or how an awareness for compliance should be anchored in the company.

It provides just as little guidance on which risks should be covered by which companies in which sectors. These evaluations—quite rightly—remain the responsibility of the company. Therefore, IDW PS 980 should only be thought of as a blueprint for a compliance management system to a very limited extent. There is a very great danger of referring to it as a construction plan rather than just a checklist.

This is a false impression that is only reinforced by the extremely varied quality of consultancy on offer on the market. The IDW PS 980 standard has itself involuntarily accelerated this development. The reason is that it does not specify that the testing of compliance management systems should be the exclusive domain of a (forensic) commercial auditor. In practice, this leads to a situation where auditors and consultants with no specialist expertise force their way onto the market and promise to certify a company's internal compliance management system according to the auditing standard at a very low price. The fact that an audit of a compliance management system is only as good as the person carrying out the audit is mostly brushed under the carpet. The promise is often formulated as follows: "We will certify the system and thus exclude the risk of personal liability." Yet the fact that any reasonably competent public prosecutor or judge has little interest in whether the compliance management system has a certificate attached to it or not is also conveniently forgotten. In serious cases, it is always the actual quality of the audit and system that is decisive. Pro-forma solutions and reports completed simply to please the client can prove disastrous in the currently prevailing legal environment. This needs to be impressed upon every manager involved with the subject of compliance.

Huge price differences do sometimes exist on the auditing market, which, in this context, are simply due to the fact that a "Big Four" auditing firm, for example, will utilize criminalistic/forensic expertise and qualified auditors during the audit to provide a totally different level of scope and quality than could be provided by a consultant located in an office around the corner.

Despite the fact that the auditing standard very clearly defines the procedures and areas to be audited, it is generally only those experienced forensic auditors who have been properly trained to carry out this type of audit that possess the required methodology and expertise to correctly interpret and professionally apply these standards. Furthermore, enlisting the additional assistance of a legal consultant can only be beneficial when auditing the design and suitability of these systems, and is certainly advisable for complex legal fields such as antitrust law or data protection law.

There is good reason behind the fact that the auditing standard was developed by the Institute of Public Auditors in Germany. In order to calculate individual measurement parameters, such as risk probability and key company figures, complex statistical models are used—which in truth can only be mastered by a properly trained specialist auditor. After all, these professionals do nothing else all day long but carry out these types of audit. This is the reason why EY compliance experts and forensic auditors only carry out the certification of a compliance management system according to IDW PS 980 in cooperation with a qualified commercial auditor. This brings together forensic expertise with auditing expertise.

Nevertheless, this does not inevitably mean that high-quality audits according to IDW PS 980 are more substantial and thus more expensive. They are merely more intelligently designed. A simple example illustrates this fact extremely well. It has been reported by some of those responsible for compliance in companies that, as part of an audit into the effectiveness of the compliance culture, they were handed a comprehensive catalogue containing hundreds of questions on the subject of "ethics in your company." It included such questions as: "Do you assume that integrity and honesty are part of everyday life in the company?" It should be obvious to everyone that any results gained from pitiful attempts like these to make corporate ethics measurable are practically worthless and will only encourage and reinforce biased opinions.

An experienced auditor would instead search for those sources that provide real information on the perception of integrity in the company. These sources could include, for example, individual case management records, the minutes from management seminars, or the frequency with which statements about this subject are released by the management board. How involved is the top management? Are training courses regularly carried out? Does the feedback from these training courses provide some insight into this area? The concept of "walk the talk" is decisive. The available documentation will generally provide a great deal more insight than a pseudo empirical management survey.

This small example is designed to demonstrate that a well-conducted audit according to IDW PS 980 is by no means a mindless and routine task. A well-conducted audit clearly defines what needs to be audited and how this will be achieved, and, of course, by definition requires auditors who properly understand how an audit should be carried out.

As hinted at earlier, the very mechanical process of querying key variables during the audit—such as the compliance culture—defines the auditing standard itself to some extent. Its clear and articulate structure, along predetermined criteria, helps the auditors to reduce the extremely complex phenomenon of "deviant behavior" to just a few specific points that can be worked through like a checklist.

The danger here exists primarily in the area of "soft" aspects of compliance such as culture and awareness. Just because employees in a company associate themselves with colorful mission statements and totally admirable ethical standards for clean business practices does not by a long stretch mean that they also act in this way in real life. Those who simply tick the relevant boxes to confirm the existence of a "mission statement" or "ethical guidelines" fall short of the mark, and ultimately have nothing worthwhile to say about the effectiveness of the compliance management system.

This is also true for any declarations made by the top management. No matter which way the situation is viewed, compliance is unconditionally and without doubt a management theme. A decisive point was already made in Chap. 2: Corrupt leaders will never control a clean company. Whether the management board really supports everything that is proposed to them about governance and compliance, or whether they find the subject tiresome can only be determined to a limited degree using an auditing standard. Moreover, there is also the fact that consultants offering audits seem to find it especially difficult to fail their clients simply because they have the impression that the company management does not show enough commitment to compliance.

This is also what was meant when discussing the fact that the IDW PS 980 standard is often made out to be something it is not. Just because the compliance culture has been evaluated as "sufficient" in the audit does not mean that only honest businesspeople are employed throughout the company. It simply means that the drafted compliance measures developed in the system correspond at least to the formal requirements found in the conceptual frameworks.

And if an audit into the effectiveness of the compliance management system is passed, this does not at all mean that there is now a guarantee that no more cases of noncompliance will occur in the company. This is also a common misunderstanding. The audit tests the effectiveness of the implemented system based upon its own design and not in comparison to a "perfect" virtual compliance management system. It merely tests whether the defined measures and processes were effective within a defined period of time.

Successful certification of the audit according to IDW PS 980 is thus no seal of quality like a TÜV sticker in Germany. The danger of this standard being taken out of circulation nevertheless exists because the audit is voluntary and not prescribed by law in any way. In this sense, the auditing standard merely provides orientation and guidelines.

Nevertheless, it does provide very good guidelines.

It only remains now to mention that the requirements and evaluation criteria applied to a compliance management system can never remain fixed even when using an auditing standard. The area of compliance is in a constant state of change because the regulatory requirements are also continuously being amended. The same is also true for the demands placed on companies by stakeholders—which are almost permanently shifting. In the context of compliance management systems, what is currently deemed "sufficient" is determined by the dispensation of justice to a much greater extent in Germany than elsewhere in the world. The current standards are continuously being determined by the personal experiences of judges and district attorneys. The converse effect is that full protection against cases of damage and personal liability can only be guaranteed if the installed compliance management system functions at a level close to perfection. Even if that were the case, there is always the possibility that the implemented controls and the other preventative measures will be judged to be "insufficient." This uncertainty has led many management boards and chief compliance officers to constantly expand their systems, thus correspondingly increasing the sheer volume of controls. It is of course only natural to want protection.

The fact that at some point business processes will start to suffer and entire sales and purchasing departments will be left paralyzed has resulted in compliance being viewed critically in many companies. Therefore, the last chapter of this book will examine how the fight against damage caused by "deviant behavior" might look in the future—from a fundamental criticism of compliance through to the concept of good corporate governance, placing the focus less on controls and much more strongly on the integrity of the individual employees.

Literature

Berthel, R. et al. (2006). *Grundlagen der Kriminalistik/Kriminologie. Lehr- und Studienbriefe Kriminalistik/Kriminologie (Fundamental Principles of Criminalistics/Criminology. Teaching and Studying Material for Criminalistics/Criminology).* Bd. 1 (vol. 1). Hilden: Verlag Deutsche Polizeiliteratur (Publishing House for German Police Literature).

Bloomberg. (2012). *UBS investigators did not have their eye on Adoboli's colleagues.* Cash. Accessed June 26, 2013, from http://www.cash.ch/news/alle-news/ubsermittler_hatte_adobolis_kollegen_nicht_im_blick-1225175-448

Burger, A., & Schmelter, H. (2012). *Internal Control für Führungskräfte (Internal Control for Management Personnel).* Munich: Oldenbourg Wissenschaftsverlag (Oldenbourg Academic Publishing House).

Dewald, A., & Freiling, F. C. (2011). *Forensische Informatik (Forensic Informatics).* Munich: Beck.

Dreher, G., & Feltes, T. (1997). *Das Modell New York: Kriminalprävention durch‚Zero Tolerance'? (The Model of New York: Crime Prevention Through 'Zero Tolerance'?),* vol. 12. Empirische Polizeiforschung Band (*Empirical Police Research Volume*). Holzkirchen: Felix.

Editorial of the Wirtschaftswoche. (2012). *Korruption, In welchen Branchen am meisten geschmiert wird (Corruption, what sectors experience the most bribery).* Wirtschaftswoche. Accessed March 22, 2013, from http://www.wiwo.de/unternehmen/industrie/korruption-in-welchen-branchen-am-meisten-geschmiert-wird/6336512.html?slp=false&p=18&a=false#image

Ernst & Young. (2011). *Der IDW PS 980 Standard zur Prüfung von Compliance-Management-Systemen (The IDW PS 980 standard for auditing compliance management systems).* Ernst & Young. Accessed June 26, 2013, from http://www.ey.com/Publication/vwLUAssets/EY_Flyer_zu_IDW_PS_980/$FILE/EY%20Flyer_IDW%20PS%20980.pdf

Faller, H., & Otte, M. (2011). *Der alte Mann und das Mehr (The old man and excess).* Zeit magazine. Accessed June 26, 2012, from http://www.zeit.de/2011/32/Wirtschaftskrise-Paul-Volcker

Federal Institute for the Supervision of Financial Services (Bundesanstalt für Finanzdienstleistungsaufsicht). (2012). *Rundschreiben 8/2012 (WA) – Besondere Organisatorische Anforderungen für den Betrieb eines multilateralen Handelssystems nach §§ 31 f und 31 g WpHG (MaComp II) (Circular 8/2012 (WA) – Special organizational requirements for the operation of a multilateral trading system according to Articles 31 f and 31 g of the WpHG (MaComp II)).* Federal Institute for the Supervision of Financial Services (Bundesanstalt für Finanzdienstleistungsaufsicht). Accessed June 26, 2013, from http://www.bafin.de/SharedDocs/Veroeffentlichungen/DE/Rundschreiben/rs_1208_wa_macomp_ii.html

Franz, P. (2004). *Grundlagen des ökonomischen Ansatzes: Das Erklärungskonzept des Homo Oeconomicus (Fundamental principles of the economic approach: A concept explaining homo economicus)* In W. Fuhrmann (Ed.), International Economics Working Paper 2004-02, University of Potsdam.

Friedman, M. (2004). *Kapitalismus und Freiheit (Capitalism and Freedom).* Munich: Piper.

Hess, H. (2004). Broken Windows. Zur Diskussion um die Strategie des New York Police Department (Broken Windows. A Discussion about the Strategy Followed by the New York Police Department). *Zeitschrift für die gesamte Strafrechtswissenschaft (Magazine for General Criminal Law), 116,* 66–110.

Hofmann, P. (2008). *Handbuch Anti-Fraud-Management, Bilanzbetrug erkennen – vorbeugen – bekämpfen (Manual for Anti-Fraud Management, Detect – Prevent – Fight Balance Sheet Fraud)*. Berlin: Erich Schmidt Verlag GmbH & Co.

Laue, C. (2002). Broken Windows und das New Yorker Modell – Vorbilder für die Kriminalprävention in deutschen Grossstädten? (Broken Windows and the New York Model – Role Models for Crime Prevention in Large German Cities?) In *Landeshauptstadt Düsseldorf*, (Hrsg) Düsseldorfer Gutachten: Empirisch gesicherte Erkenntnisse über kriminalpräventive Wirkungen, 333–436. (In *Landeshauptstadt Düsseldorf, (Publisher)* Düsseldorfer Report: Empirical Knowledge about the Effects of Crime Prevention, 333–436). Düsseldorf.

Ministry of Justice. (2011). *The Bribery Act 2010*. Ministry of Justice. Accessed June 26, 2013, from https://www.gov.uk/government/uploads/system/uploads/attachment_data/file/181762/bribery-act-2010-guidance.pdf

Moosmayer, K. (2012). *Compliance, Praxisleitfaden für Unternehmen (Compliance, Practical Guidelines for Companies)*. Munich: Beck.

Reder, M. W., Durlauf, S. N., & Blume, L. E. (2008). *The New Palgrave – Dictionary of Economics*. New York: Palgrave Macmillan (Chicago School in).

Siemens. (2008). *Gelebte Integrität: Compliance-Incentivierung (Embodying Integrity: Compliance Incentivization)*. Siemens. Accessed June 26, 2013, from http://www.siemens.com/responsibility/report/08/de/management/compliance/incentivierung.htm

U.S. Department of Justice, Criminal Division. Foreign Corrupt Practices Act (FCPA). (2013). *U. S. Department of Justice*. Accessed June 26, 2013, from http://www.justice.gov/criminal/fraud/fcpa/

Wilson, J. Q., & Kelling, G. L. (1982). The police and neighborhood safety, broken windows. *The Atlantic Monthly*. Accessed June 24, 2013, from http://www.manhattan-institute.org/pdf/_atlantic_monthly-broken_windows.pdf

A Look Ahead to the Future

5

Sustainably Reducing "Deviant Behavior" Using Business Integrity Management: The Path to Good Corporate Governance

It is not just here in Germany that compliance is probably one of the most talked about management buzzwords of our time. This makes it necessary to also cast a critical eye over the subject. What direction will the development of compliance take in the future? What pitfalls need to be taken into account when defending against corruption and white-collar crime? And what gaps still need to be filled?

After a short, critical assessment and an analysis of the empirical data, it quickly becomes clear that an understanding of compliance based on control and legal formalities can only be the first step on the road to a company attaining a sustainable corporate culture based on values. It is this culture that will automatically react against white-collar crime and corruption, driven by its inherent sensitivity to assets and values, rather like an antibody against infection. The requirement for this is truly sustainable and ethical corporate management based on the concept of good corporate governance.[1]

Therefore, this chapter will outline the basic features of good corporate governance.

5.1 Compliance in Germany: An Overview of the Current Situation

The importance of compliance has still not been realized everywhere. According to an EY survey from 2002 (see Ernst & Young 2012, p. 12 ff.), a third of the 871 business decision-makers surveyed only rated the subject of compliance as

[1] The precise origin of the term is unclear, there is no universally recognized definition in the economic world. The first really comprehensive explanation of "good corporate governance" was probably found in the Cadbury Report from 1992 (see The Committee on the Financial Aspects of Corporate Governance and Gee and Co. Ltd 1992), in which the interdisciplinary "Committee on the Financial Aspects of Corporate Governance" already defined in Paragraphs 1.1 and 1.2 what should be understood by the term "good corporate governance."

S. Heissner, *Managing Business Integrity*, Management for Professionals,
DOI 10.1007/978-3-319-12721-7_5

being of "medium importance." Despite the fact that the remaining two thirds of respondents claimed that compliance was "important" or "very important" to them, the results gathered from other more specific questions in the survey told another story. Over one fifth of those companies surveyed admitted that they had no regulations in place to deal with compliance infringements, while only a half of those surveyed even had a chief compliance officer. And training sessions dedicated to the subject of compliance had only been institutionalized in 2 % of companies.

These figures indicate that although there is some awareness about compliance themes, there still remains a great deal to be done when it comes to integrating them into the day-to-day running of a company.

5.1.1 The Control Paradox of Compliance and Its Negative Effects

It would certainly be wrong to suggest that compliance in the form of an additional set of internal company rules is enthusiastically welcomed and celebrated everywhere. Although compliance has become generally accepted as a business buzzword and is being preached almost religiously from every soapbox, many managing directors and managers view this development critically. What do these new obligations initially mean for those in positions of responsibility at companies? The real answer is lots of time and effort! In practice, it will generally be necessary to create new responsibilities, processes, and structures that never previously existed in the company.

And the establishment of a compliance management organization within a company can often bring with it significant negative effects—ones that are unfortunately not dealt with sufficiently in the relevant literature or by consultants. So it may useful to examine them in more detail at this point. Compliance management is advertised instead using terms such as increased efficiency or effectiveness. These benefits will remain nothing more than a pipe dream if the most obvious obstacles to the implementation of compliance in a company remain unresolved.

The process should begin at the most fundamental of all levels—with the individual employees and their well-being. Because what does a newly introduced compliance management system with all of its various mechanisms and controls actually do in the first instance to these unsuspecting employees? It places them all under general suspicion. And then the situation becomes much worse when some of these suspicions are actually confirmed! The reason is that white-collar crime is a control-related offense. The more people look for it, the more cases are discovered. When compliance is taken seriously it initially makes the whole organization seem more criminal than before. Or at least this is the impression that it portrays. The consequences of this control paradox[2] on the perceptions held by employees and the corporate culture or subcultures is often massively underestimated.

[2] For more on this term see Bussmann (2003, p. 41), Berg (2001, p. 101), Huntington and Davies (1999) and Palazzo (2001). Bussmann even talks of a double control paradox: Controls not only

In many companies, the compliance organization and its employees have not yet found their proper place. Especially when faced with this control paradox, reservations and resistance to these new colleagues quickly develops, with many believing that their only role is to question business processes that have functioned well for many years and to harass employees with their compliance controls.

In the worst-case scenario, the compliance department effectively develops into a bureaucratic parallel organization, with the result that its work is rejected by the existing corporate culture, while its employees become ostracized. The culture of mistrust that then develops makes it more difficult for everyone to work in harmony with each another and immediately has a negative effect on the performance of the whole organization.

What this worst case scenario can mean in terms of efficiency is easy to imagine. Compliance—which has been incorrectly developed, understood, and conveyed—can slow down functioning companies and in the most drastic cases even paralyze them. Nobody should deceive themselves when dealing with this subject. Commercial controls often have a negative impact at first on efficiency and flexibility, even if they ultimately prove beneficial later on and prevent damage to the company.

The areas of the company whose strength lies in their dynamic approach and fast response need to be particularly carefully monitored and handled. These are often ironically the areas of the company most vulnerable to corruption and criminality, such as sales and purchasing.

Typical examples could be a broker who trades in real time, or a salesperson who needs to create or change quotations and calculations at short notice. Ultimately, it is crucial to find the right balance between exercising caution and charging in at full throttle—making sure that business success is not continuously hindered while ensuring the risk of damage to the company due to noncompliance is nevertheless reduced.

This small case study already clearly demonstrates that a purely control-oriented interpretation of compliance, as it is currently implemented to a large extent, will sooner or later reach its limits. This is due to the simple fact that this type of approach cannot provide an answer to every conceivable dilemma.

It is much more important—and this will be the starting point for the final section of the book—to develop such a high level of awareness for integrity and compliant behavior that, in the best case, there will be hardly any need for a large bureaucratically managed compliance organization within the company, which, it seems, is only there to apply the brakes.

Then the compliance organization would merely be required as a consultant for the various business units—acting as a temporary corrective measure to help only from the point at which training and the employees' existing awareness for integrity stops. This model would see the compliance organization holding a much greater supporting and advisory role than it currently does in the majority of companies.

ultimately lead to the discovery of more offenses but by addressing the subject of criminal behavior some employees are encouraged to commit these offenses for the first time or to transform the way in which these crimes are perpetrated, see Bussmann (2003, p. 42).

However, when evaluating compliance it is the superficially negative aspects that often lead to it being considered a "necessary evil" and, consequently, to it not always being resolutely implemented in companies. The extent to which these pro-forma solutions can actually be dangerous for those involved is examined in the following section.

5.1.2 The Danger of Pro-Forma Solutions

Anybody who views compliance as a "necessary evil" and does not take it seriously in these times of comprehensive manager liability should be urgently warned at this point. The establishment of sustainably functioning investigative and preventative systems has long since ceased to be merely a prestige project indulged in only by those particularly dutiful people in positions of responsibility. It has become a commercial and, most importantly, legal necessity, which is now also reflected in German legislature and legal judgments.

In this evaluation, the phrase "sustainably functioning" has been deliberately chosen at this point to describe these compliance management systems. The true commitment shown by those in positions of responsibility at some companies to preventing the development of corruption and white-collar crime in the first place, or comprehensively investigating and continuously following up cases of damage so that no further misconduct is experienced, must be clearly differentiated from so-called formal compliance.

Formal compliance can result in serious consequences for managers and management board members in positions of responsibility at the latest when the preventative measures are evaluated in the course of investigations by the public prosecutor's office and subsequent court proceedings. District attorneys who deal seriously with these crimes and are also well versed with the subject matter ceased being taken in by Potemkin villages a long time ago.

The recent legal judgments issued in prominent cases confirm this fact. Anton Weinmann, former member of the management board at MAN, was convicted of aiding and abetting bribery payments because the judge was of the opinion that Weinmann had "not done enough to stop the practice of bribery" (see Editorial of the Handelsblatt 2012)—whether or not the company had a code of conduct or formally existing compliance system.

It is important to briefly clarify the situation in this case. Weinmann was not convicted because he had failed to deal with the subject of corruption in his area of the company. He had in fact done this. However, in the view of the judiciary he had not done it sustainably enough—and this should provide food for thought for every manager who thinks that they can buy their way out of any liability issues with formal compliance systems. The current trend clearly goes against pro-forma solutions.

This is also right and proper because—and this is often overlooked by some compliance consultants—the situation deals here to a large extent with criminal law. In the case of criminal law, it is not sufficient, for example, to have employees sign a contract in which they undertake not to pay bribes. The principle of so-called "subjective facts" under criminal law prevents this from being the case and looks much more stringently into the background and motives of the case to create the overall picture. Those in positions of responsibility are rated on a scale of simple, ordinary, and gross negligence, as well as conditional and absolute intent, and are then correspondingly judged. The criteria used for making decisions here are the actions of those responsible and not the forms they had the employees sign. A purely formal and legal compliance system is already hardly sufficient today if managers want to protect themselves against liability risks, never mind sustainably fighting corruption and white-collar crime and effectively protecting corporate values.

Keeping this thoroughly pragmatic and critical view of compliance as a management subject in the back of our minds, it is important to now ask what development steps compliance needs to go through in order for it to be perceived and embodied as something that adds positive value and is a real asset for the company in a competitive environment.

It is, after all, not just personal liability that plays a role in understanding compliance. Purely "formal" solutions or compliance management systems that are quite simply badly designed also damage the company in a commercial sense.

For example, this can happen when the developed measures are implemented in the incorrect place and controls are established in areas where they don't belong. Additional uncertainty will be created in business operations that can effectively cost the company a great deal of money. The same is also true for the unnecessary bureaucratization of compliance management systems. It is not without reason that particularly fast-moving company departments like purchasing and sales view compliance in many cases as an "obstacle to business." This is because unnecessary bureaucracy wastes valuable time.

And even if good compliance management systems reduce the level of bureaucracy as far as possible, the dilemma still remains. Which leads us on logically to the next step: The protection of corporate values by focusing on the integrity of employees—also with the goal of relieving the burden on compliance management systems.

5.2 The Next Step: Protecting Corporate Values with Integrity

The development of compliance management as part of the corporate strategy is still in its infancy. What has actually happened up to now in the short and turbulent history of compliance? As a reaction to the highly visible bribery and, above all, corruption scandals, reporting obligations, legal regulations, and the—accompanying—liability of managers have all been tightened. Compliance should now guarantee observance of the relevant regulations by implementing rules. Control systems have developed as a logical consequence, which aim to prevent "deviant behavior" in companies.

If we consider—as previously mentioned—this interpretation of compliance then we can only draw one conclusion as we look to the future: the introduction of controls on their own is not the solution. Controls by themselves will not sustainably protect corporate values. This is because no control can persuade an employee to sustainably and consciously act in a compliant manner. The control paradox of compliance even suggests that the opposite is actually true.

A really sustainable reduction in "deviant behavior" can solely and exclusively be promised by the integrity of the employee—from the management board to the warehouse clerk. The future task for compliance will be to establish this integrity in the company—meaning not just passively checking it exists but rather actively making it a theme throughout the company. This does not necessarily mean that seasoned managers or even management boards have to undertake an educational program that teaches them the values held by the German concept of the "honorable businessman." This would only work in the very rarest of cases. A personal understanding of integrity, sincerity, and honesty can at best only be finely adjusted.

How is it possible then for management personnel in particular to internalize and also actively embody the theme of compliance and thus to act as a role model for other employees? Without a doubt, the level of awareness for compliance in the company must be upgraded, from an unpleasant "clean-up issue" to a strategic management theme that significantly influences the value of a company.

5.2.1 Compliance as a Strategic Management Theme

The critical issue for the future does not revolve around the question of identifying the original essence of the subject of compliance. That is a question that can be quickly answered. Compliance deals with the fulfilment of legal regulations and the implementation of a consistent set of rules. A more important and fascinating issue is the question of what compliance can actually offer an organization in a positive sense, namely as a strategic management theme that can significantly contribute to the success of a company. What does noncompliance actually mean for a company? Although corruption and cartelization, for example, appear to benefit the company from a superficial perspective, they have no place in a sustainable corporate policy. In the long term, the company is not investing in quality but rather purchasing the illusion of business success. It is thus ultimately doomed to failure. Not to mention the high loss of value caused by every other form of white-collar crime being conducted in the shadows. And we are not yet even taking into account here the massive fines that can result when everything becomes public.

If a member of the management board is then heard to make comments such as "compliance simply costs money" or "business doesn't operate cleanly" then they have not understood what the critical success factors for commercial enterprises will be in 2014 and beyond, and has ultimately been miscast in the role of a business leader. Whatever they do, they will not be able to steer their company or business area in one unified direction that will sustainably guarantee business success. This is precisely how compliance also needs to be communicated and anchored in the awareness of employees—as a positive value driver for the company. Those who act with integrity within their relevant regulatory framework will reduce risk, promote a sustainable performance culture, and simply earn more money in the long term—in a modern world of business characterized by an increasing level of transparency.

Once this fact has been understood, compliant behavior will follow much more easily. This is because it can be positively incentivized in the sense of good corporate governance. In the final analysis, the formal control system with all of its legal and bureaucratic facets is transformed into a very tangible commercial motivation system that cleverly combines general and personal business success with employees acting with integrity in their business units.

The prerequisite for this is, however, that the subject of compliance is understood, accepted, and implemented in the company. It is at this point at the very latest that compliance loses its purely legal character as a control instrument and matures into a personnel management and development theme with significant implications for the corporate culture. This will ultimately prove decisive for how integrity and ethics are interpreted in the company and have an effect on the company's actual business operations.

In this transformation from a control-oriented culture of mistrust to a value-oriented corporate culture that is based on respect and trust, management personnel undoubtedly play the key role. And this begins with the chairman of the management board. The role played by the management board in setting an example to all levels of the company when it comes to "soft" themes like integrity cannot be overestimated, especially if the company is trying to formulate its own balanced vision between trust and control, or simply wants to signal that the subject is being taken seriously. If this is not the case and it becomes obvious that the management of the company does not really believe in integrity and compliance, it cannot really be expected that anything will change when it comes down to the level of the company's operative business. This "tone from the top" is in reality often the decisive factor for solving dilemmas in the business world—whether they involve crime or not.

5.3 The Requirement for Compliant Business Practices in Global Competition

Justification for taking compliance in companies seriously can also be found when examining the overall economic context. The business world is undergoing a process of globalization that is producing increasingly extensive legislation on an international stage. The strategic course has been clearly set. The international community has declared war on corruption and unfair competition, while at the same time it is becoming increasingly risky to infringe existing international agreements and laws. For example, the last major cases of corruption in Germany were ones in which this trend for greater international regulation quite simply passed the companies by. There is no case that demonstrates this better than Siemens.

Compliant behavior will not just be a bonus in the economic systems of the future, but will give companies their right to exist. Those who fail to respond to these developments will quite simply disappear from the market.

Many entrepreneurs—especially medium-sized enterprises—are too quick to consider obligations and regulations as paternalism or as a competitive disadvantage: "Everyone else is also paying bribes." "How else can we hope to compete against the Indians or the Chinese?" It is precisely at this point—when dealing with the increasing pressure placed on the Western industrialized nations by the emerging markets—that it becomes clear how important it will be in future for American and European countries to exclusively engage in clean business practices. The Western world will only be able to withstand the pricing pressure exerted by the emerging countries if they move in the direction of sustainable competition.

This begins with the selection of current projects and future objectives based on sustainable criteria and ends with functioning governance and compliance management systems. The West currently still has authority over international economic regulations and a real opportunity to actively shape them. When viewed in an overall context, the development of global ethical and corruption standards is more of a competitive advantage than a disadvantage. The better product will ultimately succeed in fair competition. Seriously promoting this type of fair play in the long term is thus by no means a disadvantage but rather an opportunity to create sustainable competitive advantages.

Yet how is it possible to develop clean business practices in corrupt countries? It would certainly be very difficult for individual companies to do much in this area, but whole industries and business groups can have greater success. This makes "collective action" probably one of the most important buzzwords in the international movement against corruption and white-collar crime. The principle behind collective action is for market participants to combine together to fight against the disadvantages resulting from corruption such as increased investment costs. The result is the gradual export of common standards and values across the whole globalized economy, implemented in the form of project-related agreements on integrity, cross-sector compliance pacts, and corresponding long-term initiatives (see Moosmayer 2012, p. 133 ff.). Either we succeed in establishing our notion of the honorable businessman across the world or Western nations will experience a dramatic fall in their level of competitiveness.

5.4 The Path to the Future: Good Corporate Governance

The really key aspects that can be learnt from daily experience with white-collar crime and the development of compliance need to be clearly formulated here once again. If the aim is to effectively protect against liability risk and a loss of assets due to "deviant behavior" then formal systems alone are insufficient. An awareness of rules, controls, and risk also needs to be integrated into the corporate culture. And this starts at the top with the management.

The prerequisite is the development of a corresponding value system, which exists in harmony with the economic goals of the company. Values are not just "nice to have," but are also fundamental requirements for the success of the company.

As a core instrument in this type of value management system, compliance is thus transformed from a concept based on controls and blockades to an active value driver and a vibrant manager of integrity. Such reasoning requires a clear understanding of an ethical corporate culture, which can be called good corporate governance—modelled on the term "good governance" from the UN, used in the 1980s when donor countries were reluctant to hand over their financial aid to corrupt governments.[3]

A similar concept applies today to shareholders in the world of business, who are interested now more than ever in long-term and stable investments. Good corporate governance is essentially a basic requirement. It may sound a little utopian to now announce the renaissance of the much-cited "honorable businessman." Yet, in truth, he has never been more in demand than he is today. Especially in international circles, the concept of the honorable businessman is fundamental to the survival of companies if we want to continue to believe in Western principles and allow them to play a role in the future.

The principles of the honorable businessman go above and beyond control, and stand for the search for better solutions. Managers with integrity do not need more control but rather less. They possess an internal compass for maintaining sustainable business practices. Developing and successively promoting this type of manager in a company is the goal of the management principle "good corporate governance." Thus, compliance becomes integrity management—meaning the targeted examination, enablement, and promotion of integrity in companies.

The management instruments required to initiate this type of change are undoubtedly already available, such as employee selection and development, training and management seminars, transparency and consistency in handling "deviant behavior," and finally remuneration and reward systems. A significant factor in the success of future commercial companies will be setting the right incentives and raising awareness for corruption, whistleblowing, and integrity so that this is always a better alternative than fraud and manipulation.

---

[3] The term can be traced back to the World Bank and various foreign aid organizations. The right to "good administration" was added as Article 41 to the EU Charter of Fundamental Rights in 2007 and came into force on December 1, 2009. In terms of good administration being a component of "good governance," the constitutionally prescribed guidelines for good administration are also binding legal definitions for good governance; see here: Article 41 Paragraph 1: the right of every person to be heard, to have access to his or her file, the obligation of the administration to give reasons for its decisions, the right to have the Union make good any damage caused by its Institutions or by its servants in the performance of their duties; Paragraph 3: Languages of the constitution; Paragraph 4.

Some people are sure to object and say: "Integrity and the concept of the honorable businessman is all well and good, but can I also earn more money in this way?" This is precisely the challenge faced by strategy consultants of the future: to demonstrate in a pragmatic and commercially realistic way how it is possible to add value by acting with integrity. This will involve promoting high performance as the goal, rather than glossing over weaknesses with risky maneuvers or constructing burdensome paper tigers.

Literature

Berg, A. (2001). *Wirtschaftskriminalität in Deutschland, Ursachen und Bekämpfung von Korruption und Untreue (White-collar crime in Germany, causes and combating corruption and breach of trust)*. Osnabrück: Der Andere Verlag.

Bussmann, K. D. (2003). Business Ethics und Wirtschaftsstrafrecht. Zu einer Kriminologie des Managements (Business ethics and commercial law. Towards a criminology of management). In: *Monatsschrift für Kriminologie und Strafrechtsreform 86 (Monthly Journal for Criminology and the Reform of Criminal Law 86)* (pp. 89–104).

Bussmann, K. D. (2004). Kriminalprävention durch Business Ethics. Ursachen von Wirtschaftskriminalität und die besondere Bedeutung von Werten (Criminal prevention through business ethics. Causes of white-collar crime and the special importance of ethics). In: *Zeitschrift für Wirtschafts- und Unternehmensethik 5* (*Magazine for Economic and Corporate Ethics 5*) (Vol. 1, pp. 35–50).

Editorial of the Handelsblatt. (2012). Ex-MAN-Manager wegen Schmiergeldzahlungen verurteilt (Ex-manager at MAN convicted of bribery payments). Handelsblatt Online. http://www.handelsblatt.com/unternehmen/industrie/anton-weinmann-ex-manmanager-wegen-schmiergeldzahlungen-verurteilt/7151984.html. Accessed: January 21, 2013.

Ernst & Young. (2012). *Enabling Compliance Welche Rolle spielt Technologie? (What role is played by technology?)* Ernst & Young GmbH. http://www.ey.com/Publication/vwLUAssets/Enabling_Compliance/$FILE/Enabling_Compliance_Welche_Rolle_Spielt_Technologie.pdf. Accessed: June 24, 2013.

Huntington, I. K., & Davies, D. (1999). *Wirtschaftskriminalität in Unternehmen (White-collar crime in companies)*. Campus Verlag GmbH.

Moosmayer, K. (2012). *Compliance, Praxisleitfaden für Unternehmen (Compliance, practical guidelines for companies)*. Munich: Beck.

Palazzo, B. (2001). Unternehmensethik als Instrument der Prävention von Wirtschaftskriminalität und Korruption (Corporate ethics as an instrument for the prevention of white-collar crime and corruption). *Die Kriminalprävention Ausgabe (The Criminal Prevention Issue), 2*(2001), 52–60.

The Committee on the Financial Aspects of Corporate Governance and Gee and Co. Ltd. (1992). *Financial aspects of corporate governance*. London: Burgess Science Press.

MIX
Papier aus verantwortungsvollen Quellen
Paper from responsible sources
FSC® C105338

If you have any concerns about our products,
you can contact us on
ProductSafety@springernature.com

In case Publisher is established outside the EU,
the EU authorized representative is:
Springer Nature Customer Service Center GmbH
Europaplatz 3, 69115 Heidelberg, Germany

Printed by Libri Plureos GmbH
in Hamburg, Germany